The Imposition of a Fake Political Settlement in the Northern Caucasus

The 2003 Chechen Presidential Election

Edited by
Tanya Lokshina in collaboration with Ray Thomas and Mary Mayer

Cover picture: Grozny, December 2004. © Tanya Lokshina

THE IMPOSITION OF A FAKE POLITICAL SETTLEMENT IN THE NORTHERN CAUCASUS

The 2003 Chechen Presidential Election

Edited by
Tanya Lokshina in collaboration with Ray Thomas and Mary Mayer

ibidem-Verlag
Stuttgart

Bibliografische Information Der Deutschen Bibliothek

Die Deutsche Bibliothek verzeichnet diese Publikation in der Deutschen Nationalbibliografie; detaillierte bibliografische Daten sind im Internet über <http://dnb.ddb.de> abrufbar.

∞

Gedruckt auf alterungsbeständigem, säurefreien Papier
Printed on acid-free paper

ISSN: 1614-3515

ISBN: 3-89821-436-2

© *ibidem*-Verlag
Stuttgart 2005
Alle Rechte vorbehalten

Das Werk einschließlich aller seiner Teile ist urheberrechtlich geschützt. Jede Verwertung außerhalb der engen Grenzen des Urheberrechtsgesetzes ist ohne Zustimmung des Verlages unzulässig und strafbar. Dies gilt insbesondere für Vervielfältigungen, Übersetzungen, Mikroverfilmungen und elektronische Speicherformen sowie die Einspeicherung und Verarbeitung in elektronischen Systemen.

Printed in Germany

CONTENTS

English editors' introduction
Ray Thomas & Mary Mayer — 9

Map of Chechnya and its neighbours — 14
Chronology at a glance — 15
Presidential election results 1997 and 2003 — 16
Dramatis personae — 17
Abbreviations and explanations — 21

1 Why this book was written
Tanya Lokshina & Sergei Lukashevsky — 25

2 The Chechen maze: Looking for a way out
Alexander Cherkasov — 30
Chronicle: December 2002 to March 2003 — 36

3 The March 2003 referendum: What difference did it make?
Alexander Mnatsakanyan — 37
Chronicle: 6 June to 20 August 2003 — 43

4 Five candidates for the presidency: Biybulatov, Bugaev, Buraev, Kadyrov and Khanchukaev
Biybulatov – Interview by *Roman Rostov* — 50
Bugaev – Interview by *Ruslan Umarov* — 53
Buraev – Searched for by *Tanya Lokshina* — 56
Kadyrov – Interview by *Ruslan Umarov* — 60
Kadyrov – Biography — 64
Khanchukaev – Interview by *Ruslan Umarov* — 67
A complaint by Biybulatov about Kadyrov — 70

	A complaint by Buraev about Kadyrov	71
	Chronicle: 23 August to 6 September	73
5	**In the end there can be only one: Removing major contenders**	
	Leonid Ruzov	80
	Chronicle: 7 to 11 September	85
6	**Malik Saidullaev: A reconaissance**	
	Tanya Lokshina	91
	Malik Mingayevich Saidullaev – Biography	96
	Appeal from the HQ of Saidullaev	97
	Chronicle: 13 September to 16 September	99
7	**The moor did his deed: Intervention by Paizullaev**	
	Paizullaev – Interview by *Ruslan Umarov*	104
	Paizullaev's HQ – by *Tanya Lokshina*	106
	Chronicle: 17 to 25 September	111
	Statement by Saidullayev's Head Of Election Campaign	118
8	**The story of Saidullaev's removal**	
	Tanya Lokshina	122
	Chronicle: 26 to 30 September	128
9	**From the life of election headquarters: Inside information**	
	Alexander Mnatsakanyan	134
	Chronicle: 1 and 2 October	139
10	**The Chair of the Election Commission before the election**	
	Interview by *Ruslan Umarov*	141
	Chronicle: 3 and 4 October	147
11	**Eve of the election 5 October 2003**	
	Tanya Lokshina	150

12	**Only good news on TV**	
	Tanya Lokshina	157
13	**Election day**	
	Tanya Lokshina	162
	Chronicle: 5 and 6 October	170
14	**Reports on violations on the election day**	175
	Chronicle: 7 and 8 October	179
15	**Did the refugees vote?**	
	Tanya Lokshina	183
	Usam Baisaev	185
16	**Book of numbers – book of the lost**	
	Alexander Cherkasov	190
17	**The Chair of the Election Commission after the election**	
	Interview by *Roman Rostov*	211
	Chronicle: 9 to 28 October 2003	212
18	**Kadyrov at the United Nations**	
	Tanya Lokshina	222
19	**Perfect stillness zone**	
	Tanya Lokshina	231
	Chronicle: 1 to 8 December 2003	256
20	**War in the Caucasus and peace in Russia**	
	Alexander Cherkasov	265
	Recent books on Chechnya	273
	Online resources	274
	Index	275

ENGLISH EDITORS' INTRODUCTION

This book focuses on the election that took place in Chechnya on 5 October 2003. Akhmat Kadyrov was elected as president – receiving 83% of the votes. Seven months later he was assassinated – in an explosion at Victory in World War II day celebrations. A bomb had been buried in the concrete of the newly built stadium. Thirteen people died. The episode epitomizes the political situation in Chechnya – a show of democracy and an act of terrorism.

The preceding presidential election was held in January 1997. The election was won by Aslan Maskhadov with 59% of the votes cast. Shamil Basaev was runner-up with 24%, and Zemlikhan Yanderbiyev came third with 10%. The clear majority for Maskhadov after a quiet campaign was a surprise for many observers. There were queues at many polling stations and voting hours were extended to 10 pm. The 1997 election was monitored. According to the Norsk Untenrikspolitisk Institutt (NUPI) there were 200 observers including 72 from the Organization for Security and Cooperation in Europe (OSCE). The head of OSCE, Tim Guldiman, declared that the election was "democratic and legitimate".

The outcome of the 1997 election was tragic despite initial jubilation. In 2000 Maskhadov was deposed. In 2004 the Russian Government put a bounty of $10 million on his head. Maskhadov was assassinated by Russian government agents in March 2005. Zelimkhan Yanderbiyev, who had been Chechen vice-president or acting president from 1993 to 1997 was assassinated by Russian agents in Qatar in February 2003. The Russian government has offered a bounty of $10 million on the head of Shamil Basaev.

The presidential election of 2003 described in this book was very different from that of 1997. There were no monitors from the Western world. The authors of chapters in this book do not describe anything like the enthusiasm that was expressed by voters in 1997. Kadyrov, with the open support of the Kremlin, was in effect self-appointed as president of Chechnya. The number of votes reported as cast for Kadyrov had little to do with reality. The election echoes Stalin's reputed declaration 'Those who cast the votes decide nothing. Those who count the votes decide everything'.

To Westerners elections are usually orderly affairs with occasional disputes over matters such as disenfranchised minorities, hanging chads, and postal voting. It may be difficult for Westerners to imagine the scale of denial in Chechnya of election procedures that are taken for granted in established democracies. It is equally difficult to imagine and not to be horrified at the scale of lawlessness in Chechnya. Two wars in less than a decade and a breakdown of civil order mean that arbitrary arrest, kidnapping, violence, imprisonment, torture, execution and other violations of human rights have become so common that they are hardly regarded as worthy of report or investigation.

It is hoped that this book, by putting on record political events in 2003, will indicate the range of problems that will have to be dealt with to stop the growth of lawlessness in Chechnya. The fake political settlement of 2003 represents a stark failure to reconcile the need to prevent terrorism with the need to allow for development of a stable and peaceful society. The political events of 2003 have maintained and exacerbated lawlessness in Chechnya. Akhmad Kadyrov's son Ramzan Kadyrov took over his father's private army and was appointed deputy prime minister in 2004. Such a growth in warlordism and the prospect that Ramzan might be appointed prime minister offer little hope of a restoration to normality for the foreseeable future. Perhaps we can learn from Chechnya's calamitous experience. It might be expected that problems that occurred in Chechnya are echoed in other countries subjected to externally imposed regime-change.

Chapters 1 and 2 give the background to this book and sketch the historical background to the conflict in Chechnya. Chapter 3 describes the referendum of March 2003 that was used to legitimize Russia's return as sovereign power in Chechnya. Chapters 4 to 9 are mostly about the candidates for the presidential election of 5 October 2003. How is it that of more than ten candidates nominated only seven got through to the election itself? How is it that just one candidate, Akhmat Kadyrov (interviewed in Chapter 4), is recorded as having received 380 thousand votes while the other six candidates only managed to get 60 thousand between them? This book aims to give some components of an explanation.

One component is that only seven got through because the three other strong candidates dropped out or were removed. President Putin persuaded candidate Aslakhanov to take another job (Chapter 5). Candidate Dzhabrailov was pressured to withdraw. The most popular candidate Saidullaev (Chapters 6 and 8) was removed by the actions of a pseudo-candidate Paizullaev (Chapter 7). Chapter 9 is about activity and inactivity in the election campaign office of a candidate who the author, for reasons best known to himself, does not identify by name. The reader is expected to work this one out (not difficult!).

Chapters 10 and 17 comprise interviews, before and after the October election, with the chair of the Chechnya Election Commission. Chapters 12 to 15 are about how the 5 October election was conducted from different vantage points – including what happened to refugees who became classified as internally displaced persons (IDPs). Chapter 16 examines the election result in the light of what is known, and what is not known, about the size of Chechnya's population.

The remaining chapters begin an examination of the consequences. Chapter 18 gives a picture of the impact of Kadyrov at a United Nations meeting on human rights. Chapter 19 gives an account of a visit to Chechnya at the time of the elections for the Duma in December 2003. Finally Chapter 20 presents a summary of the book and puts the events in Chechnya in a broader context. Does escalation of the war against terrorism in Chechnya portend parallel trends in other parts of the world? Does the growth of lawlessness in Chechnya presage a typical outcome of anti-terrorist activities?

Quite apart from such broad questions, the detail of this book is important because it presents an exceptionally well-documented account of the ways in which elections can be manipulated and corrupted. There are a growing number of countries where it is believed that elections are systematically rigged. But there are fewer countries that also have the organisational infrastructure, as Russia has, to allow for the production of evidence relevant to the scale and extent of rigging.

Russia has statistical systems that provide information on population – from censuses conducted in 1989 and 2002 and from annual statistics produced from administrative sources. The annual statistics help demonstrate the overstatement of population in the census of 2002. In reality the census result provided an indirect indication of the scale of refugee movement (see Chapter 16). But the overstatement encouraged the powers-that-be to inflate figures for the size of the electorate and for the number of votes cast. Inadvertently the powers-that-be thereby provided evidence relevant to the scale of falsification.

As well as statistical systems Russia also boasts of, or at least tolerates, a number of dedicated civil rights organisations – the Moscow Helsinki Group (Centre Demos), the Memorial Human Rights Centre and the Caucasian Knot. This book is the product of cooperative work of these voluntary non-government organizations (NGOs), and came into existence only as a result of initiatives taken and dangerous field work carried out by members of these NGOs.

The detail of the first-hand accounts given, reinforced by background population statistics, provide a kind of checklist of the many different ways in which elections can be influenced or corrupted. It could well provide a checklist for people appointed as monitors of elections held in other situations where there is any doubt that proper procedures are being followed.

The nature of the material of the book makes it difficult to maintain consistency in style and tone or even in the transliteration of Russian proper names. One reason is for that the book is the product of many eyes, ears and minds. Another is the difficulty of maintaining contact with reality in the face of contradictory accounts of the nature of reality. It would be cumbersome, for example, to report that Kadyrov *allegedly* obtained 83% out of more than an *alleged* 562 thousand votes cast in the October 2003 election. It is impossible to believe that the official figures given for the size of the electorate, for the number of votes cast and for the proportion of votes for Kadyrov are other than distorted exaggerations of reality. But we have had to report some fantasies as facts to maintain coherence in the story. The book presents as unchallenged facts many official statements – as well as the accounts of our authors and to contributions from civil rights organization and the media. It is important to keep in mind ways in which official statements may disguise reality.

The contrast between the world of officialdom and that faced by people in their day-to-day lives is illustrated in many ways in the Chronicle of Events that accompany the main text of this book. The Chronicle gives many examples of incidents of terrorism by the powers-that-be in Chechnya – as experienced by the victims and by their families. The Chronicle also gives examples of activities of law enforcement agencies designed to reduce terrorism that can be terrifying to the local population affected. There are descriptions of attempts by ordinary people to recover from the dislocation and destruction left in the wake of two wars in Chechnya. The accounts of such incidents are often juxtaposed in the Chronicle with contemporaneous events in the very different world of political decision making.

At the beginning of the book we give a few items for reference purposes. There is a map of Chechnya and its neighbours. A one-page chronology focuses on 2003, but is not limited to that year. Detail is given of the 1997 and 2003 presidential election results. A list of principal characters is included for those who like to study the cast-list. An explanatory list of abbreviations, acronyms and other terms is included for those who may not have much knowledge of Chechnya or Russia. At the end there is a list of recent books and online resources about Chechnya.

Ray Thomas & Mary Mayer
October 2005

CHECHNYA AND ITS NEIGHBOURS

Reproduced from a CIA website

CHRONOLOGY AT A GLANCE

1944–1975	Chechen population deported to Khazakhstan.
November 1990	First Chechen national congress
March 1991	Chechnya opts out of Russian presidential election.
October 1991	Dudaev became president after first non-soviet elections.
June 1992	Ingushetia becomes republic within Russia.
April 1993	Dudaev dissolves parliament and assembly.
November 1994	The first war. Russian tank incursion into Chechnya.
December 1995 – January 1996	Fighting in Gudermes, Kizlar (Dagestan), Pervomaiskoye, Grozny
April 1996	Dudaev killed.
August 1996	Maskhadov and Lebed sign peace agreement.
27 January 1997	Maskhadov elected president.
May 1997	Yeltsin recognises Maskhadov as president of Chechen republic of Ichkeria
August 1999	Chechen incursion led by Basaev into Dagestan
September 1999	The second war. Bombing of Grozny resumes.
October 1999 – Jan 2000	Russian troops invade. A quarter of a million refugees to Ingushetia.
June 2000	Russia appoints Kadyrov as head of Chechnya.
October 2002	Census of population.
23 March 2003	Referendum on Chechnya constitution.
5 October 2003	Kadyrov elected president.
7 December 2003	Duma elections.
May 2004	Kadyrov killed.
March 2005	Maskhadov killed.

A SUMMARY COMPARISON OF TWO PRESIDENTIAL ELECTION RESULTS IN CHECHNYA

Election held 27th January 1997:	Election held 5th October 2003:
Registered voters: 513,585.	Registered voters 561,817 (includes 30,000 servicemen).
Turnout: 407,699 (79.4%).	Turnout: 462,000 (82.2%).
Results:	**Result:**
- Aslan Maskhadov 242 thousand votes,	- Akhamat Kadyrov 381 thousand votes,
- 59.3% of votes cast.	- 82.5% of votes cast.
- Shamil Basaev 23.5%.	- Abdula Bugaev 5.6%.
- Zelimkhan Yanderbiyev 10.1%.	- Shamil Buraev 3.4%.
- Other candidates 7.1%.	- Other candidates 8%.

DRAMATIS PERSONAE

(Candidates for the presidency in 2003 are given two stars. Those who had been candidates but withdrew, or were withdrawn, get one star.)

Alu Alkhanov	Minister of Interior in Chechnya. Appointed president in 2004 on death of Kadyrov. Won election in 2004 in style of that of 2003.
Aslambek Aslakhanov*	Duma deputy. Presidential candidate August 2003, but withdrew in September 2003 when Putin appointed him special Aide for south Russia.
Abdul-Kerim Arsakhanov	Chair, Chechnya Election Commission. Chapters 10 and 17 comprise interviews with Arsakhanov before and after the presidential election of 5 October 2003.
Magomed Arsanukaev	Head of Saidullayev's election campaign. See p 118
Ruslan Aushev	1954 Formerly Soviet general. President Ingushetia 1993–2002
Shamil Basaev	1965– Chechen field commander. Runner up in 1997 presidential election. Led excursion into Dagestan in1999 triggering the second war.
Khusein Biybulatov**	1939– Former communist activist and Deputy in CI-ASSR. Petitioned the Election Commission about violation of his rights as candidate. See Chapter 5. Seven thousand votes.
Abdula Bugaev**	1949– Historian and academic. Deputy tp CIASSR 1990–91. See Chapter 3. Runner up to Kadyrov with 26 thousand votes.

Shamil Buraev**	1958– Agriculturist and entrepreneur. Head of the administration of the Achkhoi-Martan district.1995–97 and 1999–2003. See Chap 7. Sixteen thousand votes.
Alexander Cherkasov	A senior member of the Memorial Human Rights Group, author of chapters 2, 16, and 20.
Dzhokhar Dudaev	1944–1996. Served in Soviet Airforce becoming a General. Prime Minister of Chechnya 1991-1993. Killed by a Russian rocket that honed onto his satellite phone in April 1996.
Khussein Dzhabrailov*	Chechen Moscow businessmen. Became candidate in August 2003 but withdrew in September after talks with Putin administration.
Beslan Gantamirov	Minister for the Press until dismissed in September 2003. Supported Dzhabrailov for presidency.
Boris Gryslov	United Russia party leader and Russian Federal Minister for internal affairs.
Akhmat Kadyrov**	1951–2004. Elected Chechen President 2003. Assassinated 2004. See personal file, page 49..
Ramzan Kadyrov	1978– Son of Akhmat Kadyrov and inheritor of his army. Appointed deputy prime minister of Chechnya by Putin in 2004.
Avkhat Khanchukaev**	1954– Professor Grozny University. Established Ortsa organization. Four thousand votes. See Chapter 4.
Ruslan Khasbulatov	1947– Speaker of the Russian Parliament before it was dissolved in 1993. Returned to Chechnya in 1994 to unify opposition to Dudayev, but sidelined by Kremlin. Lost Duma seat to United Russia party in 2003.
Khattab	1969-2002. A fighter from Saudi Arabia, said to be a Wahhabi, allied to Basaev in 1999 raid on Dagestan. Killed in 2002.

Frants Klintsevich	Head of the Chechen branch of United Russia Party.
Tanya Lokshina	Author of eleven chapters. Former Executive Director Moscow Helsinki Group, Chair of Centre "Demos" (Moscow-based human rights think-tank) and journalist.
Aslan Maskhadov	1951–2005 The former general who made peace with Russia's General Lebed in 1996. Elected President of Ichkeria in 1997. Assassinated March 2005.
Alexander Lebed	1950–2002. Russian general who made peace with Maskhadov in 1996. Killed in helicopter crash.
Salambek Maigov	Former deputy for Chechnya until 1993 election, representative of Mashkadov,
Alexander Mnatsakanyan	Moscow journalist/editor. Author of chapters 3 and 9.
*Nikolai Paizullaev***	1948– Press officer for Chechen president. Folk poet. Instigated removal of Saidullaev as candidate. See Chapters 7 and 8.
Anna Politkovskaya	*Novaya Gazeta* correspondent. Author of *A Dirty War: A Russian reporter in Chechnya*, 2001.
Anatoly Popov	Acting president Chechnya during 2003 election.
Vladimir Putin	1952– Former KGB officer elected president of Russia in 2000 after promise to wipe out Chechen terrorists.
*Kudus Saduev***	Director Grosneftgaz. Six thousand votes.
*Malik Saidullaev**	Chechen born Moscow businessman. Disqualified as presidential candidate. See Chapters 6-8.
*Said-Selim Tsuev**	Deputy Military Commandant of Chechnya. Withdrew in September 2003.
Vladimir Shamanov	1962– Russian General in Chechen wars. Reported as favouring imprisonment of insurgents families and forcible repatriation of Chechen diaspora.

Ruslan Umarov	Correspondent for Caucasian Knot. Contributions to Chapters 4, 7 and 10.
Zelimkhan Yandarbiev	1951–2000. A Chechen nationalist poet who succeeded Dudayev as president in 1996. Assassinated by Russian agents in Quatar.
Sergey Yastrzhembsky	1953– Diplomat/editor appointed as Putin's aide on Chechnya and North Caucasus in 2000.
Boris Yeltsin	President of Russia until he nominated Putin as his successor in 1999.
Akhmed Zakayev	Deputy to Maskhadov. Former actor. Regarded as moderate. Russia tried to extradite him from UK for terrorist offences. Zakayev freed on bail from Vanessa Redgrave.
Akhmar Zavgaev	Brother of Doka Zavgaev. Ally of Kadyrov. Elected as United Russia candidate to Duma in 2003.
Doka Zavgaev	Head of Chechnya Supreme Soviet in late 1980s. Declared Chechen sovereignty in 1990. Replaced by Dudaev in 1991.
Murat Zyazikov	FSB General who replaced Ruslan Aushev as president of Ingusheita in 2002.

ABBREVIATIONS AND EXPLANATIONS

census	All-Soviet population censuses were conducted in 1979 and 1989. The results of these censuses and the all-Russia census conducted in 2002 are discussed in chapter 16.
CIASSR	Chechen-Ingush Autonomous Soviet Socialist Republic – the formal name in the Soviet era.
CIS	Commonwealth of Independent States. Established in 1991 by Belarus, Russia and Ukraine, soon joined by nine other former soviet states - Azerbaijan, Armenia, Georgia, Kazakstan, Kyrgyz, Moldova, Tajikistan, Turkmenistan, and Uzbekistan.
cleansing operations	Translated from zachistki. Cleansing, or 'mop-up' operations, are raids carried out by law enforcement agencies or siloviki ostensibly to identify and arrest insurgents.
CSU	Chechen State University
Dagestan	Republic to the east of Chechnya. Multicultural, relatively healthy.
FSB	Federal Safety Bureau, the successor to the KGB.
Grozny	Capital of Chechnya. Believed to have a population of more than 400,000 before the wars of the 1990s. Population 200,000 in 2002 according to census.
Ichkeria	Name adopted for Chechnya on achieving independence in 1996 after the first Chechen war.
IDP	Internally Displaced Person. A refugee within Chechnya
iman	faith, spiritual leader.
Ingushetia	Republic between Chechnya to the east and Ossetia to the west. See Vainakh.
intelligentsia	Term used widely in Russia to refer to educated people.

Khazakhstan	The birthplace of many Chechens whose parents were deported to Khazakhstan by the Russia in 1944..
law enforcement agency	The term *law enforcement agency* is used generously and ambivalently in reports quoted in this book to cover identified and unidentified forces such as the *siloviki*.
mop-up	Mop-up operation. See cleansing
mufti	An interpreter of Islamic law. Collectively the muftiat.
NGO	Non-government organization.
ORB-2	Operative and Search Bureau of the N Caucasus Dept of the Russian Ministry of Internal Affairs, a place of detention in Grozny. Visited by the Council of Europe's Committee for the Prevention of Torture in 2002 and later.
OSCE	Organisation for Security and Cooperation in Europe. Established in 1972 concerned with conflict resolution and human rights.
Ossetia	Republic west of Ingushetia.
PACE	Parliamentary Assembly for Cooperation in Europe. The parliamentary assembly of OSCE.
RFE/RL	Radio Free Europe/Radio Liberty (Prague, Czech Republic)
RNE	Russian National Unity Party. See United Russia.
rouble	In 2003 about 50 roubles made a £ sterling or 30 to $.
RSFSR	Russian Soviet Federative Socialist Republic
Russian names	Russians have a first name, a patronymic, and a family name. First name plus patronym is a common form of address – exemplified in interviews in Chapter 4.
siloviki	'the strong ones' – used to describe members of the FSB and military and other armed groups who raid, detain, torture and kill – apparently above the law.
SPS	Soyuz Pravykh Sil - Union of Right Forces.

TAC	Temporary Accommodation Centre, typically tented accommodation in Ingushetia
tiep	A clan or tribe. A traditional social division in Chechnya nowadays of uncertain importance.
UAZ	Ulyanovsk Automobil Zavod. Russian version of Land Rover or Jeep for rough country.
United Russia	'Party of power' that inherited methods of communist party of Soviet era. Established in 2001 to support Putin. Lacks policies. Gained majority in Duma in 2003.
vainakh	Name of the ethno-linguistic group to which both the Chechens and Ingushs belong
Wahhabis	An Islamic sect originating in Saudi Arabia. Believed to be, or labelled as, providing ideological support for Al Qaeda and other extremist activities.

1 WHY THIS BOOK WAS WRITTEN

Tanya Lokshina & Sergei Lukashevsky, Moscow Helsinki Group/Centre 'Demos'

Human rights defenders have monitored the situation in the Chechen Republic in recent years not just because of the continued violation of human rights and fundamental freedoms, but also because of the ambiguous legal situation in the region. There can be rule of law only if there is law to apply. In Chechnya it is not clear whether the formal law of the Russian constitution, rulings by the Kremlin, dictates by the Russian military in Chechnya or *ad hoc* decisions by the-powers-that-be in Chechnya, are governing human behaviour. There is a crisis of legitimacy.

The federal attempt to restore its sovereignty has led to continued military conflict accompanied by massive and brutal violations of human rights and humanitarian law. But when the Republic was granted *de facto* independence from the federal centre between 1996 and 1999 it could hardly be said that the government of Chechnya (or Ichkeria as it was called) was in control. The Ichkerian government was unable to defend basic human rights, prevent waves of criminal violence or effectively counter extremist groups.

Most Russian and Chechen human rights defenders firmly expressed belief that it would be impossible to conduct a free and fair election in autumn 2003. The impossibility of ensuring conformance of the election with international standards under conditions of military conflict seemed obvious. An open and fair election campaign was not possible because neither candidates nor voters could be guaranteed security. Moreover, supporters of independence were effectively disenfranchised by the federal centre from its 'political settlement'.

The impossibility of conducting a free and fair election in October 2003 was confirmed by reports of violations of election laws, massive abuse of official powers, numerous cases of violence against supporters of candidates opposing the acting president, Akhmat Kadyrov, and against election staff and their relatives. There was a faint hope that the election would be seriously contested, so giving the people of Chechnya a small window that would help establish a right to express their views. The election then might have helped to stabilize the situation in the Republic.

The events of the beginning of September, however, dispelled any illusions about the forthcoming election. Effectively a single candidate -- Akhmat Kadyrov – was imposed on voters. Those who might have competed with him either withdrew their candidacy or were withdrawn. Such tactics are not new in Russian electoral campaigns. Similar situation have existed in the Yakutia Republic, the Kursk region, the Far East, and in the Republic of Ingushetia. But Chechnya differs in principle from any other Russian Federation subject. The election in Chechnya was presented by the federal authorities as a key step towards peace following logically from the referendum held in March 2003 in favour of remaining part of Russia. The October election was presented as part of a chain of measures that would stabilize the situation in Chechnya.

Citizens should be able to express their will and should be free to nominate who they choose for public positions. They should be free to nominate even if those nominated do not express total loyalty to Russian authorities. The failure to secure a free election, with an imposed (or self-imposed) winner, did not in any way resolve the conflict in Chechnya. On the contrary, the failure exacerbated the problems that the election should have addressed.

It should be clear to all concerned that it is not possible to solve the problems in Chechnya by force. A political settlement is urgently required. But the presidential election in the republic in 2003 bore no relation to a political settlement. A president elected in such a way will not be accepted as legitimate by the Chechen people.

After the election the 'guards' of the acting president grew rapidly in number. At the time of writing they comprised between 1,500 and 3,000. That growth is a symptom of failure to establish an accepted authority. As Talleyrand said to Napoleon "One can do anything with bayonets – except sit on them".

What stability did the Kremlin achieve by selecting Kadyrov as president? They achieved stability only in terms of a continuation of the brutal policies of recent years. For several years the Russian authorities have relied on force to solve the Chechen problem and have treated the legality of their actions as a formality. Russian military actions in Chechnya, with thousands of soldiers, armoured vehicles, and bombing aircraft, were labelled as 'anti-terrorist operations'. Current interventions by the-powers-that-be are justified in terms of the same anti-terrorist label allowing for continuation of the same policy of force – but 'chechenizing' the conflict. The emphasis by the Kremlin on 'political processes' concealed both the scale of violence and the causes of violence. A democratic election in the republic would have revealed something of the complexities that were being covered up.

Kadyrov became a Kremlin favourite because of his readiness and eagerness to rule Chechnya brutally. His record indicated no fear of blood and violence. His attitude was shown in speeches right after Election Day. In an interview with *Kommersant* on 7 October 2003, Kadyrov affirmed his position with the following comments, "If I am the head of the republic, then my people should be everywhere. In the future I am going to be even tougher. Nothing else is possible; they must be totally subordinate to the president. I am not going to allow anybody to rule the Republic. If anybody still thinks this, they are sadly mistaken."

The way the legal president of Chechnya intended to act was clear. The infamy of Kadyrov's men and the growth of his personal army made it clear how these brutal policies would be implemented. The people of Chechnya, and even federal servicemen in the region, so feared Kadyrov and his men that no one could oppose him.

The brutal violations of human rights and humanitarian law made monitoring the election situation in Chechnya our civic and professional duty. Such monitoring is essential in the light of the increasing impunity of the ruling authorities associated with the lack of any recognized political opposition. We collected detailed data on the events of August – mid-October 2003 and attempted to create a full and objective picture of the conduct of the election in the situation of a continuing armed conflict.

We issued an electronic bulletin twice a week starting on 22 September 2003. The bulletins gave news of the election campaign prepared from federal and Chechen documents, from the mass media, from information from local

NGOs and from candidates for the presidential office. The bulletins included thematic articles by our monitors who travelled to the republic to get fresh evidence. In total six bulletins were published that were widely disseminated in Russian and in English among the Russian public and the international community.

A thematic section on The Presidential Election in Chechnya: Human Rights Monitoring' was open on the site of the Moscow Helsinki Group (www.mhg.ru) to feature comprehensive and daily updated data about the election in the Chechen Republic, and particularly violations of the electoral law and human rights violations.

During the period mid-October to the close of December 2003, we carefully analyzed all materials gathered in the course of the monitoring effort. We made another trip to the republic to assess post-October developments and the effects of the results of the election on the human rights situation in Chechnya.

Based on the result of this work, we bring to your attention the product of our efforts. The book gives first-hand accounts of political events in Chechnya in 2003 supplemented by thematic summaries, copies of public documents, and fragments of evidence that aim to give indications of the impact of political events, and the often violent activities of the powers-that-be, on ordinary people's lives. The book focuses on the election of October 2003 that symbolises the failure of political processes in Chechnya. Regrettably the book is permeated by the theme of unending violence and human rights violations – the context within which all political events in this region are taking place, the context within which people in Chechnya live their day to day lives.

We stress that in reality there has been no political process in Chechnya. No solution to the conflict has been found. The elections held do not indicate any kind of promise to end war in Chechnya, but are signals of failure. Our book is an open invitation to the Russian public and the international community to participate in a debate on the situation in Chechnya to find a way out from this crisis of many years standing.

Our work would have been impossible without the generous help we received from our colleagues. We thank the Human Rights Houses Network and the

International Helsinki Federation for Human Rights for their assistance in the preparation, translation and dissemination of the bulletins and of this book. We express our utmost appreciation to the Internet-media 'Kavkazsky Uzel' (Caucasus Knot at http://kavkaz.memo.ru/) for the practical and effective nature of their informational support. We are particularly grateful to our friends and colleagues from the Memorial Human Rights Centre for the information, materials and consultations they provided to us. We thank the Russian-Chechen Friendship Society for regular provision of information as well as for their direct participation in our monitoring effort. We are also happy to acknowledge that in this book we used some of the materials of the Chechen Committee for National Salvation.

2 THE CHECHEN MAZE: LOOKING FOR A WAY OUT

Alexander Cherkasov, Memorial Human Rights Centre

The Chechen problem was a focus of attention of the mass media in the 1990s, but almost disappeared from the public agenda in the 2000s. The few reports in the Russian media in recent years have maintained that the war in the Caucasus is practically over and that legitimate power has been re-established in Chechnya. Justification for any form of censorship is not discussed. Reports in the mass media generally maintain that everything important is known. The same is true of the public image of Chechnya. A few myths and oversimplified interpretations associated with this image satisfy the needs of most people's minds.

One image portrays the events of the recent years as nothing but a continuation of Russia's anti-Chechen policies that for several centuries waged war against Chechnya and that have uprooted the Chechen people every fifty years or so. But the scale of kidnappings in the period of 'independence' of 1996 to 1999 and the invasion into Dagestan that triggered the war of 1999 do not support this image of Chechen innocence. Support of this image requires recourse to provocation by the Federal Security Bureau – or to provocation by 'Zionism'.

The official point of view is that 'bandits have no nationality'. But another Russian image demonizes the Chechens. Again, plenty of support can be found from history – going back to authorities such as General Ermolov in the 19th century and earlier. This demonic image is reinforced with allegations that international conspiracies, Islamic extremism, and international terrorism have been the cause of the troubles of the recent years.

Indeed, Russian-Chechen confrontation does have deep roots – but the relationship of the two peoples is not limited to confrontation. It is hard to deny the existence of extremist and terrorist organisations, or the provocative role often played by various special services (from the British and the Ottoman Turks, to the contemporary FSB). But this can hardly explain, let alone predetermine, the events of recent years. There were other contributing factors.

Experts acknowledge this point. FSB General Mikhailov offers the following logical sequence. Chechens who returned in 1957 from Central Asia after their 1944 deportation could not find employment. There were no vacancies in industry. Mountain villages, unpopulated for thirteen years, had become desolate. To provide accommodation for those who returned, two districts north of the Terek River were added to the Chechen-Ingush Republic. But when industrial construction did start in Chechnya in the 1980s, the response included an ecological protest movement that soon became a national movement. From there, through numerous intermediate stages, General Mikhailov draws a direct line to the second Chechen war. According to the General, there were no other options – everything was predetermined.

Mikhailov's explanation is based on correct assumptions but is developed into untenable theory. Another example of this kind is 'the theory of the pipe' that explains the conflict in Chechnya (and in the Caucasus, in Asia, and through much of the world) in terms of a struggle for oil deposits and oil transportation lines.

Historical factors, the activities of special services and other seemingly inescapable events have contributed to the conflict in Chechnya. But otherwise the factors that helped create the conflict fall within normal political and governmental activities. Popular political movements and decisions by politicians have contributed to the conflict. These movements and decisions indicate that there was some choice, and hence some opportunity to allocate responsibility for what happened. History cannot be altered. But we can try to understand it and learn from it.

The history of the Chechen wars at the turn of century cannot be described on a few pages. This chapter aims only to provide brief notes on matters we consider important in order to understand what is happening in Chechnya today. There is a kind of continuity in the relevant federal politics since 1990. These events have one thing in common – they result from decisions taken in terms of the political considerations of the moment, rather than from any attempt to deal with a complicated socio-economic problem.

In the 1980s the political crisis in the USSR was brought about to a great extent by an economic crisis. It manifested itself in major and minor developments. There was, for example, a reduction in investment in the agricultural and industrial sectors. Earlier a buoyant construction industry had helped prevent large-scale unemployment. But a decline in construction in the 1990s in rural areas deprived Chechens of the opportunity to get jobs as construction workers. Tens of thousands of young men who would have left the region to work elsewhere in Russia or the CIS started to compete for jobs in Chechnya – so creating a pocket of unrest.

Attempts to resolve socio-economic problems led to an ecological protest movement that became a political and separatist movement. A growing awareness of Chechen self-identity, as noted by Solzhenitsyn, and growing political literacy among the population supported this development. Many Chechens were reading the underground publications by their famous compatriot Abdurakhman Avtorkhanov.

The Chechen national movement in 1990-1991 was fuelled by differences between Gorbachev and Yeltsin. The Soviet Union in its confrontation with the leadership of Russia sought support from the Autonomous Republics. In response Yeltsin offered the regions as much sovereignty 'as they can take.' Led by Major-General Jakhar Dudayev, the first Chechen national congress was convened In November 1990. Immediately after that, the legislative body of power – the Republican Supreme Soviet (of Chechnya) headed by Doka Zavgaev adopted a declaration of the republic's sovereignty. In March of 1991 the Chechnya Supreme Soviet refused to take part in the All-Russian referendum on the introduction of the position of the president of the Russian Federation.

That was the beginning of Chechnya's refusal to be involved with any All-Russia voting, which lasted for many years. Throughout Russia existing power structures, already doomed, were trying to deal with local opposition. In other republics new local leaders appealed to Moscow as to a referee in their struggle with the existing power structures. Only Chechnya of all the Caucasus republics declared secession from Russia.

At the same time, that is, during Doka Zavgaev's rule in the late 1980s, the exodus of the Russian-speaking population from Chechnya started. The enhanced status of the core nationality was accompanied by Chechens taking over top jobs. Unemployment was also driving Russians out of Chechnya. Criminal pressure grew against those not protected by tribal or family ties – that is against the non-Chechen population.

Those gradual processes were replaced with spasmodic ones after 19 August 1991. Zavgaev who had supported the Coup was overthrown on 6 September by the Dudayev National Congress, and on 27 October presidential and parliamentary elections were held in Chechnya, and Dudayev became president.

The struggle for power in Moscow led to incoherent responses to developments in Chechnya. The Supreme Soviet of the Russian Soviet Federative Socialist Republic (RSFSR) did not approve of Yeltsin's edict imposing a state of emergency in Chechnya. The attempted intervention in October 1991 displayed a lack of coordination among law enforcement agencies and armed forces. Another attempt to send troops to Chechnya was made in November 1992 under the pretext of settlement of the Ossetia-Ingushetia conflict. Russian Vice-Premier Egor Gaidar managed to prevent the war at that time. But in the autumn of 1993 Moscow was preoccupied with other things and Chechnya was not on the list of priorities. They were again dividing power in Moscow.

The relationship between Moscow and Grozny stalemated. A solution could be found only at the negotiation table. Legal contradictions did not support any clear resolution between the federal centre and the separatists. Economically, the Dudayev regime did not differ much from other regions of Russia – there was no privatization, for instance. Dudayev's entire budget was used up minting Chechnya's own currency in 1994 (many other 'red belt' governors in Russia also dreamed of having their own currency). In October 1993 Dudayev congratulated Yeltsin on his victory over the Supreme Soviet – after having done away with his own parliament several months earlier. Some kind of settlement could have been reached at this time as happened in the case with the Republic of Tatarstan. But negotiations between Russia and Chechnya faded.

Meanwhile, power structures were deteriorating in Chechnya. Various armed formations acquired legal status. Crime was on the rise. This trend should have been countered. But federal enforcement agencies were going in a different direction. They were actively making use of the separatist enclave in their own interests, as a kind of 'off-shore zone' for special operations. For instance, during the war in Abkhasia Russian airborne troops and special task units (*spetsnaz*) trained Shamil Basaev's battalion.

The victory of the Communists and Zhirinovsky at the Russian parliamentary elections in December 1993 put the Chechen problem back on the federal agenda. Having suffered a defeat in their ideological confrontation with 'National-Patriots', the federal power decided to follow suit and become 'stately' – by restoring control over the mutinous province – and by so doing improve its deteriorated ratings.

The Federal plan envisaged negotiations in the context of forceful pressure and support for the anti-Dudayev opposition. But six months later special services gained control over the operation and the very concept of negotiations was forgotten. Now it was the territory of Russia that saw the formation of illegal armed detachments. The spiral of the civil war was spinning faster and faster. After an abortive assault on Grozny in November 1994, a full scale war broke out. On 11 December federal troops entered Chechnya. The rest is relatively well-known [see books on Chechnay listed on p 245].

The death toll of the first and second Chechen wars amounted to approximately 70,000 civilians and nearly 12,000 servicemen and staff of federal enforcement agencies. Exact figures are not known. Only human rights activists counted civilian casualties. Military losses are classified. The military maintain that the victory had been taken away from them by Russian politicians bribed to hamper troop operations. The three truces in the first Chechen war (in February and March 1995 and in June 1996) can be explained, as can the whole war, in terms of internal political reasons. President Yeltsin had to make an address to the state Duma, Yeltsin had to host foreign guests coming to commemorate the 50th anniversary of the Victory in the Second World War, and finally Yeltsin had to win the presidential election in July 1996. Two other alleged stolen victories (in Budennovsk in June 1995 and in Grozny in May 1996) – when some kind of peace was established for six months and three years respectively – were failures only in the sense that political leaders took responsibility for negotiating peace.

In the second war nobody was hampering the generals but the schedule of the advance into the territory of the republic was similar to that of the first war, and it cannot be said that Russia has achieved a victory.

The official point of view is that on 5 October 2003, Akhmat Kadyrov was voted president. And that had to be the end of the Chechen conflict – all the rest is irrelevant. It is hard to agree with that argument.

Free and fair elections were impossible during the conflict. There was a *de facto* state of emergency and threats of terror on the part of the 'death squads.' The election campaign itself was tuned to uphold Kadyrov. Kadyrov's real opponents – the separatists – had been withdrawn from the race. Then his serious competitors – Malik Saidullaev and Khussein Dzhabrailov – were also eliminated. The administrative resources of the Chechen government were used to support the acting president. Journalists and human rights monitors who were in Chechnya on October 5 noted a low turnout of voters. But according to the official protocols, nearly all voters participated in the election, and nearly all cast their ballots for Kadyrov. The declared number of voters was based on the 2002 census results that substantially overstated the size of the population. The Parliamentary Assembly for Cooperation in Europe (PACE) and the Organisation for Security and Cooperation in Europe (OSCE) chose not to observe the election, and the UN Human Rights Committee noted that the election did not meet relevant international standards.

However, the federal authorities assert that after 5 October Kadyrov acquired legitimate status as president of Chechnya, with the republic being one of the subjects of the Russian Federation. The future will show if the issue of Chechen separatism has been resolved in this new reality. But the armed conflict in Chechnya is not over. In Chechnya itself a roadside war goes on, clashes continue, people get killed and 'disappear.' The war is not confined to the limits of the republic – the December 2003 events in Dagestan testify to that. And explosions in a commuter train in Essentuki on 5 December, and in the Manezh Square of Moscow prove that the terrorism issue is far from being resolved.

A few months prior to the all-Russia parliamentary elections of December 2003 the Chechen problem disappeared from the front pages. It is impossible to win two elections separated by four years under the same slogan of a 'small-scale victorious war'. By 2004 it was apparent that the term 'small-scale' did not apply any more than does 'victorious'. There is a pressing need to analyze the situation in and around Chechnya, to look for a way out, to have a public debate. If we continue to hold on to a tangle of myths, rather than to Ariadne's clew, we shall never find a way out of the maze.

Chronicle of Events: December 2002 to March 2003

15 December 2002 RF president Vladimir Putin signed decrees 'On Approving Regulations for Holding a Referendum in the Chechen Republic on the Draft of the Chechen Republic Constitution, and on the Draft Laws of the Chechen Republic,' 'On Election of the president of the Chechen Republic' and 'On Elections to the Parliament of the Chechen Republic.'
kavkaz.memo.ru

23 March 2003 A referendum was held, and according to the RF Central Election Commission figures, 95.37 % of its participants voted for the draft law of the Chechen Republic 'On election of the president of the Chechen Republic.'
kavkaz.memo.ru

3 THE MARCH 2003 REFERENDUM: WHAT DIFFERENCE DID IT MAKE?

Alexander Mnatsakanyan, freelance journalist

I remember January 1995 watching federal soldiers throwing loaves of bread into a crowd of Chechen women and elders like a bone to a dog. I realized then that the objective of this war was not a matter of seizing territory or killing enemy soldiers. The key objective was to degrade the civilian population so that they become ready to accept any power – domestic, foreign, or even extraterrestrial – as long as that power ensures order, food and protection. In this regard, 23 March 2003 was the last day of the second Chechen war. The Chechen people came to vote at the referendum. And they accepted the new constitution. There wasn't any real choice.

The Chechens were cheated. There was no alternative draft constitution. There were no draft laws for electing the president and parliament. But we live in Russia. Neither the spirit nor the letter of the law is important, just the political reality. The Chechens were indoctrinated so that they seemed to believe the slogan 'referendum means peace'. Ninety-six percent voted "yes" with a 95% turnout – a surfeit of votes. An acquaintance from one of the local election commissions, reported that the instruction 'from above' was that the turnout figure should have been in the range of 75-85%. But the reported results provided support for assurances given to Moscow that voters' eagerness had exceeded all expectations. OK. At least this is almost a true statement.

But something else caused doubts – the uniform distribution of the electors' eagerness. Regarding the largest village in Chechnya – Shali – there are no questions. The inhabitants of the former domain of late field commander Aslanbek The Big (Abdul Hadjiev) filled the polling stations to overflowing. Everything is clear with regard to Urus-Martan that is historically loyal to Russia. High turnout is perfectly understandable in the Cossack villages of Naurskaya, Shelkovskaya, Znamenskoe, Isherskaya, and in the Goragorsk district – the north of the republic has always been pro-Russian. It is easy to understand the 97% in Sharoi district – there are only 1,500 local people living there and it is not them who make the turnout. Four thousand Russian soldiers are registered in the district and entitled to vote there. Small wonder that by 10 am the turnout had reached 47%. The same explanation could apply to the mysteriously high turnout of the electorate in Vedeno district that houses the second largest grouping (after Khankala) of Russian troops. There is little difficulty in explaining the 90% turnout in Grozny – voters could come from Khankala, from Kadyrov's bureaucrats hand-fed from Moscow, from police, from state security staff and their spiritual next of kin.

But the results for Nozha-Yurt, Itum-Kalinsky, Achkhoi-Martan, Kurchaloi, Argun and Sunzha districts are remarkable. Why did they vote? Did locals really vote? In order to answer such questions we either have to believe the official information, that 'life in Chechnya is getting back to normal' or we had to have visited the republic at least a week before the referendum. I did the latter.

My friends from a human rights group have shown me the data from an opinion poll conducted in the beginning of March. We cannot refer to its results officially since it has been carried out by non-professionals. But it gives an idea of the situation. In early March, 80% of recipients indicated that they did not want to participate in the referendum. In the column 'Why' we find such answers as, "If I write the truth they will pay me a call one night and spend a magazine-full of Kalashnikov on me," "We deserve only to be killed – that is the opinion and attitude of Russia." They didn't want to, but they came to polling stations nevertheless. Like Dostoyevsky's famous Sonechka Marmeladova, 'sobbing and reaching for the sky... because there was no other way.'

In a refugee tent camp a 52-year-old mathematics teacher, Khizir, from Grozny, looking up from washing his feet, stated that he would definitely participate in the referendum. "There is no choice, you understand. We need law, any law. You cannot live otherwise. It can't be any worse. Existing laws are ignored, and there is no guarantee that new ones will be observed. So what's the difference? If we vote, we have the moral right to ask why the constitution is not observed. But there should be some accord with the insurgents anyway. If there is a conflict it is essential to sit at the table and talk to your adversary."

Two or three tents further down the path an old man, Ali, is sitting. He is a refugee from Urus-Martan. Ali gets riled and his unshaven chin jerks while he is struggling with Russian words, "What referendum? Why a referendum? We haven't seen humanitarian aid for four months now. They brought some the other day but said that it is going to be distributed after the referendum. I believe they will be judging by the results. But I am an old man. You cannot scare me with famine."

Later on it seemed clear that there was no direct linkage between food and the referendum. But people in refugee camps in Chechnya have other ways of understanding things. Ten years of war develop an intuition and help master the Aesopian language. Everybody understands that if you ignore the referendum, if you fail to get registered, you may run into numerous problems. In a refugee camp the problem may consist of not getting the humanitarian aid. It may be your life that is at stake.

Indeed, life in Chechnya is getting back to normal. It is like the story of a tramp who was about to commit suicide out of desperation in a public toilet. But he found a cigarette butt on the floor and an unfinished bottle of beer on the window sill. He took a puff on the fag, took a swig of beer and thought 'Life's getting better!'

My friends from Grozny were grateful for the referendum – in the near future they will have electricity practically the whole day, unjustified quibbles at the checkpoints will stop, and maybe people will cease to disappear. The federal checkpoints turned surprisingly polite and even (a miracle!) scaled down their tariffs for passing through the maze of checkpoint concrete blocks. Mini-van taxi drivers were able to bring their fares down by 20–25%. What's more, the drivers became so bold that they started to go from Nazran in Ingushetia to Grozny directly passing through the notorious Kavkaz-1 checkpoint instead of the long road via the north of Chechnya.

But you'd be better off if you take a longer route through Goragorsk anyway. The barely navigable road is unchanged, but the checkpoints are more passable (they did not check my ID though I looked very much an easterner and wore a beard). You can see the pretentious official slogans *'The referendum means a better future for Chechnya!' 'The referendum will bring peace!'* 'We *shall all leave our homes to vote in the referendum!'* (This one is fixed on a completely empty five-storey apartment block.) There is even a witty one – *'Come to referendum, your first invitation!'*

Among those slogans we read a protest graffito alongside the Staropromyslovskoe highway: *'Ichkeria needs no Jewish referendum!'* Good God, why Jews again? What do they have to do with this? Though, if you give it a second thought... Chechens have never displayed great love towards Jewish people, and the flavour of Islamic opposition to Russia does not assume profound affection towards the children of Zion. Possibly, some disenchanted public relations worker made up his mind to place this anti-advertisement for observers and journalists to see.

In the evening, when darkness sets in, the city becomes almost quiet. People watch TV, drink tea. Sometimes they hear the explosion of a grenade launcher (later they will come to know that the target was the polling station and that the grenade did not go wide). Assault rifle bursts. Gas flares are roaring. Dogs are barking.

It became even calmer in the morning of 23 March. Grozny appeared to be deserted. There were not more than 20–30 traders in the marketplace. Practically no minivan taxis. But there were at least 10–15 gunmen from the Chechen police at each polling station.

In the centre of Grozny, near the ruins of the drama theatre, there was a block-long double line of senior citizens. Everybody was silent, they didn't shout any slogans. Each of them was holding a piece of green material inscribed with a protest against the referendum and bearing a coloured photograph. The photos looked as if they came from the files of a criminal case – corpses dismembered, corpses intact, old corpses, fresh corpses, corpses in the ground, corpses on stretchers. Sometimes the photos showed live faces – those who had just disappeared.

"There would have been more of us," says Visit Umarov from Novye Atagi, "but all the checkpoints were blocked this morning. A lot more wanted to come but they were not allowed to. My son has been missing since 8 March. In the morning, at about 11 am two UAZ jeeps entered the yard, one white, one blue, carrying a mixed team of masked Russians and Chechens. They took my son away. Jot it down: Bislan Umarov, born in 1977."

Gradually some women get involved in the conversation, "Write it down. Gikalo district was shelled on the 21st. Two women were injured, four houses destroyed." "Write it down, near Germenchuk at the checkpoint they burned a car with people last night". "Yes, on the 21st in Germenchuk they arrested the Kurbanovs, two women and two men and in our Novogroznaya two dead bodies were found, unidentified, one old, the other fresh." "In Lin Chiri-Yurt ... jot it down..." "Write down the information about Berdykel..." "Twenty people were arrested at the checkpoint near Assinovskaya."

This handful of Chechens, who do not realize how happy they are, and who face anything but a bright future, did not in any way hamper the triumph of a controlled democracy. The same day at 4 pm – that is even before the official ending of voting – the CIS observers got together in the Central Election Commission building. The head of the delegation Yuri Yarov, Executive Secretary of the CIS, noted that the presence of the military had been justified and in no way impeded the free expression of the will of the people. Everybody signed the document offered by Yarov stating that voting had been free, people were acting on their own free will and that there had been no violations. According to those present, the only problem was the lack of ballot papers because of an unexpectedly high turnout of voters at some polling stations. Who could have doubted the extent of friendly feelings of a former Soviet republic towards Russia's will?

There was a mixture of vision and blindness in the officials' observation of election behaviour. Officials saw queues for voting in deserted Grozny. They saw happy and enthusiastic people. But they somehow overlooked the fact that apart from 400 registered voters the voting booth was attended by 500 'newcomers'. They ignored the fact that a French journalist took part in the voting after he produced his French (*sic!*) passport. They did not notice that scores of people, for the sake of an experiment, were voting as 'new arrivals' at several polling stations. They failed to see a huge armed redneck standing right behind a person watching closely what he was writing on the ballot paper. I saw that with my own eyes.

The only person concerned with these irregularities and violations was the elections department head of the OSCE, Mr Balyan, who was present at the Central Election Commission meeting. He noted the presence of armed men at the polling stations. He did not miss the Chechen mothers' pickets in downtown Grozny. But he made the reservation that such things were admissible in this complex situation.

While talking to me Mr Balyan remained as diplomatic as before, "Of course the number of armed men at the polling stations was unjustifiable. But nobody was breaking up the illegal rally. It is a good political sign. We are not here to root out faults but to help the democratic process. The voting will be a success if it starts a transition from the power of arms to the power of law." Mr Balyan stated that he was in Chechnya not as an OSCE observer but in his personal capacity. The European Community distanced itself from the shame of this referendum. But it is not quite clear why civilized Europeans who are well aware of the situation do not go further. Westerners do not have a means of influencing their Russian counterparts. But each of them as an individual could at least refuse to shake hands with Putin, or what is simpler, refuse to shake hands with Rogozin.

In fact the new constitution was designed for the sake of Mr Balyan and his colleagues from the international community. Under the then valid Fundamental Law of the Chechen Republic of Ichkeria any elections must be postponed till the end of war. Maskhadov should have been regarded as the legitimate president for as long as Russian troops were present in Chechnya. Russia spent at least 70 billion roubles to deprive Maskhadov of his legitimacy. But the return on that investment may happen to be zero.

A Chechen resistance fighter whom I met in Grozny (let's call him Salaudi) is not going to lay down arms, "I do not believe those figures, and neither do you, right? And nobody does. I did vote. And many of our men voted. I voted for the constitution. I fight only at night, but in daytime I appear as a law-abiding person. They know me and if I do not vote they will ask 'why'? So should I tease them? Our votes will not change anything. Observers know that the referendum is dishonest. And Putin knows it, and Russian generals know that. But it is not 'what people know' that is important; it is 'what they do.' Mercenaries kill us, and we shall be killing them."

The most terrible thing is that Salaudi says all this without any passion, quite matter-of-factly, in a calm and descriptive way. At the end he adds, "Wasn't the Russian constitution enough for them? The Russian constitution also states that one mustn't kill, rob, torture. It is good that we have a new constitution. Now Russia needs to observe it. But it is a trap for Russia because Russia does not care about the constitution. What if we elect Maskhadov under this new constitution, or even, God forbid, Basaev? Shall we have another referendum? Even though voting means nothing to us..."

Salaudi is an intelligent person. He understands everything. And he repeats the key slogan of the Soviet dissidents without knowing it – "Observe your constitution!" Salaudi realizes that nobody cares about the voting. The referendum, presidential election, war, peace, mop-up operations, and special targeted operations – all these will happen irrespective of the will of the Chechens, be they with Kadyrov, Maskhadov or anybody else.

Chronicle of Events: 6 June to 20 August

6 June 2003. The state Duma passed a resolution declaring an amnesty in the Chechen Republic in connection with the adoption of the constitution of the republic. Eligible for the amnesty are individuals who have committed socially dangerous acts on the territory within the borders of the former Chechen-Ingush Republic from 12 December 1993 through to the day when the resolution of the amnesty declaration came into force, who have terminated their participation in the unlawful military formations or have voluntarily given up their arms and military vehicles by zero hours 1 September 2003. The amnesty was applicable both to the members of unlawful military formations and to the participants of the counter-

terrorist operations – servicemen of the Federal troops and officers of the law enforcement bodies. According to the mass media reports (Anna Politkovskaya, *Novaya Gazeta*, No 65, 'Guard of the old-timers,' etc), the pardoned offenders are being actively recruited into the security service of the acting president of the republic.
Kavkaz.memo.ru

20–25 June. 'Validata' polling service conducted a public opinion survey. To the open-ended (i.e. without any given reply options) question 'If the election of the Chechen Republic president were to be held next Sunday, who would you vote for?' The majority of the respondents gave 12 names. The following names received the biggest scores: Malik Saidullaev (20.1%), Ruslan Khasbulatov (19.2%), Aslambek Aslakhanov (17.6%), and Akhmat Kadyrov (12.5%).
kavkaz.memo.ru

4 July. President Vladimir Putin signed into law Decree No 729 'On the Election of the first president of the Chechen Republic'.
Kavkaz.memo.ru

17 July. The Public Opinion Foundation published the results of a poll showing that over 75% of Chechens intend to take part in the upcoming election.
Strana.Ru

24 July. President of the RF Vladimir Putin during his meeting with the leadership of Chechnya said that the head of the Chechen administration Akhmat Kadyrov was appointed member of Russia's delegation to the United Nations for a period of one year.
Strana.Ru

24 July. Minister of the Interior and Chairman of the Supreme Council of the United Russia Party Boris Gryzlov said that the United Russia Party decided to support Akhmat Kadyrov in the forthcoming election for the Chechen president.
Strana.Ru

25 July. President of Milan business concern, Malik Saidullaev, officially notified the Chechnya Election Commission about his decision to run for president of the republic.
Kavkaz.memo.ru

25 July. Aide to the RF president Sergei Yastrzhembsky said that the Kremlin does not and cannot run its own candidate for the Chechen president. "We hope that the winning candidate in Chechnya will enjoy the fullest possible support of the Chechen people and voters," stressed Mr Yastrzhembsky, appearing in a live broadcast of the Echo of Moscow radio station. "We do not want the legitimately elected president to be a weak president without a power base among his own people," he said. "If that happened, it would mean that the federal centre would again have to solve many problems from Moscow. The fed-

eral centre would not be able to delegate responsibilities to Grozny," he added. "It is extremely important for us that this election is held in an honest way, under normal conditions, that those individuals who are standing for the presidency are given equal opportunity to present their views inside Chechnya and that we pass this test flawlessly. It is very important that Chechnya should get a real leader capable of resolving problems, rather than a president 'with feet of clay'" stressed Mr Yastrzhembsky.
Strana.Ru

31 July. According to the Echo of Moscow radio station, the former chairman of the Supreme Soviet of Russia Ruslan Khasbulatov made a statement expressing his intention to run for the president of Chechnya.
Strana.Ru

1 August. The Chechen Republic prosecutor Vladimir Kravchenko signed a resolution advising his office to oversee legal compliance during the election campaign for the president of Chechnya. "Given the need for continuous supervision from the prosecutor's office over compliance with the requirements of the decree of the RF president on the election of the Chechen president, all the officers of the prosecutor's office will be advised to provide necessary legal assistance to the electoral commissions of all levels, to take part in the meetings of those commissions and to work at the polling stations," said Mr Kravchenko. "The prosecutors will check the legitimacy of decisions for their compliance with the federal election legislation and the law of the republic, and will take the measures available to the prosecutor's office if any violations are identified," explained Mr Kravchenko.
Strana.Ru

4 August 2003. The acting president of the Chechen Republic Akhmat Kadyrov officially notified the Chechnya Election Commission about his decision to run for president of the republic. A day earlier Mr Kadyrov had made a statement to that effect in his 'native' village Tsentoroi of Gudermes district. Mr Kadyrov's statement was delivered at a meeting that brought together several hundred Chechen religious leaders, as well as Muslim leaders from the neighbouring regions of the North Caucasus. Mr Kadyrov stressed that he considers himself to be "called by the Almighty and by the people to finish the process of Chechnya's revival, to uproot the causes of the crisis that continue to claim the lives of innocent citizens".
Strana.Ru

5 August 2003. The acting president of the Chechen Republic Akhmat Kadyrov, who on 3 August publicly announced his decision to run for president of the republic, took leave from office for the period of the election campaign and signed a decree appointing the chairman of the Chechen Republic cabinet Anatoly Popov as temporary acting president of the Chechen Republic for the period of the election campaign.
Kavkaz.memo.ru

On 5 August 2003 the body of a local resident, Akhmed Khamidovich Dzhamaldaev, born 1958, was found with multiple wounds on the field of the Ataginsky state farm in the village of Starye Atagi of Grozny rural district. He had worked as a watchman guarding the state farm's fields. After examining the body and the place where the man died the local residents came to the following conclusion: Dzhamaldaev found an object he had never seen before (probably it was a mine), took the object and knocked on it with a hammer, as a result of which the object exploded in his hands (the remnants of the object remained on the dead man's hands). Dzhamaldaev's relatives took pictures of the dead man and the place where he died. Next day Dzhamaldaev was buried in the village cemetery.
Memorial Human Rights Centre

6 August. Akhmat Kadyrov stated that the future Chechen president should unite the Chechen people that have been plagued by conflicts for a long time. "The message of bringing unity to the Chechen people and peace to the republic has become the key message of my campaign. I will come out with this message to the voters during the campaign meetings due to start across Chechnya in the nearest future," he stressed.
Strana.Ru

6 August. Chairman of the cabinet and temporary acting president of Chechnya Anatoly Popov addressing a meeting of the members of the republic's cabinet of ministers and heads of local administrations stated, "The president of the Russian Federation assigned us a mission to hold a democratic election in Chechnya and to elect a worthy, courageous, brave and respected leader who would be capable of leading the republic in this difficult time. I'm sure we will accomplish that mission."
Strana.Ru

7 August. Presidential candidate Malik Saidullaev stated in Moscow that all candidates running for the president of Chechnya are willing to put up a joint front in their election campaign against Akhmat Kadyrov. Mr Saidullaev said further that he had met practically all the presidential contenders as well as "those candidates who have not yet been registered." He mentioned in particular Beslan Gantamirov and Ruslan Khasbulatov. "One of us is bound to go into the second round," said the businessman confidently. "We have agreed that we will throw our weight in the run-off behind whatever candidate besides Kadyrov gets the most votes. It may so happen that we will come to realize that it is impossible to win the current election in an honest way. In that case we agreed that we will make a joint statement and step out of the election process, because we will consider the election campaign invalid," said Mr Saidullaev. In his view, in order to hold an honest election, it is necessary to bring in as many international observers as possible. "No effort shall be spared to make the election in Chechnya truly democratic," stated Mr Saidullaev. He believes that all the people in Chechnya are for holding elections, including those, who are in illegal military formations. "They do not spend their time only in the mountains; they also

live in towns and villages and they will go to the polls," said Mr Saidullaev, answering journalists' questions.
Strana.Ru

On 8 August, in daytime, the servicemen stationed on the territory of a former mill opened fire at a Zhiguli car with three village residents, when the car was entering the village of Starye Atagi of the Grozny rural district. As a result Khjasan Samrailovich Sanarbekov, 45 years old, was seriously wounded and subsequently died. Local residents described the incident as follows. In the afternoon Sanarbekov and two other villagers were coming home in a Zhiguli car (the licence number is unknown). Sanarbekov was sitting in the rear of the car. When the car went through the 'snail' and passed the commandant's office the soldiers fired several shots in the air. The car stopped and the driver got out, but the soldiers waved them on.

The military commandant's office is located on the outskirts of the village where a mill used to be. About a year before, the commandant's office was in the village itself but after it was fired at several times at night, it was relocated to the mill on the outskirts of the village. On the road which passes by the mill they laid concrete blocks, a so-called 'snail,' to cause cars to slow down, but there is no stationary checkpoint as such.

When the car was approaching the first bridge (approximately 500 m from the soldiers) several shots were fired at the car from the mill and Sanarbekov was seriously wounded. His two friends tried to take him to the village hospital but Sanarbekov died before they got there. According to the residents of the village the military deny their involvement in the incident saying that no shots were fired from their territory. The prosecutor of the Grozny rural district came to the place of the incident but it is not known if a criminal case has been opened. Khjasan Sanarbekov's death left three children orphaned.

Residents of Starye Atagi complain that in the evenings (when people are coming home from the city) the military come out to the road and, under the pretext of checking documents, hold up cars causing long lines of cars to form. This so-called document checking lasts for an hour and a half and it is carried out regularly, particularly after the killing of Anzor Bashirov in the village (the villagers say that he was an FSB officer).
Memorial Human Rights Centre

9 August. The Vesti Respubliki newspaper published the prices charged by the state TV and Radio Company of Chechnya for the production and placement of the election advertising in television and radio broadcasts. Production of a three-minute advert on the local television – 15,000 roubles; the same length spot on the radio – 11,500 roubles; organisation of a 'round table discussion' with the participation of two or more candidates – 2,500 roubles per minute on the air. In the first ten days of the election campaign one minute of TV prime time broadcasting in the evening will cost just 3,500 roubles, while the last pre-

election day the price will rise to 6,000 roubles. (The current rouble to $ rate was approximately 29:1.)
Strana.Ru

11 August. The Minister of the Press, Information and Mass Media of Chechnya, Beslan Gantamirov said his ministry will provide equal opportunities for campaign advertising to all presidential candidates. "We will work in the campaign period in strict compliance with the laws 'On the Mass Media' and 'On the Election of the president of the Chechen Republic.' All candidates regardless of their political views or party affiliation will be offered equal conditions, space in the printed media, and airtime," said Gantamirov.
Strana.Ru

12 August. Shamil Buraev, resident of the village of Achkhoi-Martan, notified the Chechnya Election Commission about his decision to run for president of the republic. In June 2003 Mr Buraev was relieved of his duties as head of administration of Achkhoi-Martan district.
Strana.Ru

13 August. State Duma deputy of the RF Aslambek Aslakhanov made public his decision to run for the president of Chechnya.
Strana.Ru

14 August. The Minister of the Press of Chechnya, Beslan Gantamirov, made a statement at a press conference in Moscow saying that he will take an active part in the election campaign by "backing the candidacy of Khussein Dzhabrailov."
Strana.Ru

14 August. The temporary acting president of the republic Anatoly Popov stated at a press conference in Moscow that "the election in Chechnya will be the fairest among all the regions of the Russian Federation ... According to the law on the mass media, the campaign for the president of the republic will start on 5 September," explained Mr Popov. "All the candidates will have equal opportunities. First, we will hold a draw and then distribute the space in the printed media and free airtime."
Strana.Ru

20 August 2003. The Chechnya Election Commission closed the period of accepting registration documents from candidates for president of the republic. The required number of petitions has been submitted to the commission by the following candidates:
Akhmat Kadyrov, head of the Chechen Republic administration;
Malik Saidullaev, businessman;
Khussein Dzhabrailov, first deputy general director of the Russia Hotel (Moscow);
Avkhat Khanchukaev, professor at Grozny University;
Kudus Saduev, deputy general director of the open joint stock company Grozneftegaz;
Shamil Buraev, ex-head of the Achkhoi-Martan district administration;

Said-Selim Tsuev, colonel, deputy military commandant of Chechnya;
Zaindy Movlatov, ex-army;
Ruslan Zarkiyev, journalist of a local newsletter Svoboda.
Election security deposit has been made by the following candidates:
Aslambek Aslakhanov, state Duma deputy of the RF;
Khussein Biybulatov, former deputy prime minister of Chechnya.
Strana.Ru

In the night of 20 August 2003 several of Grozny have seen pogroms staged by unidentified people dressed in camouflage uniforms and masks. According to the deputy Chechen minister of interior Sultan Satuyev, "late in the night they broke into houses, battered members of the families and loudly vowed that they would kill them if they didn't vote for Akhmat Kadyrov at the polls." An investigation has been opened for the purpose of identification and apprehension of the offenders. But the authorities called the incident a pre-planned provocation against the acting president of Chechnya Akhmat Kadyrov. Kadyrov went on record with a rhetorical question, "Do you believe that I am such a fool as to urge my supporters to break into people's homes and batter them saying 'we are Mr Kadyrov's people and we will kill if you vote for another candidate?" The provocation label given by the authorities is scarcely credible and Kadyrov's elliptical response is hardly relevant. 'Mr Kadyrov's people' have become notorious throughout the republic by their arbitrary aggression. The claim of provocation points to methods that are reminiscent of the communist era.
INTERFAX; Polit.Ru

20 August. The official representative of the Regional HQs of the counter-terrorist operation in the North Caucasus, Iliya Shabalkin, made a statement, saying that Aslan Maskhadov has received 3 million dollars "from abroad" to disrupt the upcoming 5 October presidential election in Chechnya. "According to the evidence received from detained militants," said Mr Shabalkin, "this 'task-oriented tranche' will be used to organize terrorists and sabotage acts against civilian objects and the innocent population."
Strana.RU

4 FIVE CANDIDATES FOR THE PRESIDENCY: BIYBULATOV, BUGAEV, BURAEV, KADYROV AND KHANCHUKAEV

CANDIDATE KHUSEIN GEZIHADJIEVICH BIYBULATOV

Interviewed by Roman Rostov, kavkaz.memo.ru

Khusein Gezihadjievich, would you tell us a little about yourself ?

I was born on 21 March 1939 in the village of Tsotsi-Yurt in the Kurchali district of the Chechen-Ingush Autonomous Soviet Socialist Republic (CIASSR). I am a graduate of the Rostov Finance and Economic Institute, the All-Union Correspondence Food Industry Institute, and the Academy of Social Sciences. My first job was at the Argun sugar refinery. Then I worked at the Djalka state farm in the village of Shali. I was First Secretary of the Nozhai-Yurt CPSU District Committee. I was elected deputy of the Chechen-Ingush republic twice and was Deputy Chairman of the Council of Ministers and of the CIASSR state Planning Committee Chairman.

I held leading positions in the CIASSR and in the Russian government. In 1996-1997 I was Co-Chairman of the Russian-Chechen Joint Commission for Political Adjustment of Relationships between the Russian Federation and the Chechen Republic. I am a candidate of economic science. I was awarded a medal for Military Valour.

Why did you decide to propose yourself as candidate for the republic's presidency?

Recently a label has been stuck on the Chechens – that we solve everything through power and money, illegal money. I want to prove to the world our people solve everything by intelligence. The Chechens are not stupid. I will give you an example. In Soviet times 75% of Chechens applying for postgraduate studies succeeded, while the proportion for other regions barely exceeded 50%. I hope to prove to the entire world that money does not settle everything and the label stuck on us when the so-called *zhelezniki* won in 1991 is just a myth. There are a lot of politically literate people among the Chechens, worthy patriots of the nation, who can make a considered choice. That is probably the main reason for me to stand for the presidency.

Let me remind you that none of the politically literate people had a chance in 1991, in 1995, or, most recently, in 1997. The election campaigns were conducted for just one man, who, unfortunately, was well armed.

Who are your voters? Who will vote for you?

My voters are all the Chechen people. And I do not divide my people into peaceful and not peaceful. I try to solve the problem of peace in Chechnya only by peaceful means. We have been trying to bring peace back to Chechnya by force for ten years. But time has shown that we can't get what we want by force. If we keep setting the Chechens against each other, the war will last another twenty years. My programme differs from the programmes of those who think that peace can be brought to Chechen only with guns in their hands.

How do you evaluate the current situation in the Chechen Republic: the 'Chechnya-Ichkeria' dilemma and the situation with the opposition? Does it influence the situation in the republic?

Of course it influences the situation. Those who struggle for Chechnya's independence with guns in their hands are certainly not right. We have to have political struggle, not for independence, but for normal coexistence. Russia is a very rich country with two-thirds of world natural resources on its territory. We can live well at peace with Russia. I am an economist and I have confidence in what I say. I try to convince those who call themselves 'fighters for independence' of this.

If you win the election, what will be your first steps?

I have no doubts about my victory. I think 65 to 75% of the republic's population will support my candidacy. The first step will be to establish peace. Negotiations are essential so that people will give up their weapons. I hold that only legitimate police should be armed. Everybody wants to live in peace. Those who want to work will work. Let those who want to study do so. The economic restoration of the republic can be started only after all these things.

Who do you consider to be your principal rival in the election struggle?

Akhmat Kadyrov. And Abdula Bugaev to some extent.

What is your attitude to the events of the last ten years?

I think international military aggression was committed in Russia. The aim of it was to undermine the economic and military strength of Russia and Islam. Huge money was allotted for it. Everybody has known for a long time who finances such activities.

A plan and scenario on how to weaken Russia were worked out long ago. So-called Wahhabi cells were established. And we are seeing the result today. I have been researching this matter for some time. My report is to be published shortly. I have been a participant in developments since 1 November 1994. They all have taken place before my own eyes. I was a member of Dudayev's government, and of Yandarbiev's. I know all the ins and outs of this war, and it has no relation to independence or to Islam.

How is your election campaign going? Have there been any difficulties and surprises in the course of it?

Unfortunately, yes. I can communicate with my voters only through the media: TV, radio, and papers. I have no other means. People are afraid to go to meetings because there are so many armed people about. Only Kadyrov can meet with voters. As for the mass media, there have been setbacks. My speeches were taken off the air twice.

What was the reason for it?

They said I had been sharply critical of the situation in the Chechen Republic. I consider some of the powers-that-be were playing their dirty tricks.

Khusein Gezihadjievich, thank you for your interview. We wish you good luck in the forthcoming election.

CANDIDATE ABDULA MAKHMUDOVICH BUGAEV

Interview by Ruslan Umarov, kavkaz.memo.ru

Would you tell us a bit about yourself?

I am Bugaev Abdula Makhmudovich, born in Chechnya in 1949. I graduated with honours from the historical faculty of the Chechen-Ingush State University in 1973. I am married with a son and a daughter.

From 1967 to 1969 I worked in the system of consumer cooperation of the Chechen-Ingush Autonomous Soviet Socialist Republic (CIASSR). From 1978 to 1990 I was a lecturer at the Chechen-Ingush State University. From 1990 to 1991 I was a deputy of the CIASSR and chairman of the Standing Commission for Nationalities and Inter-ethnic Relations of the CIASSR Supreme Council.

From 1995 to 1996 I was first deputy chairman of the government of the Chechen Republic and in 1996 became Deputy of the National Assembly of the Chechen Republic. From 1997 to 2000 I worked in the commercial sector, and from June 2000 to February 2001 became First Deputy head of the administration of the Chechen Republic.

Why did you decide to stand as a candidate for the presidency?

In order to use my knowledge and experience to achieve peace and happiness in Chechnya.

Who are your voters?

The intelligentsia, political sympathisers, my contemporaries ... all those who care for peace, lawfulness, and the spiritual in Chechnya.

How do you evaluate the 'Chechnya-Ichkeria' dilemma, the state of the opposition and its influence on the current situation? How much does official information presented by the central media differ from the real state of affairs in the republic (your view and the view of the media)?

The 'Chechnya-Ichkeria' dilemma as such does not exist for me. The situation requires responses that meet political realities. It is obvious to me (it was and it still is) that the division between Chechnya and Inguishetia is short-sighted, to put it mildly. Unfortunately, as is well-known, the divide and rule principle prevailed.

That stage is over. Opposition to Russia is a serious force influencing the situation in the republic. But the information presented by the national media (with rare exceptions) does not give a picture of the real state of affairs in Chechnya. Not everything is as smooth as seen from the outside. Only the surface is presented. There is a need for thorough analysis of the situation and its multi-dimensional components.

What will be your first steps if you win?

Pacification of the situation. Peace in Chechnya is not just a condition without war. Achieving peace in 'post-war' Chechnya is a bigger job. And it can be achieved without outside interference.

The Chechen people need to persuade the federal centre (make them understand – if you want) that the need for PEACE is imperative. The next step is to realise peacemaking potential by national diplomacy...

Can you say a little about your election programme? What, in your opinion, will be the results of its realization in the republic?

My programme is the achievement of a settled peace. The rule of law – the dictatorship of the law. The restoration of the economy and social sphere – not federal targeted programmes, but short-range programmes to resolve immediate and urgent problems. The revival of spirituality and morality.

Who do you consider to be your main competitor?

Voters' passivity. The disillusion and political apathy resulting from the cleansing operations ('zachistok'). The contenders for the post of the president.

Large scale extra-legal use of administrative resources in favour of Akhmat Kadyrov.

How do you estimate your odds for success?

They are good enough.

What features of your election campaign, in your opinion, will help you to win?

It is not excessively ambitious or pretentious.

How do you estimate the present election campaigns of the other candidates?

They vary in direction but none is particularly striking.

Do you believe the votes will be fairly counted?

There are serious worries, not unfounded, that district administrations will use unfair methods to proclaim Kadyrov president of Chechnya on 6 October.

What is your attitude towards the counter-terrorist operation? Has it changed since it began?

I regret that appropriate constitutional order has not been established in the Chechen Republic as a result of the counter-terrorist operation.

How is your election campaign going? Are you meeting difficulties and surprises?

The serious difficulty is that the administration of the Chechen Republic, with the obvious support of the federal centre, is ranged against the modest efforts of most of the candidates, including me, and is indifferent to human rights organisations.

CANDIDATE SHAMIL DOUSSIYEVICH BURAEV

Searched for by Tanya Lokshina, Moscow Helsinki Group/Centre 'Demos'

Getting ready for a trip to Chechnya, I told my colleagues that I wanted to visit the headquarters of the candidates for president. I received all kinds of advice. "Try to find candidate Khanchukaev – he is someone on the faculty of the University of Grozny, but nobody knows anything much about him". "Visit Kadyrov's headquarters for the sake of objectivity". "The most interesting characters are Bugaev and Buraev. Especially Shamil Buraev – he is supposed to be in the opposition. On the other hand, it won't be a problem to meet up with Bugaev, but Buraev is a different story. You'd be crazy to go all the way to Achkhoi-Martan..."

Achkhoi-Martan is exactly where I ended up. I wouldn't have risked going by myself but some friendly people offered to take me there, and the rest of my itinerary proved to be a letdown. For starters Khanchukaev could not be found anywhere in Grozny University. The administration said that he was based in Building No 3 in the biochemistry department. They had no idea that he was running for president. And generally, they could not tell me anything significant about him. The visit to Building No 3 did not yield any results – Khanchukaev was not there at the time.

In Kadyrov's headquarters there was also no luck. The public relations interest was sacrificed to the needs of security and counter-terrorism. My ID documents were not picturesque enough. Kadyrov's staff would not let me in without more impressive papers. And candidate Bugaev was travelling and his HQ personnel could not be located. They seem to have gone underground, and they could not be located. Disappointed by these barren developments, I was very happy to be given a ride to the headquarters of Shamil Buraev. Indeed, it was an offer impossible to resist.

As we entered Achkhoi-Martan, election posters and banners became visible *'Shamil Buraev is our president!'* *'Honour and dignity – Shamil Buraev.'* Just words without pictures and with little variety – but plentiful. Headquarters. Fence. Inner yard. A few security guards. I am taken into the house – a hybrid of a reception area and a small conference hall. Five men enter – four in suits, one wearing a high sheep hat. They sit down, forming a semi-circle. Lord, which of them is the candidate? It turns out – none of them!

The candidate himself has gone to Moscow to give a press conference at the Interfax Agency. But the headquarters officials are at my service and willing to provide information. The chief of the headquarters Uvais Elzhiev is here as well as three authorized representatives of the candidate and the local iman (spiritual leader).

The first authorized representative takes the floor. "This is not an election, but a ball game with only one goal. All of the mass media campaign for Kadyrov, the political parties in Chechnya, especially United Russia and SPS, campaign for Kadyrov. Shamil Buraev has filed a lawsuit to the Supreme Court for infringement of the campaign rules and usage of administrative resources by Kadyrov. But the proceedings are delayed without reason being given. Shamil Buraev personally has been told that nothing will be decided before 10 October, when the election is already over. Furthermore, Buraev, who was always the guardian of peace in Achkhoi-Martan [incidentally, in the previous couple of days different people told me that Shamil Buraev is not popular in the district], was relieved of his duties as the chief of the district in the summer of 2003. All election centres were disbanded and reoccupied by persons, who have family ties to the new, pro-Kadyrov chief of the administration." etc. etc.

At the end of his monologue, the orator chops the air with his hand and proclaims, "You know what the locals say here in Achkhoi-Martan? Let them even bring a Negro! We, they claim, will vote for a Negro and for anyone, as long as it's not Kadyrov!" His gaze is burning, searching for compassion. I nod gravely, trying to keep a poker face. Indeed, poor people – what must they endure...

After this, all those present have their say, strictly turn by turn. They don't interrupt each other. And all speakers tell more or less the same story.

The iman brings a breath of fresh air into this verbal rondo. He speaks in Chechen and for the first couple of minutes I pleadingly look at those present for a volunteer translator. A volunteer is swiftly found. I cannot be sure that the translation is adequate, but he speaks about Kadyrov, Shamil Buraev and Wahhabism.

"As a spiritual leader of the district, I state that if Kadyrov remains in power, then he will breed Wahhabis of a kind that this district has never seen before. We, the clergy of the district, collaborate with the headquarters of Shamil Buraev; we have a specific programme, and we teach traditional Islam and oppose the spread of Wahhabism and of Wahhabist literature. But the realization of our programme is hindered by the mufti of Chechnya and the administration of Kadyrov. We are in negotiations with the insurgents. We have agreements with many rebels that they will put down their weapons if Kadyrov leaves".

The issue of relations with the rebels is picked up by the final speaker – another authorized representative of Shamil Buraev. "Our main goal is the unification of the Chechen people through the creation of employment. The youth would come back home and would live peacefully if they had employment."

In conclusion, the authorized representative repeats the already voiced metaphor about a ball game with only one goal, points out that one candidate is being forced on the people, and adds that the situation with Maskhadov in 1997 was the same. He looks to me expectantly as if for some sign of approval. It seems to me that the situation with Maskhadov was somewhat different, in fact vastly different, and the 1997 elections don't even come close to this colourful performance...

But my head is already spinning, so I change the topic to stay on the safe side, and ask, as if incidentally, "You sent out announcements that on the 13 September, last Saturday, Shamil Buraev held a meeting with the electorate and 10 to 15 thousand people were expected. How did it turn out? Did a lot of people come?" Of course this is a trick question, it is known from reliable sources – I asked around – that the meeting indeed took place, but the mighty masses of Buraev's supporters never arrived. The authorized representative excitedly raises his voice, "Indeed there was a meeting with the electorate. It was a great meeting. Ten thousand people came. And you know what the people from everywhere – from Naur, from Nadterechny – are saying? Let him even be a Jew! We'll vote for a Jew, as long as it's not for Kadyrov!"

On this pinnacle of racial and ethnic tolerance I parted with the representatives of the headquarters and started my return journey, recalling a punch line to a long forgotten joke. "Poor thing. Not only is he a Negro, but a Jew as well…". Our country remains only too Soviet, ladies and gentlemen!

A personal file on Shamil Buraev, a candidate for president of the Chechen Republic

Shamil Buraev was born on 28 January 1958 in the village Achkhoi-Martan of the Achkhoi-Martan district of the Chechen-Ingush Autonomous SSR. In 1974 he completed secondary school in the Achkhoi-Martan district. In the same year, he enrolled in the State Agricultural University, which he completed in 1981, having specialized as a zoological technician. For more than 10 years he worked in agricultural production in the Achkhoi-Martan district. In the beginning of the 90s, he successfully began activities as an entrepreneur in Moscow. In the period between 1995 to 1997 and 1999 to 2003 he held the position of the head of the administration of the Achkhoi-Martan district. He was decorated with an Order of Courage on 5 June 2000 by the order of the president of the Russian Federation. Under his management, in 2001 the workers of the Achkhoi-Martan district held first place in agriculture throughout the republic, in 2002 first place in the improvement and the replanting of the area and second place in agriculture, as well as first place in the organisation of the relocation of the population. Relieved of duty from his position in 2003 by the order of Kadyrov, acting president of Chechnya, Shamil Buraev is enrolled in a distance learning division of the Russian Academy of government Service specialising in regional management. Married with three children.

(from kavkaz.memo.ru)

CANDIDATE AKHMAT ABDULKHAMIDOVICH KADYROV

Interview by Ruslan Umarov, kavkaz.memo.ru

Akhmat Abdulkhamidovich, why did you decide to nominate yourself as candidate for the Presidency of the Chechen Republic?

It was not an easy decision for me. I am not too excited to be placed in the thick of these tragic events. But it was me who generated the line of opposition to the thugs, terrorists and religious extremists. I initiated this fight long ago and if I refused to participate in the election, I would fail all those who counted on me, followed me and believed in the possibility of restoring order in the republic.

Our people voted for unity with Russia, for the territorial integrity of Russia and for a peaceful, stable and safe life. People believed me. I could not fail them. At the meeting of elders who came to Tsentoroi from all parts of the Chechen Republic I was asked to run for the presidency. Their main concern was to bring an end to banditry, terrorism and religious extremism and restore peaceful, stable and secure life in Chechnya. And they promised to support me. The people of Chechnya are tired of arbitrary rule.

Who are your voters?

My voters are first and foremost the people of the Chechen Republic who encourage and support all my initiatives. The referendum confirmed that. My thoughts and cares coincide completely with the aspirations of ordinary people and it cannot be any other way. I come from a religious family. None of my relatives ever occupied high posts. I come from the people myself; I am well aware of how people live, what they think and what they dream about.

I meet with different sections of the population – farmers, workers, intelligentsia, youth, retired people, office employees, teachers, doctors and I always find their support. They are my voters.

What is your perception of the current situation in Chechnya: the dilemma of Chechnya-Ichkeria and the situation with the opposition and its effect on the current situation? To what extent does the information presented in mass media correspond to the real situation in the republic?

The situation in the republic still remains difficult. I have expressed my concerns about the disappearance of civilians in Chechnya in letters to the heads of the federal law enforcement ministries and to the office of the general prosecutor of Russia. Unidentifiable people in camouflage carry out raids on peaceful residents. Their relatives fail to find out what has happened to them. This is a highly destabilizing factor. Currently we are planning to implement several measures to put an end to that. These raids hurt the republic and hurt me.

As far as the Chechnya-Ichkeria dilemma is concerned, the March referendum gave a clear answer to this question. The Chechen Republic is a constituent part of the Russian Federation. Chechens voted for unity with Russia. That is the story. Unity with Russia is the will of the Chechen people.

Information presented by journalists in central mass media differs. Those who pay the costs of publishing newspapers and supporting TV and radio companies set the tone of these publications. Some media (I do not want to mention names) tend to highlight the events in Chechnya only in dark colours presenting only a negative perspective; others try to be more objective adding some light colours. But life does not consist of just two colours, it is diverse and multicoloured.

What real steps will you implement in case of your victory?

I will be involved in the same activities as before, establishing peace in Chechnya and restoring economic and social activities. I will be implementing the political processes leading to peaceful solutions in Chechnya. The president of Russia, Vladimir Putin, fully supports me.

Tell us about your election programme. Is it possible to realize it?

My election programme is realistic, but comes from the hopes and aspirations of the people. It is not huge and has three main themes. By the way, I wrote about these in my recent dissertation on the settlement of Russian-Chechen relations. Three main points of the peace settlement are stressed in the dissertation and in the programme. First, we are a part of Russia and have to have trust in the federal centre. Second, there must be reconstruction of all economic and social institutions with financial and material support from the federal centre. Third, all our natural resources, including oil, must be at the disposal of the republic so that we can in part use our own resources in the process of economic and social reconstruction.

I reminded Mr Kasyanov, Chair of the Russian government, about this once again, and also asked for economic, financial, tax and other privileges. If Moscow does not provide this and continues to finance the reconstruction work in the republic at existing levels the republic cannot be restored from the ruins in the short run. I expressed this directly to Mr Putin and Mr Kasyanov, and they assured me that privileges would be granted. As far as the question of distribution of powers between the Russian Federation and the Chechen Republic is concerned, a specific person responsible for these matters has been appointed in the administration of the RF president, so this issue will be solved.

Who you consider to be your main rival?

Nobody. I see only one candidate for the presidency of the Chechen Republic – Kadyrov. Today a weak leader cannot gain a firm hold in the republic. One needs here a person, who, when necessary, is courageous enough to stand against armed thugs.

We have been living by the law of the jungle for 11 years – the law of the wolf pack, where the strong unmercifully suppress the weak and the unprotected. Unfortunately, we all got used to it. Now we need someone who can take responsibility to call people to order and follow accepted norms of behaviour. He has to have a sober head and pure thoughts. That implies that he has to take decisions thoughtfully, not in a hurry, be sensible and kind, but at the same time when necessary and when it comes to violations and crimes, he should be able to show determination and firmness.

I do not know of any other person who can fulfil these responsibilities. When registering as a candidate with the Election Commission, I said that I would give up my intentions to stand for the presidency if such a leader appeared and the people supported him. If such a leader appeared I would support him myself.

How do you estimate your chances for success?

The people want a peaceful, stable and secure life. I want the same. The election is our historical chance. I trust my people. And I will abide with their choice.

Which distinctive features of your election campaign will help you to win?

I have already given an answer to this question. I come from the core of my people. I know my people's pain, hopes and aspirations. The people take me as I am – I never left the republic; all my family stayed in Chechnya during the military action. The people see and appreciate it. I know what should be done and how to do it. And my main task is the security of the people, the revival of the Republic, the wealth of my nation. These are the key points of my programme.

What do you think about the election campaign of other candidates?

I said from the beginning: equal conditions and equal opportunities should be created for everybody. I always follow this principle.

Do you expect a fair count vote calculation?

I do not think it can be any other way. I trust the members of the territory and district level election commissions. I trust the management of the Chechnya Election Commission. And hundreds of monitors will observe the voting. So I do not think there will be foul play.

What is your attitude to the counter-terrorist operation? Has it changed over the time?

I take your point. My attitude to the counter-terrorist operation was always straightforward and has never changed. When illegal formations of Khattab and Basaev invaded Dagestan, I was the first to voice a protest against it. Terrorism, thuggery and religious extremism have no nationality. We have to combat this evil. The other thing is that we have to do it without endangering the lives of the peaceful population.

Have you faced any difficulties or surprises during your electoral campaign?

Difficulties and surprises are everywhere. All our life consists of them. Especially in Chechnya. But I have got used to solving difficult problems, so it is not new for me. I am aware that I endanger my relatives, friends and my supporters by announcing uncompromising war against terrorism, thuggery and religious extremism. But it is not possible to establish a peaceful, stable and secure life in Chechnya without it. And this is what I want for my suffering people – a peaceful, stable and secure life. And, if the Almighty is willing, we'll get our way.

Biography – Akhmat Kadyrov

Akhmat Kadyrov, Head of administration of the Chechen Republic, former mufti of Chechnya.

Born in 1951 in Khazakhstan, with the family coming from the village of Tsentoroi of the Kurchaloi district of Chechnya. Comes from a religious family, his father and five uncles are religious figures. Comes from the Benoi teip (the largest teip or Chechen tribe). Is a representative of the most widespread vird (religious brotherhood) of Kuntahadji of the Sufi Kadiri Order. In 1980 the district administration of Gudermes sent him to study at the Bukhara Miri-Arab Madrasah where he graduated. In Bukhara he studied with the present chairman of the Board of Russian Mufti, Ravil Gainutdin. Later Kadyrov graduated from the Islamic institute in Tashkent.

Kadyrov became deputy iman [spiritual leader] of Gudermes. In 1989 Kadyrov initiated the creation of the Islamic Institute of Northern Caucasus in the village of Kurchaloi (founded in 1991), and headed the institute till 1994. In 1990–1991 Kadyrov studied at the Shariat faculty of the Jordan University. He returned to Chechnya after the declaration of independence by the republic in autumn 1991, and became an active figure of the religious office (Muftiat) becoming deputy mufti of Chechnya under Arsanukayev.

In 1994 Arsanukayev went abroad (for medical treatment), and Kadyrov took up his post. In 1994 Kadyrov took part in the war against federal forces on the side of the Chechen fighters. When Arsanukayev refused to back jihad, radical Chechen leaders decided to replace him. The congress of 1995, organized with the participation of the Alims of five highland districts of Chechnya and field commanders Basaev, Yandarbiev and Maskhadov, elected Kadyrov the mufti of Chechnya. There were no other candidates for the post since Kadyrov was the only eligible person who backed the idea of jihad. Since he was not a legitimately elected mufti, he was regarded as a sort of 'war mufti.' With the support of field commanders he organized an extensive campaign against the mullahs of Arsanukayev's muftiat.

Kadyrov participated in negotiations between Aslan Maskhadov and Alexander Lebed in Novye Atagi in August 1996. In 1996 Kadyrov convened a congress of Alims in Grozny and suggested that they should elect a different mufti (because he regarded himself as a war leader in religion), but the Alims elected him again. Kadyrov actively supported Aslan Maskhadov, standing for struggle against religious extremists and demanding a ban on Wahhabism.

Since 1997 two unsuccessful assassination attempts have been directed against him. According to the Kommersant-Vlast weekly, he took part in an attempted coup in Chechnya on the wave of anti-Wahhabi feelings in June 1999. A secret meeting attended by all the heads of the Ichkeria law enforcement agencies elected Kadyrov to be a war amir. According to Shariat, the war amir was to replace the secular president. But Magomed Khambiev, the commander of National Guards, and Aidamir Abalayev, the Minister of Internal Affairs, remained loyal to Maskhadov, and the coup failed.

Kadyrov denounced the incursions of field commanders Basaev and Khattab into Dagestan and demanded that Maskhadov declare them to be outlaws. In August 1999 Maskhadov's decree dismissed him from the post of mufti but Kadyrov did not accept that decree. In September 1999 he declared his insubordination to the president of Ichkeria and his readiness to support the counter-terrorist operation of federal forces. In October 1999 Kadyrov, together with the field commander brothers Yamadaev, declared the Gudermes and Kurchaloi districts to be a "territory free from Wahhabis". The Yamadaev brothers and Kadyrov played a crucial part in the peaceful transfer of control over Gudermes and most villages of the Gudermes and Kurchaloi districts to Russian forces.

In November 1999 the Russian government regarded him as an alternative to Maskhadov in negotiations with the Chechen Republic. On 30 November 1999 the Board of Muftis of Russia asked the government of the Russian Federation to protect the Chechen Mufti who had been called an enemy of his nation by Aslan Maskhadov on 28 November. On 15 March 2000 Kadyrov supported the introduction of direct presidential rule in Chechnya to last for one or two years, "after which there ought to be an election of the president of the republic." As for the head of the republic, Kadyrov said that "the leader is to be a Chechen who has been living in Chechnya and lives there now. As for those, who watched the developments on TV from Moscow, let them go on watching it." As for his own candidacy, the mufti said without false modesty that "he will take up this job. I will take it up for the sake of my people in order to put an end to the outrages."

On 12 June 2000 Kadyrov was appointed the head of the administration of the Chechen Republic. He planned to resign from the post of the mufti in connection with this appointment. Only three heads of 18 Chechen districts supported Kadyrov's appointment. Soon after this appointment the heads of 12 Chechen districts sent an appeal to president Putin asking him to dismiss Kadyrov. The letter, signed by 44 members of the interim Chechen administration, claimed that it was impossible for them to cooperate with the former jihad leader.

Kadyrov's ceremony of inauguration was delayed twice (16 and 19 June) as Kadyrov refused to come to Gudermes if his authority was not presented to him in person by Viktor Kazantsev, the representative of the Russian president in the Northern Caucasus. The ceremony took place only on 20 June. On 22 August 2000, Kadyrov resigned from the post of the Chechen mufti when Akhmat Shamayev was elected to this post.

In September 2000 Kadyrov visited the USA where he participated in the work of the World Forum of Religious and Spiritual Leaders.

On 31 October 2000 Kadyrov's escort came under shelling from federal forces. In January 2001 Kadyrov proposed a withdrawal of forces from Chechnya on the grounds that the "military phase of the counter-terrorist operation was completed," and the army complicated the post-war situation. On 24 January 2001 he agreed to head the board of directors of the Grozneft oil company. On 10 February 2001 he was appointed to the government of Chechnya. On 14 February 2001 during his meeting with Kalamanov, the special representative of the Russian president, Kadyrov said, "from now on Chechen authorities are not going to allow independent activity by humanitarian organisations" because some organisations "speculate on the problems of Chechnya, on the blood of its people" (Interfax, 14 February 2001).

In March 2001 Kadyrov opposed convening the Congress of Chechen people initiated by Aslanbek Aslakhanov, the deputy of the state Duma. On 16 April 2001 he signed a decree banning any congresses, meetings, and other mass events "until the situation in the republic is fully stabilized." Kadyrov's son Ramzan works as a personal bodyguard of his father; in May 2000 he suffered from shock resulting from an assassination attempt, and, on Putin's suggestion, a special flight of the Russian air force carried him to the Burdenko Moscow hospital for examination. On 18 January 2001 there was another attempt on Ramzan Kadyrov's life. (from kavkaz.memo.ru)

CANDIDATE AVKHAT KHANCHUKAEV

Interview by Ruslan Umarov, Caucasian Knot

Would you tell us something of your background?

I was born in Khazakhstan in 1954. Returning to the homeland, I graduated from secondary school in Grozny in 1970. Then I entered the Chechen State University (CSU) and graduated from the chemical and biological faculty. I had an internship at the Leningrad Chemical and Pharmaceutical Institute, so I started my scientific work as a student. I worked as a junior member of the teaching staff at the CSU, then as a school teacher. I returned to the CSU in 1980 and have taught there since that time to this very day. I graduated from the construction faculty of the Grozny Oil Institute while in employment. In 1997 my associates and I founded a public organisation, the Coordinating Council *Ortsa* (Anxiety), and I began to get involved with public activities. This work made me a politician in part.

Why did you decide to become a candidate?

Through my public activities I participated in the preparation of the draft Chechen constitution contributing to a number of educational and human rights measures. I believe that I can contribute to a resolution of the problems of the republic.

Who are your voters?

They are a variety of people, from agricultural workers to scientists, students and other young people. I am predisposed to the intelligentsia.

How do you see the current situation in the Chechen Republic?

Of course today's situation cannot be compared to that of two or three years ago. The cost of restoring order in the Chechen Republic has been reduced, but is still there. Explosions and shelling continue and there is still no lasting peace. We have a complicated tangle of problems. The situation is influenced by internal and external factors and is linked to a chain of geopolitical matters.

We have to make a proper analysis. The situation in Chechnya will not normalize quickly or painlessly. There must be dialogue.

The Chechnya-Ichkeria dilemma belongs to Russia's politics. It is not an internal invention of Chechnya. We remember that Boris Yeltsin switched on the green light for Ichkeria. The deputies of Ichkeria are fully aware of the current situation. We can talk with any representative of Ichkeria who is open to dialogue, excluding only those who do not accept dialogue, or diplomacy, and who are oriented only towards violence.

Are the mass media objective in their treatment of Chechnya?

The mass media from the outset created an image of Chechens as the enemy. Today, when we try to find civilized ways to develop, the media should not focus exclusively on problems. For example, without any proof, TV broadcast that Chechen Prime Minister Anatoly Popov had been poisoned. There needs to be more trust. The media should report on constructive developments.

What will be your practical steps if you win the election?

We shall extend and maximise the area of civil agreement. We will not divide society into Kadyrov's supporters and Maskhadov's supporters. Governors leave, people stay. The division of the nation into camps of supporters detracts from necessary concord. Representatives of Ichkeria can be taken into the Chechen government. Let there be a coalition for a period of transition. When we build up the state system, we will be able to speak about the development of policies.

What are the basic features of your election programme?

First of all, I intend to obtain a concession from the federal centre for preferential terms for Chechnya for 5 to10 years. I mean the creation of a special zone to encourage businessmen, such as our neighbours had. It might be an offshore zone or privileges in the use of energy resources. It might mean supporting investment and privatization, and the profitable use of local resources and so on. It is necessary to speed up the creation of employment. Local organisations must be participants in local tenders and so on.

Who do you consider to be your principal rival?

Akhmat Kadyrov, I think.

How do you estimate your odds for success?

I am a pragmatist. The main thing for us has been to publicise our vision of the situation and problems. Our programme could be carried out by any president.

What is special about your programme?

We have limited financial resources. We depend upon on live contacts with electors.

How doe you see are the election campaigns of the other candidates?

I do not see any breaches. I've got no complaints.

Do you believe the votes will be fairly counted?

Yes, I count on it. The situation requires that everybody behaves responsibly.

What is your attitude towards the counter-terrorist operation in Chechnya?

It is misleading, to put it mildly, for the military, politicians and journalists to call the events in Chechnya a war.

As to methods, I will remind you an old joke. Two people meet in jail. One man asks the other, "What are you doing time for?" The answer is, "For robbery." "What is your term?" "5 years. And you?" "For poaching. 15 years." "Why is your term so long?" "Well, I was stunning fish: killed two carp and three divers."

That is how things are being put to order in Chechnya.

Are there any difficulties in the course of your election campaign?

No. I even declined security services. On principle. I find a common language with everybody, even with opponents.

A complaint by Biybulatov about Kadyrov

(Documents from the Election HQ of Candidates for the president of Chechnya, 3 September 2003)

To Mr Arsakhanov, A-K.B. Chairman of the Election Commission of the Chechen Republic

On facts of prosecution and violation of the law 'On the election of the president of the Chechen Republic' by candidate Khusein Biybulatov. Numerous violations of my rights as a candidate for the post of the president of the Chechen Republic have taken place since the start of my election campaign and the violations have continued. The most significant are listed below.

1. My supporters, Ms L.A.Edelkhanova who is in charge of financial issues and my aide Mr V.M.Israilov were stopped at the checkpoint in the entrance checkpoint of the Central Election Commission and not allowed in for the period from 25 August to 29 August 2003. The officer explained that they had been given an order not to allow anybody into the Central Election Commission because of a quarantine.

2. At about 1 am in the night of 31 August/1 September 2003, three shots were fired with a machine-gun over the house where I was spending the night in the home of my aide in the village of Tsotsin-Yurt.

3. At 2 am the same night an armed man, dressed in camouflage, driving a Zhiguli car (model 95), appeared at the house of my second cousin, Mr Boltiyev, Akhmed Tashykhadzhievich, who lives near the home of my parents in the village of Tsotsin-Yurt, house No. 2 in Zarechnaya St. The man called Mr Boltiyev outdoors and warned him, saying, "If you let Biyboulatov Khussein again into your house and do not remove his headquarters, you will have problems." To the question "Who are you?" he answered, "It's none of your business, I have warned you." And then he left.

4. I received a letter from the Minister of Interior of the Chechen Republic (A.D.Alkhanov) (A photocopy is appended hereto) with a request to inform him about the location of my electoral headquarters and whether I have any guards, the model of my car and other data. I told them that I have no guards and asked them to resolve the issue of my safety and allow me to enjoy the support of the law and ensure my safety myself. He answered that he was not given any such directions and that he would not ensure my safety.

In view of the aforesaid and in view of the special conditions in the Chechen Republic, I ask you to address the top management of the country and the Republic with a request to resolve the issue of my safety as a candidate for the post of president of the Chechen Republic as quickly as possible and to create for me equal conditions with other candidates without any prejudice to my rights – as envisaged by the legislation of the Chechen Republic and the Russian Federation. I made the appropriate deposit to the Election Commission of the Chechen Republic and I have received a certificate acknowledging my candidacy; but I lack the prerequisites envisaged by the law to hold my election campaign.

At the same time I ask you to give your legal assessment of the above facts.

Kh. G Biybulatov, candidate for the post of the president of the Chechen Republic

A Complaint by Buraev about Kadyrov

Document Provided by Election HQ of Candidates for the president of Chechnya 12 September 2003 Claim of Mr Sh.Buraev, candidate for the post of the president of the Chechen Republic to recall the registration of Mr A.Kadyrov, candidate for the post of the president of the Chechen Republic. To the Supreme Court of the Chechen Republic, 42 Idrissova St., city of Grozny

Claimant: Mr Buraev, Shamil Doussiyevich, candidate for the post of the president of the Chechen Republic

Defendant: Mr Kadyrov, Akhmat Abdulkhamidovich, candidate for the post of the president of the Chechen Republic

Complaint Petition:

On cancellation (removal) from registration of Mr Kadyrov, Akhmat Abdulkhamidovich, candidate for the post of the president of the Chechen Republic. Pursuant to Article 31, part 2, of the Law of the Chechen Republic 'On Election of the president of the Chechen Republic,' a candidate for the post of the president of the Chechen Republic, who has been registered by the Election Commission, is obliged to take leave for the period of the election campaign and to refrain from using his or her of administrative levers in implementing his or her election campaign.

The said provision of the Law is being grossly breached by Mr Kadyrov, candidate for the post of the president of the Chechen Republic, and the following facts provide clear evidence of this:

1. Mr Kadyrov, acting president of the Chechen Republic and a registered candidate for the post of the president of the Chechen Republic, has only formally taken leave. He interferes in the activities of various state bodies, instructs them on decision-making, reports to the president of the Russian Federation and the head of the government of the Russian Federation on the decisions he is taking, including information about the course of the election campaign. These activities are confirmed by news items broadcast by the ORT First Federal TV Channel in their Vremya programme on 11 September 2003 at 21 hours.

In the first news item Mr Kadyrov was reporting to Mr Putin, president of Russian Federation, about the measures he was taking to pay compensation to the citizens of the Chechen Republic for their lost housing and property, and in doing so, he also expressed his judgment about his chances in the election campaign. In the second news report Mr Kadyrov was meeting the president of the Russian Federation and the Chairman of the government of the Russian Federation, and they were also talking about the situation in the Chechen Republic. The first news report was later repeated in the Vesti-Plus programme in the RTR Rossiya TV Channel.

The aforesaid confirms the fact of the formal nature of the retirement of Mr Kadyrov for his vacations, demonstrates the favourable attitude of the higher officials of the Russian Federation towards Mr Kadyrov, candidate for the post of the president of the Chechen Republic, and is nothing but pressure on public opinion in relation to the election of the candidate effecting the course of voting.

The above news reports may remain in the consciousness of the population of the Chechen Republic. The population, having suffered from missile and bombing attacks, are given the idea that if they fail to elect Mr Kadyrov the missile and bombing attacks would continue. Such attacks are regularly taking place now in the mountainous parts of the Chechen Republic. Demonstrations of the loyalty of the top management of the country towards Mr Kadyrov as a candidate for the post of the president of the Chechen Republic, and obvious support by them of his candidature, breach the rights of other candidates for the post of the president of the Chechen Republic, and encroach on equality of information distribution and election campaigning. A similar situation can be seen in the mass media of the Chechen Republic that refer to Mr Kadyrov as president of the Chechen Republic, although the election has not yet taken place.

2. Mr Kadyrov's use of his administrative levers is also confirmed by the fact that the government of the Chechen Republic is holding its sessions in the regions of the republic, and that it co-ordinates and matches them to the period of informing the electors and the pre-election campaign. At each such session the ministers and other officials appeal to the voters to cast their votes for Mr Kadyrov.

Mr M.Dashoukayev, First Deputy of the Chairman of the government of the Chechen Republic, head of the Chechen regional branch of the political party Soyuz Pravykh Sil (SPS or Union of Right Forces), took it upon himself to make an illegal decision of the party regional branch to support the candidature of Mr Kadyrov together with other party members (officials of state agencies) while touring through the republic. SPS are demanding the unconditional support of the candidate Kadyrov, threatening otherwise to dismiss the heads of districts and agencies from their posts.

The illegality of the decision of the regional SPS party branch lies in the fact that only the Supreme Political Council of the SPS Party is authorized to take decisions on someone's support or to recommend its regional branches to support a candidature of this or that candidate.

3. Right on the eve of the election, under the direction of Mr Kadyrov, in all district capitals, so-called 'security agencies' were created numbering from 100 to 400 persons. These agencies are not included in the framework of the official law enforcement or executive bodies. They are not maintained by the state, and their material provisioning is made at the expense of enterprises of the districts. They have their arms and technical means; all are dressed in camouflage, their main aim being to demonstrate the power of Mr Kadyrov and to exert an illegal pressure on the population during the election campaign with the purpose of inducing the electorate to vote for Mr Kadyrov.

I hereby ask that the Court interrogate Mr M.Dashoukayev as a witness, retrieve the materials from the 'Vremya' TV programme and from the Vesti Russian TV Channel, and interrogate as witnesses among those who have watched the said broadcasts. Please ask the heads of district administrations to inform you of the presence of armed people in their districts, who are not parts of the Ministry of Interior or the FSB (Federal Security Service), and please also seek confirmation from the said agencies.

With the account of all the aforesaid, taking into account that Mr Kadyrov, candidate for the post of the president of the Chechen Republic, is grossly breaching the principles of equal opportunities in the election campaign, is using administrative levers in his election campaign, by using the officials, whom he had appointed, and also being guided by sub-item 'b' of item 3 of Article 73 of the Law of the Chechen Republic 'On Election of the president of the Chechen Republic' and item 2 of Article 75 of the Federal Law 'On the Main Warranties of Election Rights and the Right to Participate in Referendums of Citizens of the Russian Federation,'

I hereby ask:
1. For the removal of Mr Kadyrov from registration as candidate for the office of the president for gross violations of the laws 'On Election of the president of the Chechen Republic'. Violation has included usage of his official position in holding campaign and putting out propaganda for his candidature, recruiting officials of state agencies and state bodies to the campaign and propaganda in favour of his candidature,

Claimant: Buraev, Sh D., candidate for the office of the president of the Chechen Republic.

Chronicle of Events: 23 August to 6 September

23 August. The suburbs of the Serzhen-Yurt village in the Shali district came under yet another artillery attack from the positions of federal forces in the town of Shali, near the territory of a former military base. Local residents spent the whole night in the basements of their houses. Several houses were seriously damaged in the attack (holes in roofs, windows shattered and doors brought down). Partly destroyed was the house of a famous ac-

tor Dagun Omaev at 104, Aslambek Sherilov Street. Shell-splinters killed a cow in the neighbouring house of Barznukaevs.
Russian-Chechen Friendship Society

26 August. At 7.00 am an incident fraught with casualties among civilians occurred in the village of Serzhen-Yurt in the Shali district in Aslambek Sherilov Street in the southern section of the village. A Russian federal force armoured personnel carrier sped through the village in the direction of the Vedeno district, almost running down a group of women taking their cattle to graze. Without slowing down the armoured personnel carrier roared into the yard of the Nasukhanovs' house. The carrier brought down the wall and came to a halt in the bedroom of Askhab Nasukhanov. Askhab, his wife and three small children survived by a miracle. They hardly had time to recover from shock, when the carrier backed up, pulling down the fence. It then sped off in the direction of the Vedeno district. As a result of this visit of the military, part of the house was destroyed and property in the house was rendered useless.
Russian-Chechen Friendship Society

26 August. Abdul-Wahid, mufti of the Vedeno district, and his bodyguard were killed in the village of Elistanzhi. According to villagers, at night a group of armed Chechens took them from the house and one of the killers read out some sort of an order, the mufti was then shot dead and his bodyguard stabbed to death. Villagers point out that Abdul-Wahid was a close friend of Akhmat Kadyrov, head of the Chechen administration.
Russian-Chechen Friendship Society

26 August. Speaking at a joint session of the boards of the ministries of interior of Russia and Belarus the Russian Minister of Internal Affairs Boris Gryzlov stated that security throughout the election campaign in Chechnya would be provided at appropriate levels. "The law enforcement bodies have had experience of conducting similar socio-political events, namely the referendum," said the Minister, "That time we managed to ensure the security at polling sites and have prevented 11 terrorist attacks."
Strana.Ru

27 August. In the village of Valerik in the Achkhoi-Martan district agents of the local military commandant's office arbitrarily arrested Wakha Idigov, 50, in his home and drove him away to an unknown destination. At the time of his arrest he was sick in bed. According to relatives, Wakha Idigov was taken hostage because of his son Ramzan Idigov whom the federal forces considered to be a guerrilla. When arrested, Wakha was told that the only condition for his release was his son's surrender to the military authorities.
Russian-Chechen Friendship Society

30 August. The Chechnya Election Commission registered the following 11 presidential candidates:

Aslambek Aslakhanov, the RF State Duma deputy;
Khussein Biybulatov, advisor to the director of Electrogorsk Power Plant Safety Research Centre;
Abdula Bugaev, temporarily unemployed;
Shamil Buraev, ex-head of the Achkhoi-Martan district administration;
Khussein Dzhabrailov, first deputy general director of the 'Russia' hotel (Moscow);
Akhmat Kadyrov, acting president of the Chechen Republic;
Nikolai Paizullaev, poet, employee of the press-service of the Chechen Republic acting president;
Kudus Saduev, deputy general director of open joint stock company Grozneftegaz.
Malik Saidullaev, president of Milan concern;
Avkhat Khanchukaev, professor at the Grozny State University;
Said-Selim Tsuev, colonel, deputy military commandant of Chechnya.
Beslan Gantamirov and **Ruslan Khasbulatov** who initially expressed their intention to take part in the election gave up the idea of getting nominated to run for president.
kavkaz.memo.ru

1 September. The ITAR-TASS news agency quoted Akhmat Kadyrov who predicted a virtually 100% turnout of voters at the polls in the Chechen presidential election. According to Mr Kadyrov "a vigorous political advertising campaign is underway in the republic one month before the election day." He noted that "at the time of the referendum on the new constitution of Chechnya political advertising campaign was conducted only by the plebiscite group, but now all 11 campaign HQs are engaged in such activities throughout the republic".
Strana.Ru

1 September. A correspondent of the Information Centre of the Russian-Chechen Friendship Society met with Uvais Elzhiev, head of the pre-election headquarter of Shamil Buraev in Achkhoi-Martan. According to Elzhiev, the rules for the pre-election procedure are being violated by the administration of the Achkhoi-Martan region, which supports the acting president, Akhmat Kadyrov. Materials by Buraev do not reach the public, because they are confiscated from the news-stands. The regional TV refuses to give time to Buraev to introduce his political programme. Buraev has not received the promised bodyguards yet. "It is very difficult to work in such unlawful conditions," Uvais Elzhiev said.
Russian-Chechen Friendship Society

1 September. At 2.00 am on 1 September 2003 armed people in military uniforms burst into the house of the Migiev family in Stepnaya Street in the village of Orekhovo in Achkhoi-Martan district and took away their only son – Imran Migiev (born in 1964). The next morning the body of Migiev was discovered some 50 metres away from his home. He had been stabbed to death with a hilted bayonet. According to villagers, Imran was a

peaceful person who delivered water around the village in his own car and was in no way engaged in military resistance to the federal forces.

1 September. In the eastern suburbs of the town of Gudermes, near a filling station, some 150 metres from the location of the local police Chechen Friendship Society department, the body of Aslan Shakhidovich Usmaev of the village of Tsentrovaya was found. On one of his legs he had an Ilizarov device. It was later discovered that Usmaev had undergone an operation in the Gudermes city hospital No 2. On 31 August, at midnight, armed people in masks arrived in an UAZ and stormed into the hospital kidnapping Usmaev and a friend of Usmaev's looking after him in the hospital. The same night Usmaev's friend was released. The murder was not reported to the law-enforcing bodies.
Memorial Human Rights Centre

2 September. Akhmat Kadyrov sent a motion to the RF State Duma asking for the prolongation of the amnesty deadline for the participants of illegal Chechen military formations till 5 October 2003 (i.e. the date for the election of the president of the republic), arguing that "not all of the militants eager to accept the amnesty had a chance to do it, and they should be given more time."
Newsru.com

On 2 September Kh.Dzhabrailov announced that he had withdrawn his candidacy. According to mass media reports this act had been preceded by Kh.Dzhabrailov's talk with the RF president administration head A.Voloshin or some "lower ranking" official.
kavkaz.memo.ru

On 2 September lots were cast at the Election Commission of Chechnya to share free republican TV time.
Strana.Ru

2 September 2003. Saipuddin Tsitsayev, head of the administration in the village of Chechen-Aul near the capital Grozny was killed at dawn. Unknown armed people in masks stormed into Tsitsayev's house, dragged Saipuddin into the yard and shot him dead. A criminal case has been initiated for the murder; the investigation is being conducted by the police of Grozny rural district.
Russian-Chechen Friendship Society

3 September. Not far from the village of Kulary in the Urus-Martansky district, Russian soldiers detained a person named Akhmed Magomedovich Katraev (born in 1977), a resident of the village registered at 7 Sovetskaya Street. The military claim that a mine was found in Katraev's car. Representatives of the village administration and his fellow-villagers are sure it was a setup. According to the police, the car of the detained person had been looted by soldiers.
Russian-Chechen Friendship Society

On 3 September the Press Ministry headed by B.Gantamirov and the Ministry on Nationalities were disbanded and merged into the Ministry on National Policy, Information and Foreign Relations. Taus Dzhabrailov, former Minister of Nationalities and at the same time the manager of Kadyrov's election campaign, was appointed head of the new ministry. On 11 August Gantamirov stated that his Press Ministry will grant equal terms and conditions to all candidates, and on 13 August he informed journalists that he would support Kh. Dzhabrailov.
kavkaz.memo.ru

On 3 September the Minister of Chechnya on National Policy, Information and Foreign Relations Taus Dzhabrailov said that in the Lenin district of the city of Grozny unidentified persons beat up Boki Amaev, a member of the Chechnya Election Commission. According to Dzhabrailov, Amaev was attacked by several men. Amaev was taken to hospital with concussion and bruises. The police of the Lenin district are investigating the incident.
ITAR-TASS; Kavkaz.Strana.Ru, Gazeta.Ru; RFE/RL

On 4 September the village of Sernovodsk of the Sunzha district of the Chechen Republic hosted the meeting of the government of the Chechen Republic. A.Popov, Chairman of the government, chaired the meeting. The meeting was attended by the following ministers: internal affairs, education, agriculture, housing and communal services, the republic's Procurator, as well as heads of administration of Urus-Martan, Achkhoi-Martan, Sunzha districts of the Chechen Republic. The meeting discussed reports of some ministers, heads of district departments, as well as issues related to compensation payments. Besides that, instructions were given regarding the nomination of a joint candidate for the forthcoming presidential election. No specific name was mentioned but the name of Kadyrov was implied. The road between from Grozny and Sernovodsk was guarded by police posts and other law enforcement agencies.
Memorial Human Rights Centre.

On 4 September the Chechen TV and radio company building was blocked by the police and FSB. According to Zaur Eskirhanov, deputy director of the Chechen TV and radio company, journalists were not allowed to leave the building for their assignments because the TV company director had been fired. Journalists of the TV and radio company stopped work and filed applications to quit their jobs as a token of protest against the liquidation of the Press department and the firing of the TV and radio directors.
Newsru.com

4 September. At around 4.45 am agents of an unknown law enforcement agency of the Chechen Republic arrested and drove away Irskhan Khaditovich Edilkhanov (born in 1984) living at 5 Melnichnaya Street in the village of Khamby-Irze (Lermontovo) of the Achkhoi-Martan district. According to Khadid Edilkhanov, the father of the detainee, as many as 10

armed people in masks and military uniforms stormed into the house early in the morning. Waving their guns, they threw all the residents of the house on the floor with their faces down, seized Irskhan, tied up his hands and put a bag on his head. After that they took him out of the house and into a grey UAZ-452 vehicle without number plates. Some of the neighbours tried to stop the kidnappers and block their three cars, but the agents opened fire above the people's heads and escaped. Two hours later Irskhan Edilkhanov's relatives reported the incident to the local police and the District department of the Federal Security Service but were told that no arrests had been performed by the agents of these services and no information on the case was available to them. Edilkhanov's relatives have no clue as to the reasons for Irskhan's arrest. According to them, he has never been part of any illegal organisation; had recently passed a medical commission of the Interior Ministry in order to start work in the police force of the Achkhoi-Martan district.
Memorial Human Rights Centre

On 5 September the Grozny TV and radio company cancelled the scheduled presentations by four presidential candidates as part of TV free time sharing. This followed the liquidation of the Press department and the firing of Beslan Gantamirov, Minister of the Press, by the edict of the acting president of Chechnya Anatoly Popov.
Newsru.com

On 5 September armed detachments of the security service of the acting president of Chechnya took control of the TV and radio company of Chechnya and the editing offices of republican newspapers and print shops.
kavkaz.memo.ru

On 5 September the Vesti Respubliki newspaper published an article about the firing of the Commission secretary E.Vakhitov. The cause for the firing was a report by B.Amaev, election commission member, stating that Vakhitov was M.Saidullaev's relative. Saidullaev is a candidate running for Chechnya president. The Election Commission is the place… where people get beaten up / Instead of a topical satire/ (Vesti Respubliki No 70-71, September 5, 2003).

On 5 September the Mayor of the town of Shali ordered his subordinates to liquidate the election headquarters of M.Saidullaev in the city. He also banned any election propaganda for this candidate running for presidency in this city. According to the press service staff of Saidullaev, a candidate running for president of Chechnya, S.Kaimov, head of staff of Saidullaev's election campaign in Shali district, and Saidullaev's agent A.Askhabov started to receive death threats.
Memorial Human Rights Centre

On 5 September the Central Election Commission of Chechnya cancelled Kh.Dzhabrailov's registration as a candidate for Chechnya presidency.
kavkaz.memo.ru

On 6 September in the city of Grozny OMON (special task police unit) and PPS (street patrolling police) of the Chechen Republic, on orders from the Ministry of the Interior of the Chechen Republic, began to destroy posters and banners with Saidullaev's portraits.
M. Saidullaev's Press Service

5 IN THE END THERE CAN BE ONLY ONE: REMOVING MAJOR CONTENDERS

Leonid Ruzov, freelance journalist

Yesterday the infamous date of 11 September acquired further significance. On the same day as Felix Dzerzhinsky was born, and the Twin Towers came crashing down, the hope for a fair presidential election in Chechnya came to an end. The Election Commission may well carry out its procedures properly on 5 October. But this will not be sufficient to repair the damage.

Chechnya had been set to produce a fascinating action thriller. But it took just a day for the character of future political events in Chechnya to change. The successors to the KGB over-ran the sacred borders of Russia. What in Chechnya had been a thriller, became an exciting whodunit, has now become a comedy of the absurd.

The struggle for power in Russia is like a dogfight under a carpet. Thanks to the new Russian election law, journalists are not allowed to write about candidates for election. We got a lucky break because nearly all of the candidates have dropped out of the electoral race. Without breaking the law we are now able to name those who HAD BEEN serious contenders in Chechnya. We were finally able to talk about Malik Saidullaev, Aslambek Aslakhanov, and Khussein Dzhabrailov.

Yesterday, the Supreme Court of the Chechen Republic ruled that Saidullaev had to be removed from the election ballot. Yesterday Aslakhanov cancelled his visit to the University of Grozny and "with great thanks" announced that he would be accepting an offer to become president Putin's aide for the south of Russia. On 2 September Dzhabrailov withdrew from the race after talks with Putin's administration officials. The promise of a thrilling final became a one-horse race. We might imagine a scene from *The Highlander*, where the Council of Watchers has 'chats' with the various challengers to decide who will be their champion to fight Duncan McLeod. Those the Council deem unworthy are sent off on other missions or withdraw from the contest.

You might think that these three candidates removed themselves because of lack of administrative resources. But it is more likely that disappearing candidates are the public and visible part of private and hidden processes. Putin's first administration was buoyed up by the second Chechen war. But there was no obvious public issue to give legitimacy to Putin in 2003. An uncertain peace settlement provides no such support. Perhaps a new enemy could be found?

What is meant by 'settlement' and how we got there has always been disputed. The public had always insisted that an election should come before any peace agreement. This demand made negotiations between the Russian government and Maskhadov, the president elected in 1997, a pivotal part of the formula. But the Russian government has repeatedly maintained that Maskhadov is not the president. That deadlock seemed bound to change with the election. The question of who is leader of Chechnya would be settled.

That is how it seemed until 12 September 2003 when Sergei Yastrzhembsky, Putin's aide on Chechnya, unexpectedly recognized the separatist Ichkeria government. On the same day everyone's favourite, Isa Temirov, now 'vice-speaker of the parliament of Ichkeria' (he was also called 'acting speaker'), announced at a press conference in Moscow that it had been decided on 5 September 2003 that Maskhadov was no longer the Ichkerian president. As the story went, Maskhadov had contravened the Ichkerian constitution, because he had misappropriated power and impermissibly introduced Islamic Shar'ia law, thereby undermining the Ichkerian constitution. Maskhadov therefore was guilty of a serious crime.

The author of this chapter does not possess Athenian wisdom, and has not attempted to determine the standard set forth by these Ichkerian legal documents. Nor does he recommend that other people attempt this. Simply put, these documents are full of vagueness and contradictions. Equally unclear are the circumstances of the decision making on 5 September (the eve of the twelfth anniversary of the independence of Ichkeria). It is not known where the resolutions came from, whether there was a quorum, or who called the meeting to order. Speculation about the meeting had been flying around since August, putting particular strain and stress on the deputies set to attend, and on their families.

There is also something of a mystery about who allowed Temirov to become the speaker and take the place of the missing Ruslan Alihadjiev. Indeed, what was Temirov doing at the press conference in Moscow, given that he was involved in Basaev's raid on Budennovsk for which he is under indictment? The person most likely to have the answers to these questions would be Vagap Tutakov, Maskhadov's representative who was allowed back into Chechnya from Europe by Russian officials this very week. However, Tutakov was indisposed at the time of these events. The security services had been detaining him in a hotel since the morning of 11 September.

The most interesting feature of the internal Ichkerian intrigue is the reaction of the federal government. Yastrzhembsky's recognition of the Ichkerian parliament's impeachment of Maskhadov according to the Ichkerian constitution contrasts with Yastrzhembsky's long-standing insistence that Ichkeria did not even exist. The situation is reminiscent of the stories told about Sir Isaac Newton who, after re-ordering how we think of the universe, is said to have reverted in his old age to an obsession about the possibility of a universe ruled by warring demons and angels. Perhaps in the Chechen case, the 'flip-flop' is even starker. If Yastrzhembsky recognizes an independent Ichkerian state, might there need to be two Chechen presidents chosen on 5 October? One for the Federal subject-republic and one for the Ichkerian one?

Taking a higher level view we could say that whereas Maskhadov's legitimacy was indisputable in 1997, it was open to question by 2003. Maskhadov's inability to stop crime waves and kidnappings, to stop the Dagestan incursion in 1999, and the Moscow theatre hostage-taking in 2002, undermined the legitimacy of a sovereign Ichkeria. How much legitimacy remains? Might the Maskhadov representative, Salambek Maigov, fired for not condemning the acts of terror this summer, be the straw that broke the camel's back?

The one thing that is clear is that the legitimacy of Kadyrov, the current acting president, is even less certain. An opinion poll carried out by the Sergei Khaykin Institute shows that neither Kadyrov nor Maskhadov is regarded by Chechens as the head of Chechnya. In such a situation, any leader who comes forward and is trusted by the people would be a blessing, or at least better than the situation that we have now.

How did Kadyrov get to the top of the electoral list? He was an army chaplain for the separatists in the first Chechen war who identified extremists and terrorists as Wahhabists. He may thereby have involuntarily become an ally of the federal forces at the start of the second Chechen war. To the Russian government it must have seemed easier to label Wahhabists as the enemy rather than Chechens who wanted separation from Russia. In the middle of 2000 Russia chose to deal with Kadyrov rather than go through the politically difficult process of having to deal with 'moderate' separatists and radicals. One possible negotiator on these more difficult paths, Ruslan Alihadjiev, simply disappeared. Another, Turnal Ali-Atgeriev, was arrested and died in prison.

When things of this kind happen, eventually someone has to pay the piper. In the second half of 2000, a new large-scale guerrilla war began that has continued through to this day. At the same time, the reliance on Kadyrov, this Chechen chosen immortal, did not fade away but grew. The most recent example of this was the Chechen amnesty that Kadyrov was able to apply to all those fighters who would take up arms on his behalf and become his security detachment.

There is the old saying, 'If you borrow a rouble, then the borrower is indebted to the lender. If you borrow a million roubles, then the lender becomes dependent on the borrower.' Russia may have thought it was lending a rouble, but within a year or two found that the loan had escalated and that Kadyrov had become an uncontrollable satrap in his own province. Kadyrov took control of budget expenditures (including monies for restoration of buildings) and for the creation of legal fighting forces, far wider than that granted to Dudayev, Maskhadov, and Basaev taken together. And all this was done with full official backing from the Kremlin.

In many ways, the current Chechen administrative scheme looks a lot like being caught in a pyramid scheme. Yesterday it was easy and there was nothing to lose. Today it is turning out to be expensive. Tomorrow the costs may become catastrophic. And so what are federal forces going to do? For a long time the head of Chechnya has been a thorn in the federal forces side, independent and uncontrollable. So, when are the Russians going to balk, and how are they going to do it?

The election of 5 October may have seemed a good opportunity. An opinion poll had shown the acting president Kadyrov's approval rating was low and falling, as even his security forces engaged in banditry. The fall in popularity is surprising considering the tendency in times of upheaval for people to cling to whatever signs of authority exist. It might be a charade to hold an election during a civil war and under a state of emergency. But it might bring a change of power. One way to get rid of Kadyrov and his praetorian guard would be to have him lose an election. Maybe, this would not force him to put down his arms, and a small war against him might also be necessary, but at least there would be an impressive pretext.

The favourite who could have replaced the acting president in the election might have been Saidullaev, for he is known to have helped his clansmen in Chechnya financially as well as in other ways over the last four years. In December 1999 he seems to have stopped the Shamanov-caused chaos in his native town of Alkhan-Yurt. Saidullaev was not the only person running for election. There were also two other well-known figures on the list of candidates, the businessman Khussein Dzhabrailov and Aslambek Aslakhanov, the member of parliament. These two figures would surely have drawn votes off Saidullaev. If this was the plan, then the withdrawal of both these candidates (see above) could be seen as the unfolding of the Kremlin's envisioned architecture for Chechnya's future.

The same plan seems to have included election monitoring – a project voiced by the presidential Commission on Human Rights. Five hundred human rights activists were sought for monitoring the voting and the results, but both Russia and Chechen human rights communities rejected the idea. The idea is still being floated by Ella Pamfilova, chair of the presidential Human Rights Commission. Forcing candidates out of the race on one side and earnestly trying to have the election fully legitimized by international standards on the other side makes an interesting combination.

The nullification of Saidullaev's candidacy by the Chechen Supreme Court on 11 September seems not to have been part of the plan. This was very much a local decision. It is true that the Election Commission agreed with the decision of the court. We may already have seen the reaction of the federal government. On the same day as the court ruling Putin met publicly with Kadyrov to discuss how compensation for demolished houses would be spent and to demand that the money no be stolen. Kadyrov listened and agreed to order the return of stolen funds that had already been paid out. If this was not a form of election campaigning it did at least indicate the official government position.

We can of course wait. One can hope for miracles, and this is exactly what some human rights defenders are doing, those who are still planning to do election observing. It will be a miracle if Chechens come to the ballot boxes on 5 October. But we are no longer dealing with stories of a genre that allow miracles to happen. All story-lines from the past in Chechnya are action thrillers, heroic fairytales, and crime fiction. The federal government does not change horses in mid stream, so we are not going to revert to these story-lines until the race is done.

The scheme to change the power structure in Chechnya using elections was fraught with danger from the beginning – particularly because the powers-that-be had to deal with their parliamentary and presidential elections at the same time. Such plans, risky and uncertain as to their outcome, could not have had universal support at the Kremlin, and so what do we have?

We are left in Chechnya with an empty set. The producers have simply walked off. The only reason for viewers to stick around is if they want to catch the sequel to this movie about Kadyrov. Beware though, only stay if the types of movies you enjoy are tragi-comedies in the style of the absurd.

Chronicle of Events: 7 September to 11 September

On 7 September the district election headquarters of Malik Saidullaev, presidential candidate, were fired at in Samashki. As was reported by the election headquarters personnel, the guards returned fire, killing one of the attackers. The guards found a guard's ID of Akhmat Kadyrov, another candidate, on the dead body. The chief of staff of the Saidullaev headquarters maintains that he informed the police immediately. But neither the police nor the prosecutor's office confirmed the report. Deputy Prosecutor General of the Republic Vladimir Chernyaev stated that since the beginning of the election campaign there had

been no complaints about violations on the part of the candidates, and he promised that he would promptly respond if such complaints were filed.
Kavkaz.Strana.Ru; Gazeta.Ru; Polit.Ru; INTERFAX

7 September. In the middle of the night on 6 September, the town of Urus-Martan came under intensive artillery fire from the positions of a federal forces unit. A local resident reported over ten explosions of shells of various calibres. Residents of Urus-Martan spent the night in the basements trying to calm down their frightened children. Several houses in various parts of town were damaged (shattered window panes, damaged roofs). A shell hit a house on the junction of Gagarin and Nekrasov Streets. Luckily, there were no casualties because the house had been partly destroyed back in 2002 and had been deserted ever since. No casualties were reported.
Russian-Chechen Friendship Society

7 September. Five local residents were arrested by the Russian federal forces in the village of Chiri-Yurt in the Grozny rural district. According to some sources, two of the detainees were abandoned on the outskirts of the village after being severely tortured and beaten up. The whereabouts and destiny of the other three detainees are unknown.
Chechen Committee for National Salvation

8 September. Local residents of the village of Elistanzhi in the Vedeno district reported the kidnapping of their fellow-villager Danilbek Gunukbaev, 70 years of age. The old man took his cattle to graze on the outskirts of the village and never came back. His relatives organized a search party but to no avail. They turned for assistance to the local military commandant's office. The military, however, refused cooperation saying that a unit of paratroops was on a mission in the district and no steps could possibly be taken before the end of that mission.
Chechen Committee for National Salvation

On 8 September unidentified gunmen set off a grenade at the entrance to the office of Saidullaev's headquarters in Dagestanskaya Street almost killing Magomed Arsanukaev, head of the election headquarters of Saidullaev.
Kavkaz.Strana.Ru; Gazeta.Ru; Polit.Ru; INTERFAX

On 9 September in the Staropromyslovy district of the city of Grozny, in the Katayama area on Zhukovsky Street, gunmen, presumably from the security service of Kadyrov, in cars without licence plates (windows were covered with stickers displaying a portrait of Kadyrov) stopped Bislan Khayauri for an ID check. After the inspection, they shot him dead with assault rifles. Then they blocked the neighbourhood where the house of the Khayauri family was located. Having fired at the house the gunmen broke in and destroyed and stole property from the house. The father of the late Bislan Khayauri is a coordinator of the election headquarters of Malik Saidullaev. Katayama's inhabitants believe that Bis-

Ian's assassination and house looting were acts of deterrence and revenge on the part of Kadyrov's supporters, against those who back Saidullaev.
Memorial Human Rights Centre

9 September. A landmine exploded in Grozny at the junction of Kassiora and Tukhachevskogo Streets. As a result, five people were injured — three policemen and two civilians (a man and a woman) who happened to be nearby. They were all taken to the city hospital No 9.
Russian-Chechen Friendship Society

9 September. Three women were killed and three children injured in an explosion of a home-made landmine in the village of Assinovskaya in the Sunzha district. The women were Mart Makhauri, 45 (a mother of eight children, two of whom were sick), Rosa Adayeva, 41 (a mother of nine, including a baby of nine months) and one more woman (a still unidentified refugee). Rosa Adayeva was the mother of the three injured children (two girls and one boy). The family were on their way from a tomato field. Hassan Adayev, the husband of Rosa Adayeva, was driving the tractor with the women and the children in the tractor carriage. When they approached the location of the former sovkhoz (state farm) weighing facility, near a bus stop, a mine exploded under the tractor carriage. Two women were killed on the spot while the others were rushed to the hospitals in the village of Ordzhonikidzevskaya (Republic of Ingushetia) and the town of Urus-Martan. At the scene of the explosion a plastic bottle was discovered with a remote control and wires going to the side of the road. The mine had been planted right on the road. A de-mining unit located at the village of Assinovskaya arrived at the scene of this terrorist attack. They defused a similar mine that failed to explode. A criminal case was initiated by the prosecutor's office of the Sunzha district of the Chechen Republic.
Memorial Human Rights Centre

On 10 and 11 September the Krasnodar centre of social studies with the Gorod TV and radio company conducted opinion surveys that showed that 65% of respondents in Grozny would take part in the election on 5 October with 19% still undecided. Answering the question, "Have you decided for whom you will vote at the Chechnya presidential election?" Fifty percent gave positive answers, 34% gave negative answers, and 16% refused to give an answer. The following percentage of people managed to recognize the candidates: Aslakhanov 67%, Biybulatov 0.1%, Bugaev 2%, Buraev 28%, Saduev 0.1%, Saidullaev 32%, Kadyrov 94%, Paizullaev 5%, Khanchukaev 3%, Tsuev 2%. At the time of the survey Aslakhanov, Saidullaev and Tsuev were still on the list of registered candidates.
kavkaz.memo.ru

10 September. At 8.55 pm Chechen guerrillas took over the local TV centre in the village of Sernovodsk in the Sunzha district. Magomed Astamirov, director of the local TV centre, threatened with a weapon, was forced to play a videocassette brought by the paramilita-

ries showing an address by Maskhadov and scenes from the first and second wars. After the screening Seid-Magomed Islamov, the leader of the armed group, called on the villagers to give armed resistance to the "Russian invaders and their local administrators". According to Madina Musayeva, an internally displaced person living in the temporary placement centre (PVR), a group of 15-20 assailants blocked off an area of the campus of the agricultural college. Some of the guerrillas went into the college building. Several forced their way into the local TV centre while another group was about to break down the door of the office of the Memorial Human Rights Centre. Residents of the PVR managed to talk the paramilitaries out of breaking into the office.

At the same time another group of paramilitaries blocked off the electric power plant substation on the agricultural college campus to prevent a power blackout. One more group of paramilitaries opened automatic and bazooka fire on the local police station. No casualties were reported either among the assailants or the policemen. The police building is reported to have suffered only insignificant damage.

The fourth group of the paramilitaries destroyed Kadyrov's local pre-election headquarters in Nagi Asyeva Street. In Lenina and Kirova Streets they fired their guns and shouted "Allah Akbar!" telling onlookers to go home and watch the local TV channel. After that, meeting no resistance from the Russian law enforcement agencies, the paramilitaries went away. The overall attack was carried out in an efficient and calm manner and was coordinated with the help of walkie-talkies. The same night, paramilitaries also visited the village of Assinovskaya where they strolled along the streets shouting "Allah Akbar!" and shooting at random. According to witnesses, the paramilitaries filmed their activities on video. The activities of all these armed groups seemed to be very well planned.

Memorial Human Rights Centre

10 September. Chaotic gunfire was reported around 11 pm in the Avtarkhanovsky (Leninsky) district of the town of Grozny. The fire originated from the sixth microdistrict, parallel to the Kirov Avenue. Bullets were whining between the residential high-rise buildings hitting the walls of apartments. Residents of the district spent the night in fear, lying on the floor and being afraid to come near a window. According to residents, the fire came from the federal forces checkpoint at the end of the sixth microdistrict. Luckily, there were no casualties.

Russian-Chechen Friendship Society

On 11 September president Putin received Kadyrov, acting president of Chechnya on leave because of his participation in the presidential election. They discussed compensation payment organisation to cover expenses related to lost houses. The meeting report was telecast on central TV channels.

kavkaz.memo.ru

On 11 September State Duma Deputy Aslambek Aslakhanov withdrew from the race for presidency of Chechnya. Among the reasons he gave "impossibility to conduct regular election campaign." Chechnya still faces a tense situation, "there are no proper conditions for the campaign," he stated. "It was not an easy decision. I was pondering over it all night, consulting with my staff. As a result, I made up my mind to withdraw," he stressed. Then he added that "no pressure was exerted" by anyone.

At the same time, Aslakhanov noted, "I didn't want to be deprived of the registration as a presidential candidate that's why I pulled out." Aslakhanov reported that the local election commission found several faults in his documents. He had failed to fill in the column 'citizenship' in the questionnaire, failed to file his income declaration, and there were discrepancies n his address. Aslakhanov submitted his documents to the local election commission for registration on the very last day.

"Purely technical errors brought me and Malik Saidullaev to court," said the deputy. "I was supposed to get my income declaration from the Duma secretariat, but Saturday is not an office day. Besides I am a state servant and I live only on my salary and I am not involved with any profit-making organisation. According to the law a state servant does not have to complete the income form. Regarding my home address – one digit in the house number happened to be wrong. The outcome of the election had been predetermined two months before that. Aslakhanov said sadly. "I don't want to play at a one-actor theatre." Putin, in his turn, in a telephone conversation offered Aslakhanov a position as his aide on Chechnya and the South of Russia. "I agreed to this proposal, if the president doesn't change his mind, " Aslakhanov. He added that it was a team decision which he had discussed (and which had been put to vote) with his staff consisting of 28 persons. Aslakhanov emphasised that the offer had been flattering. "I believe I was the first Chechen to be offered such a high position," he said.
Strana.Ru; Newsru.com

On 11 September the Supreme Court of the Chechen Republic cancelled Saidullaev's registration because of violations of the regulations for signature lists. The relevant complaint was made by another candidate, Paizullaev, press service employee of the acting president of Chechnya.
kavkaz.memo.ru

11 September. One of the microdistricts of the Leninsky district in Grozny was completely blocked off. In some areas the cordons were much stronger than usual, documents were checked and even agents of the Ministry of Internal Affairs and other law enforcement agencies were not allowed to pass. The police referred to an order of the Minister of Internal Affairs on passport registration checks. No reports are available on the number of detained people or the number receiving administrative punishments for violating the passport regime.
Russian-Chechen Friendship Society

11 September 2003. In the depth of night the village of Makhkety in the Vedeno district came under artillery fire from the Russian federal forces. According to local residents, some private houses were damaged with shell-splinters shattering window-panes and damaging roofs. No casualties among the civilian population reported.
Chechen Committee for National Salvation

6 MALIK SAIDULLAEV: A RECONAISSANCE

Tanya Lokshina, Moscow Helsinki Group

It is strange to find yourself here for the first time when you have read so much about the place, when you know it so well in theory that every name speaks to you. The world of words is suddenly filled with life. The September sun makes the landscape soft, fields spread on both sides of the road. Suddenly you doubt that the war has been really raging here for so many years… The idyll is broken by the military transport, by the men in camouflage and masks, seated on the armoured personnel carrier. I thank them for a timely reminder.

The Kavkaz-1 military checkpoint on the road to Chechnya welcomes the traveller with a slogan painted in white on a block of concrete, 'Stop! Transport Patrol! RNE!' (RNE being the acronym for the strongest Russian nationalist party – Russian National Unity). The welcome is extended with an appeal 'Glory to Russia! RNE.' One cannot but feel proud for our mighty Motherland…

We are driving to Alkhan-Yurt, the ancestral home of the prominent Moscow businessman Malik Saidullaev whose registration as a candidate in the Chechen presidential election was voided on 11 September. The man himself is in Moscow at the moment. But his election campaign centres are still working in the Chechen Republic, and his brother Milan, who flew from London abandoning some major business project there, is keeping a close watch on the situation. Milan wants to get information on the pre-election situation in Chechnya, and on the pressures felt by Malik Saidullaev's supporters.

The 'ancestral home' is hidden from curious eyes by high iron gates. The gates open and we are let into a spacious yard crowded with strikingly tall and handsome men in camouflage – all carrying automatic rifles. The house itself looks like a castle. A small one, but a castle indeed. Everybody takes off their shoes on the snow-white steps that look like marble. The floors of the terrace sparkle with the same marble whiteness. We are seated on a large soft sofa and wait in silence. I don't know what exactly we are waiting for but prefer to refrain from asking questions.

After a couple of minutes there is movement in the yard. The guards step aside and a dark burly man with a short black beard and the inevitable camouflage comes up to us. He exchanges embraces with the newcomers, shakes hands with me and takes a deep armchair nearby. Resting his hands on his knees and never quite raising his eyes, he begins to speak quietly and monotonously. His voice is emotionless, almost toneless. The guards quietly approach the staircase and sit on the steps listening to their leader with silent respect.

I will not cite the whole monologue, which was sometimes broken by my questions, because the speaker did not say anything really new. It basically amounted to the following.

"The cancelling of Malik Saidullaev's candidacy is an arbitrary act that demonstrates the federal centre's support of the acting president. Kadyrov's men commit outrages [we know much about it from the coverage of the Chechen election campaign by the central media]. The Supreme Court of the Russian Federation has yet to make its final decision concerning the appeal of Malik Saidullaev, but the local television keeps emphasizing that Saidullaev is out of the election race, and sometimes even adds that he withdrew his candidacy HIMSELF, because he understood that Kadyrov is the only possible president for the Chechen people. The situation is critical. Beatings, violence, murders happen every day, especially where Saidullaev's staff in local offices and in the campaign headquarters are concerned. [He cites several examples which have already been reported in the news.] Roads are mined. A mine was set on Saidullaev's route when he travelled to Grozny. All cases have been sent to the Prosecutor's Office but nothing has been done to investigate them. The Minister of the Internal Affairs of the Republic deliberately delays investigation.

"And the people support Malik Saidullaev. The people will not support Kadyrov. Young people are flooding to the campaign centres to join the personal guard of Saidullaev. Nobody is recruiting them, they come on their own. Seven thousand people are already on a waiting list to join Saidullaev's personal guard. If Kadyrov becomes president, Saidullaev would need protection, and they are going to form a wall around him. Do you see the situation?"

"Do you mean that, if Kadyrov becomes president and Malik Saidullaev is not allowed to participate in the election, a civil war is going to break out?" I cut in, tired of absorbing his lengthy speech. "No!" The candidate's brother suddenly looks up. "We cannot have any civil war in this republic. That would be the end. We just have blood feuds."

'No matter what you call it – if it walks like a duck...' I think to myself. But there is neither the time nor the wish to start an argument. "I'd like to see your main headquarters in Grozny, talk to the staff, to see some of the documents you mentioned. You spoke of the polls which were conducted to estimate the public support for Malik Saidullaev. Can we see them?"

"Why are we sitting here then? Let us go".

Milan Saidullaev jumps up. The guards rise to their feet in one motion. We go out to the back yard with the security staff trailing behind us. A standard village outhouse is in one corner of the yard. The opposite corner has a cage with two huge furry bears rubbing their muzzles against the grating. One is reminded of Kirill Trokurov's estate from Pushkin's famous story 'The Captain's Daughter,' but our host resembles another character – the protagonist – from the same literary masterpiece.

The host gallantly throws open the door of his shiny Mercedes with tinted, almost black windows. The windscreen boasts a huge portrait of Malik Saidullaev with a clean shaven face and thoughtful gentle eyes. The candidate's brother takes the wheel and two men take the back seat. All three in one synchronized gesture get out their pistols and set the locks. The guards jump into their jeeps. I happen to glimpse a bazooka – hadn't been that close before. A thought flickers through my mind that in the event of a mine on the road the bazooka would be useless...

We race on wildly, accompanied by three jeeps with security men. The jeeps display the candidate's posters; automatic rifles jut out of the windows. In Alkhan-Yurt cars hoot to welcome us and swerve to the side of the road, people wave their hands. The streets are decorated with posters featuring the candidate, his slogans. Inscriptions on the walls scream that 'Malik Saidullaev is our president!' Posters, banners, slogans – everything is in Russian. Milan Saidullaev hoots in response explaining that he is not Malik, of course, but he is welcomed as his brother's representative.

We rush onto the Rostov-Baku highway. Saidullaev's men drive in the middle of the road literally throwing everybody else to the side. An hour ago, I saw how the federal servicemen travel on their personnel carriers, it was just the same. Evidently, this is the way of the armed people here.

We enter Grozny a few minutes later. The ruins of houses flicker past. There is almost no city here: there is nothing that we usually call a 'city.' I had seen many photographs of Grozny. My colleagues had told me that the scale of destruction in Chechnya's capital can be compared to Sarajevo or the most severely destroyed German cities after World War II. But photographs and stories cannot prepare oneself for the real Grozny which manages to be dead and alive at the same time. "Are you here for the first time?" Milan Saidullaev asks with a hint of mockery. I nod silently.

The headquarters, located near the Oil Institute, is a small fortress. A familiar crowd of armed people wearing camouflage meets us in its yard. I enter the premises and we are introduced. They explain that the election campaign is a farce, and, if Malik Saidullaev is not allowed to participate, it will be a total farce, and that the election is actually an operation of some special task force.

Saidullaev has twenty-six campaign centres, including centres for work with young people and centres for contacts with religious leaders. The centres in Gudermes and Kurchaloi operate underground. Saidullaev cannot campaign now, but his campaign centres are active. "What do you mean? Are they quietly collecting signatures?" "No" "What happens then?" "People bring them. Today we already have 70 thousand signatures to support Malik." "Did the people bring them themselves?" "Certainly!"

I ask to see signature lists, and they give me a fresh stack of them. The column featuring addresses shows the same block: Nos. 8, 8, 8, 9, 9, etc. So, individuals from all the dwellings in the block came to sign the list in an organized way? I don't know why the campaigners do not admit that they visited every dwelling, but it is useless to discuss it with them...

The head of the campaign refers to an anonymous source that claimed that Kadyrov's people had conducted a survey that covered a thousand people in Grozny. The survey, conducted before the withdrawal of Saidullaev's and Aslakhanov's candidacies, showed that only 3% of the voters were going to vote for Kadyrov. Saidullaev's polls (he used village teachers as interviewers) conducted before Dzhabrailov and Aslakhanov left the race, revealed the support for the candidate between 65 and 70% and today it exceeds 80%. I ask for the data of the polls. It turns out that it "is not quite processed" yet. I hear stories about attacks on campaign centres, on their workers, and on like-minded people. I hear stories about their readiness to protect their candidate and to be ready to defend themselves at all times.

Leaving the house I suddenly run into one of my Moscow colleagues crossing the yard. We felt as happy to see each other as if we were old friends who had not seen each other for a dozen years. Casual acquaintances from the 'other life' are always delighted to meet you here. It is as if you have arrived from another world, or as if they had come to be part of this world and you are an unexpected guest from the world of the living. I am not quite sure which of the two metaphors fits best. I explain to him why I came to Chechnya. "And what are you doing here?" He responds, "I was offered a job at Saidullaev's election headquarters and refused. Then, they asked me if I did not want to help Chechnya get rid of Kadyrov. I thought about it and agreed". Do I understand his motives? We hug each other and part.

On my way back, I examine the motley campaign materials of Kadyrov. Banners are everywhere saying, "We need a strong president – vote for Kadyrov!" "Kadyrov: pure intentions, strong power!" I see posters with the same slogans and bright portraits of the acting president of the Chechen Republic. And here is the famous enlarged photo where Putin and Kadyrov shake hands. We travel along the streets of the devastated city with Akhmat-Hadji Kadyrov everywhere around us. With Putin. With a tractor. Against a background of mountains.

Well, "Do you want to work at Saidullaev's election headquarters?" is one thing, and "Do you want to help Chechnya get rid of Kadyrov?" is quite a different story.

MALIK MINGAYEVICH SAIDULLAEV – BIOGRAPHY

Chairman of the Directors Board of Milan Concern. Chairman of the Fund for Humanitarian Aid to Chechnya.

Born 5 October 1964 in the village of Alkhan-Yurt of the Urus Martan district of the Chechen-Ingush Republic. Brought up in a family with many children, has nine brothers and eight sisters. In 1971 entered secondary school No 2 of Alkhan-Yurt and graduated in 1981. After secondary school went to work in Khazakhstan. In 1981 started work on a construction site, later worked in a meat processing factory. Then he served in the Soviet Army. In 1985 worked as a laboratory assistant in the physics section of the Chechen-Ingush State University named after L.N.Tolstoy. Studied at the evening department of the physics faculty, then at the correspondence department of the economic faculty.

In 1986, when the Gorbachev thaw began, he started in business. In 1989 he became acquainted with Herman Sterligov, president of the Alisa company who offered him a partnership in the business. With the support of businessman Artyom Tarasov, Saidullaev created his own Milan Company four years later and took up lottery business, including The Russian Lotto at the Russian TV channel. At present Saidullaev has more than 60 thousand employees. The 'empire' of Milan, besides the Russian Lotto, includes the Milan beauty salon, the Kon i Pyos restaurant, Goodwill Science and Production Company, AO Lan Centre for Construction Technologies, Genii M Science and Technology Company, and other firms.

Saidullaev comes from the influential Benoi teip (Chechen tribe), as does Akhmat Kadyrov (This does not prevent Saidullaev from criticizing Kadyrov sharply). Saidullaev tried to become a deputy of the State Duma at the 1995 election with the federal list of the Kedr electoral association, but the association failed to reach the 5% barrier. In 2001 Vladimir Putin's awarded Saidullaev both the 300th Anniversary of Russian Navy medal and the Participant of Combat Actions decoration. Since 1998 Malik Saidullaev has participated in the activity of the Union for People's Power and Labour movement. In October 1999 he was elected Chairman of the State Council of the Chechen Republic.

Saidullaev proposes that direct presidential rule be introduced in Chechnya with the head of administration having the rank of a vice-premier of the Russian government. According to his forecasts, it is possible to bring the social and economic sphere of Chechnya up to the level of 1990 in two or three years when it would be necessary to conduct legitimate democratic elections. In Mr Saidullaev's opinion, the head of the Chechen Republic should have full authority in the Republic, including the right to coordinate the activities of the army (when its main units are withdrawn), law enforcement agencies, and representatives of federal ministries and agencies. As he puts it, it is necessary to develop a "complex economic programme featuring a strict schedule of financing and short-term monitoring." Mr Saidullaev believes that a part of the profit from the sale of Chechen oil should remain in the republic in the course of two or three years. Besides that it is necessary to conduct a dialogue with the representatives of different Chechen parties and movements, of the muftis, elders, intellectuals, and of the diaspora located outside Chechnya.

Saidullaev believes that Chechnya should become a full-fledged subject of the Russian Federation, and in advancing the constitutional process in the republic. In Saidullaev's view Maskhadov's participation in the presidential election in Chechnya could help to determine the proportion of the Chechen population that supports Maskhadov. Saidullaev admitted that he had helped Chechen fighters when they came to him. He explained that it does not mean financial help provided to the fighters, he means aid, including medical aid, provided for their relatives. Saidullaev claims that his men were able to disrupt completely a system that was providing financial aid to Chechen fighters from various organisations in Turkey. Saidullaev's family members (a sister and a brother) were victims of kidnappers. Saidullaev is married and has two children. (from kavkaz.memo.ru)

Appeal from the HQ of Saidullaev to President Putin, 16 September 2003

To: Mr V.V.Putin, president of the Russian Federation. Copy to: The government of the Russian Federation. From: Workers of the headquarters of the Sunzha District, of Stanitsa Assinovskaya, village Sernovodsk, Susaev, R.S., head of the headquarters of the Sunzha District of M.Saidullaev, candidate for the post of the president of the Chechen Republic

For you – it is a political game. For us – a chance to get out of chaos. Is there really a presidential election in Chechnya?!

APPEAL

The events of 13 September 2003 have forced us to write this letter. We find ourselves witnesses at the epicentre of the electoral processes of the presidential election in the Chechen Republic. We see and know, as no others can know, what is happening in the districts of the Chechen Republic. And we are ready to sign this letter and to take responsibility for setting out the facts in this letter.

Mr Kadyrov and his supporters are intimidating the population by means of physical violence. The heads and managers of all agencies and organisations have been threatened with dismissal and prosecution for any active or passive refusal to support and campaign for Akhmat Kadyrov as candidate for the post of the president. Kadyrov's supporters manipulate electoral procedures to push forward their candidate by every possible legal and illegal means.

The supporters of Malik Saidullaev were not allowed to open electoral headquarters in any state-owned building in the districts of the Chechen Republic, although they had no problems in finding vacant rooms. In response to our questions for the reasons, the administrators responded laconically, "An order has arrived from the Kadyrov's HQ banning your access to rooms. If we disobey we are in danger of losing our jobs and of prosecution."

Kadyrov's armed formations use violence and murder as weapons against the supporters and workers of Saidullaev's headquarters. There has been kidnapping and 'disappearances' of people. Groups of Kadyrov's men have been roving through Chechnya harassing our colleagues and supporters! The mass media of Chechnya and the Russian Federation lie openly, and use commercial services to broadcast and publish misinformation about other candidates.

Kadyrov's supporters captured workers of Saidullaev's headquarters in the villages of the district, took them to unfrequented places, where they were tortured and forced to dig their own graves. This fact was testified by Mr Amagov (Idris Khusanovich) who was captured and taken away while campaigning for Saidullaev. During its short period of existence five workers from our headquarters, including Arbi Saiev, Lema Isigov, and Idris Amagov, were subjected to various degrees of violence and psychological pressure by those who had seized and taken them outside the Sunzha District.

During the daytime in various regions of Chechnya, Kadyrov' men conduct zachistkas and unauthorized detentions of citizens. During the night hours machine-gun fire comes from the windows of Kadyrov's headquarters. According to the information that we have this is done in order to create a negative attitude among the law-abiding citizens of the regions of the Chechen Republic towards the headquarters and supporters of Malik Saidullaev. Kadyrov supporters hold that such actions of intimidation and terrorist operations belong to Saidullaev. They say: "You see that Saidullaev. You will see violence and wrongdoing by him and by his supporters. Saidullaev and his people use gangster methods to try to achieve their aims. And Kadyrov and his election supporters are suffering!" These allegations are supported by video commercials, showing how supportive authorities, elders and heads of many organisations are towards Akhmat Kadyrov.

In fact those who tried to object and oppose Kadyrov, were dismissed from their posts and are still being persecuted. The remaining of them, in answer to our question about their civil position, confessed. "We were intimidated – by blackmail or by threat of death. Others were bribed. But on the election day we shall vote for Saidullaev".

The peacemaking and patronage activities of Mr Saidullaev are known at all levels of Chechnya society. It is alleged that many of the signatures we have gathered in favour of Mr Saidullaev are not valid. We doubt that is true. But it is a fact that the team of Mr Kadyrov could not get the required number of signatures in favour of their candidate, so they got them under the name of Saidullaev! The candidature of Malik Saidullaev is associated with stability, peace processes and the readiness of insurgents to stop military actions and acts of sabotage.

In the summer of 2003 it was declared at an international conference that Chechnya was on the verge of the so-called 'Lost War' formula. One of the main reasons why the insurgent forces of Ichkeria were ready to lay down their arms and to accept amnesties and rehabilitation were the guarantees of Malik Saidullaev. Otherwise, they were ready to continue the war. Kadyrov's role has been a factor causing special aggression. The fact that Chechnya has made a step towards a civil war is an irrefutable fact. And the only neutralizing force for this opposition was Saidullaev. Having become president, he could become a guarantor for the elimination of the causes and consequences of the civil military conflict.

Unfortunately, many Russians and the heads of various echelons of power do not realize and do not understand that Malik Mingayevich Saidullaev is not only a guarantor of peace, prosperity and creation in Chechnya, but also a guarantor of stability in the Russian Federation as a whole! He is a symbol of public order and well-being throughout Russia. Saidullaev is not a loner and is not motivated primarily by self-interest. Because of this he has many supporters in the Russian Federation and in other countries. Saidullaev's appeal, set out with his associates, declares to that in Russia "It is now time to escape from collapse and chaos!"

Mr Saidullaev is of a generation and from a galaxy of people who will drive society, the economy and international relations in a positive direction. There is plenty of evidence to support this fact, and there is no need to spell it out. This generation are known by their deeds. But the fact that the president of the Russian Federation, Mr Putin, pays no attention to this matter looks at least strange! Failure to notice people oriented along the similar mentality, means not to have any idea on what can bring Russia into peace and prosperity.

Susaev, R.S.

Signatures of 240 members of the headquarters of the Sunzha District of the Chechen Republic – villages of Sernovodsk and Assinovskaya.

Chronicle of Events: 13 September to 16 September

13 September 2003. According to the report of local residents, Khasan and Apti Alaudinov disappeared in the forest at the edge of the Makhkety village, Vedeno district. That morning the brothers went on their tractor into the forest to fell firewood for winter and did not return. When relatives searched the forest, they found the tractor but did not see any traces of Khasan or Apti. When the family of Alaudinov asked for help at the military unit located in the vicinity of the Makhkety village, they were told that a paratroop unit was conducting an operation here and no search was possible until the operation is over.
Chechen Committee for National Salvation

14 September 2003. In the centre of Grozny, in the building of a former supermarket the mutilated body of 28-year-old Aslambek Dikayev, resident of Duba-Yurt, Shali district, was discovered. Local residents report that the corpse retained traces of brutal torture. Evidently Dikayev was the victim of an extra-judicial killing on the part of some enforcement agencies.
Chechen Committee for National Salvation

15 September 2003. About 2 am in the village of Avtury in the Shali district unknown armed people in masks and military uniforms shot to death Isa Magomedovich Musayev, born in 1971, living at 14, Titova Street. Late at night there was a knock on the door of the Musayev's house. His wife Manash Abubakarova, born in 1973, thought it was an ID check by the military and opened the door without asking who it was. Four armed men in masks entered. They went straight to the room where Isa Musayev was sleeping, forced him out of bed and put him up against a wall. They did not ask any questions, they did not want to see any documents – they shot Isa to death and hurriedly left the house. Manash Abubakarova with an 18-month old baby in her arms tried to protect her husband but one of the assailants grabbed the baby from her and threw him on the floor, roughly pushing Manash against the wall injuring her shoulder. According to Manash Abubakarova, two of the assailants were Chechens and the other two were Russians. There were some people in the street but she could not tell how many. Not long before his death, Musayev started to work as an extra-departmental guard in the town of Shali.
Memorial Human Rights Centre

15 September 2003. Two people were shot dead and two heavily wounded at 13.30 pm in an attack in the centre of the village of Sernovodsk in the Sunzha district where four policemen were having lunch at the Markha Café opposite the district administration building in Sovetskaya Street. Those policemen had been sent to the Sunzha police station from the town of Barnaul in the Altai Region six months prior to the incident. According to eyewitnesses, while the policemen were having lunch under the tent round the corner of the café trailer, two young men of about 20 years of age came from the territory of the adjacent water tower. One of them was carrying a sports bag on his shoulder. They went round the trailer and opened fire from a sub-machine gun that they took out of the bag, emptying the magazine. After that they put the gun back into the bag and strolled in the direction of Rechnaya Street. Witnesses insist that while one of the men was shooting, the other one was filming the scene on video. At the time of the attack there were people in front of the district administration building. However, these involuntary witnesses of the attack were shocked by what they had just seen and did not take any steps to detain the assailants.

Villagers who happened to be nearby hailed a shuttle service minivan and rushed the wounded policemen to the local hospital, where they were given first aid. Some time later an ambulance took the policemen to the central district hospital in the village of Ord-

jonikidzhevskaya (Sunzha district, Republic of Ingushetia). According to a nurse, one of the wounded policemen said that it was local policemen who shot them. The bodies of the two dead policemen were left at the scene of the crime until the arrival of FSB agents from Achkhoi-Martan and Grozny. One of the killed policemen, a major, was deputy chief of police for public security. The villagers had a very high opinion of the policemen. They said: "They were calm in carrying out their military duties and even provided assistance in the issue of passports to the local people." In the temporary placement centre (PVR) they provided advice to internally displaced people on issues of temporary registration.
Memorial Human Rights Centre

15 September 2003. Residents of the village of Avtury in the Shali district reported that armed people in masks had kidnapped from his home Mokhmad Saidayev, 40, father of five small children. According to relatives and acquaintances, Saidayev was a well-known religious activist respected by his fellow villagers. It is not yet known who stands behind the kidnapping of Mokhmad Saidayev. In 2002 Saidayev's 15-year-old son, who suffered from a severe form of a psychiatric illness, was shot dead by the Russian federal forces.
Chechen Committee for National Salvation

16 September 2003. After 9.00 am agents of the FSB of the Achkhoi-Martan district carried out a mop-up operation to check compliance with address registration requirements in the village of Sernovodsk in the Sunzha district. The operation was in response to an armed attack on Russian policemen the day before. The agents arrived in Sernovodsk in an armoured personnel carrier, an UAZ-452 and an UAZ-469, all vehicles having number plates. Some of the agents were in masks. During their raid of the village they were accompanied by Lom-Ali Khildikhoroev, a district policeman. Leaving the APC near the police station building, the FSB men moved around the village in the two UAZ cars. The UAZ-469 stopped in front of the building of the secondary school No 3. Four of the FSB men went inside and detained, in front of the class, Movli Zaindinovich Batalov, an eighth-grader.

The other group of the agents moved to M.Gorky Street, where they detained Bekkhan Vakhidovich Sulaev (born in 1983). According to relatives, Bekkhan lived at home during the whole war and there was no evidence of any illegal activities by him. His older brother was killed during the operation in the village of Komsomolskoye (March 2000). Both detainees were taken to the building of the Sunzha police. Three hours later Batalov was released. According to the boy, the interrogators were interested in the whereabouts of his older brother Kazbek. Sulaev was released at about 6.00 pm. He was asked questions about his whereabouts during the second war and whether he had heard anything related to the killing of the policemen. Neither of the two detainees were beaten, offended or humiliated during the interrogations.

At 4.30 pm a resident of the village of Samashky Musa Nazirov, a third-year student at the Agricultural College, was detained on the Agricultural College campus and taken to the police department. Reportedly, he was arrested for irregularities with his address registration, although he had on him both his passport and his student's record book. He was detained by armed people without masks identifying themselves as agents of the security service of Kadyrov. They had come to the village in four grey UAZ vehicles with number plates.

The agents randomly stopped several people in the yard of the college and near the faculty building and checked their documents. The detention was performed without rudeness and the detainee was told that he would be taken to the district police department where "everything would be clarified and he would be released." However, several staff members of the Agricultural College went to the police: Nadezhda Shamsoltovna Madagova (Deputy Director for Educational Work), Sergei Kuzmich Popov (Chairman of department), Bavdi Magamaev (Deputy Director for Administrative and Economic Activities), and Sultan Irbaiyev, who provided guarantees with respect to their student. After their intervention Nazirov was released.

Memorial Human Rights Centre

16 September 2003. A member of the armed Ichkeria formation, with the family name Yandarbaev and his nineteen-year-old niece were killed in the morning in the Novie Atagy village, Shali district. Half an hour earlier Yandarbaev had come to visit his brother's family. His brother had been killed in 2000 in a helicopter shoot-out at Shali. Suddenly eight armoured UAZ vehicles stopped at the house and people in camouflage uniforms surrounded it and opened gun-fire. At that time Yandarbaev's sister-in-law, her nineteen-year-old daughter, his two-year-old grand-daughter and his paralyzed grandmother were in the house. The attackers did not call on Yandarbaev to surrender and made no attempt to spare the women. The young girl was hit instantly hit (later eleven bullet wounds were found in her body). Yandarbaev moved the paralyzed old lady to the floor, covered her with cushions and then urged his sister-in-law to flee through the window. She took the young child and started running. The attackers shouted after her, "We let you live only because of the little bastard!" Then Yandarbaev opened fire, wounded two of his attackers but was killed. The attackers made his neighbour take his gun and his documents. Then they put the body onto a truck, searched the house, and stole money.

Memorial Human Rights Centre

16 September 2003. A mutilated corpse was discovered on the outskirts of the village of Bachy-Yurt in the Kurchalovsky district. The corpse was moved to the mosque of the village of Ilaskhan-Yurt in the Gudermes district. On the same day relatives identified the dead person as Shamil-Hadji Abusoltovich Elmurzaev, born in 1968 who had lived in a newly-built residential complex on the south-eastern outskirts of the village of Ilaskhan-Yurt. Much evidence of torture was to be seen on the corpse with broken legs and the arms. Traditionally, Chechens show the body of a dead person to relatives after cleansing,

but the body of Shamil-Hadji was in such a state that he was buried without being shown to his female relatives. A week earlier Shamil-Hadji had been arrested in a coffee shop in Grozny by agents of local law enforcement agencies. Shamil-Hadji was a member of the armed formations of the Chechen Republic of Ichkeria but applied to Kadyrov for amnesty. According to relatives, he was assured of the possibility of being granted amnesty; however, he was later arrested and disappeared.
Memorial Human Rights Centre

On 16 September Vladimir Putin signed his edict on Aslambek Aslakhanov's appointment as RF president's aide.
Strana.Ru

7 THE MOOR DID HIS DEED: INTERVENTION BY PAIZULLAEV

CANDIDATE NIKOLAI PAIZULLAEV

Interviewed by Ruslan Umarov, Caucasian Knot

Would you tell of your background?

I was born in Grozny in 1948. I've got higher education. I am an engineer-architect by profession. Now I am a leading specialist of the Chechen acting president's press service, and an active participant in social and political events in Chechnya.

Why did you decide to propose yourself as candidate?

I know the people well because I am one of them. I worked as a loader and a carrier. I made my living by the sweat of my brow. I deeply sympathize with my fellow countrymen and believe that only a man who came from the ordinary people can effectively serve them. And I am ready for it.

Who are your voters?

The most downtrodden people, those who live below the poverty line, those who have lost their relatives, the humiliated and the insulted. These groups are great in number.

How do you estimate the current situation in the Chechen Republic? I'd like to focus on two things: the Chechnya-Ichkeria dilemma and the situation with the opposition and its influence...

In my opinion, the belligerents should have reached a logical point – some kind of agreement as a basis for further negotiations. As long as Ichkeria and Russia have not come to such an agreement we must make our choice. We cannot stay in a suspended state without an authorised government. When chiefs quarrel, the innocent, and especially the young, get bloodied. Chechens want peace and are ready for the election. There is no alternative way forward and no opposition to the election.

To what extent are reports in the central media subjective in their coverage of Chechnya?

There is no objectivity. Everything said or written is turned against us.

What will be your first practical steps if you win the election?

To regularise relationships with Russia, so that Chechnya and the Chechens are treated in the same way as other subjects of the Russian Federation. To use all possible means to alleviate poverty and to protect the poor from violence by means of firm control over all security agencies.

Would you say something about your election programme?

The priorities of my programme are to find the 'disappeared' at any cost, to stop the illegal detention of citizens, to transfer the military away from the republic, to get rid of sentry posts, to get migrants back, and so on.

Who do you consider to be your principal rival?

Kadyrov.

How do you estimate your odds for success?

We have close contact with the people. We feel understanding and support. If there is a second round, I am sure I will reach it. If the election is decided in the first round, Akhmat Kadyrov will surely be the winner – taking into account his campaigning advantages.

What are the distinctive features about your election campaign?

Our meetings with people – something that other contenders can hardly boast of.

What is your estimation of the election campaigns of the other contenders?

Of course, all the contenders have different resources, but TV appearances and press reports are assigned uniformly according to schedule.

Do you believe the votes will be fairly counted?

No, I don't.

What is your attitude towards the counter-terrorist operations? Have they changed with time?

These operations are conducted with many gross violations of Russian law. I don't see any major changes over time.

Have you experienced any difficulties in the course of your election campaign?

We have not found obstacles from insurgents or opponents. There are no noticeable difficulties.

CANDIDATE PAIZULLAEV'S HEADQUARTERS

Tanya Lokshina, Moscow Helsinki Group/Centre 'Demos'

If you travel to Chechnya specifically to assess the pre-election situation, you cannot but visit the candidates' headquarters. And that's exactly what I was planning to do, having reached Grozny on a grey rainy Thursday 18 September 2003, with less than three weeks to go until Chechnya's presidential election. The local paper Terskaya Pravda declares that the "nation-wide election...of the first president of free Chechnya will become chronicles in the history of the Chechen people and will be studied by our descendants". I hope that while studying these extraordinary events, 'descendants' with various views, will not ignore my humble observations.

It took me quite a while to find the Department of Commerce in a tumbledown city. Actually the word 'tumbledown' is not strong enough to describe Grozny. There are some buildings in the city that, miraculously, are still standing. Grozny cannot be said to have been completely levelled to the ground. And arriving at a dilapidated stairway to the second floor, I found what I was looking for – the sign 'Headquarters of Nikolai Paizullaev'.

The visit to Mr Paizullaev was top of my agenda for a number of reasons. Paizullaev is a leading specialist in the press office of the acting president of Chechnya, Kadyrov, so it appears as if he is standing against his own boss.

There were no signs of his campaign in Grozny, but this might not mean very much. Except for the ubiquity of Kadyrov posters, no significant indication of election activity was apparent in Chechnya by 18 September. Another reason for seeing Paizullaev was that it was he who had initiated the de-registration procedure again Malik Saidullaev – the only serious rival to the current head of the Republic in the pre-election steeplechase – after such barriers as Aslambek Aslakhanov and Khussein Dzhabrailov had been successfully eliminated.

In general, this candidate is an enigmatic and contradictory character. It turned out to be impossible to get in touch with him personally on that particular day. Paizullaev's phone number was not included in the list of candidates for the Presidency and I did not have the time to look for alternative means of contacting him to arrange for a meeting. However the impossibility of talking with the candidate in person did not upset me too much; as far as the election is concerned, a lengthy conversation with the head of the headquarters can be much more informative.

Having entered the room, I blurted out the standard opening speech, "Moscow Helsinki Group, the oldest and one of the strongest of human rights organisations now active in Russia, is seriously concerned with the pre-election situation in Chechnya and intends to find out to what extent the electoral rights of citizens are being complied with."

A tousled middle-aged man with shining dark eyes asked me with genuine surprise:

"So, you have come to see me?"

"If you are the head of the headquarters, then I have come to see you."

"Yes, I am," he introduced himself, "Movsar Kagirmanov. And you've really come to speak to me? What about?"

"Well," I twittered, "You are running the election headquarters, working with voters. I wonder how you see the pre-election situation, whether your team is facing problems".

"Wait a second. I will call the staff, so you can see everyone. Hey, come over here! All of you! Someone has come to talk to us!"

This war-cry of the chief of the headquarters revealed such genuine rejoicing that I suspected I was the first visitor in the whole history of this establishment. As if with a wave of a wand, the room was filled with people, and more than a dozen pairs of eyes gazed at me in expectation.

"So, now everybody is here," Kagirmanov began the conversation. "And do you know the name of our candidate?"

"Nikolai Paizullaev," I answered horror-struck, trying to think up the best way to get out of this madhouse. All the people around the table nodded in accord.

"Absolutely right," Kagirmanov acknowledged, "And here is his portrait. This is a gift for you."

A middle-aged man in a suit stared at me from the glossy poster. He bore a pensive romantic look and an imposing grey moustache.

"And how many centres does the candidate have in all? How did you complete the collection of signatures?"

I was told that there was nothing else but the headquarters where I was sitting at that moment. But there were district representatives and most of them were present in the room. A total of 13,580 signatures had been collected. Kagirmanov revealed that he was not just the head of the headquarters but also the head of the Charity Foundation 'Mother's Call' registered as long ago as 1995. Apparently, people involved in the Foundation activities were also the ones collecting the signatures in support of Paizullaev. The headquarters staff are involved in this Foundation in one way or another.

This was the one tiny streak of normality in our conversation. Then, having reached out to me across the table, Kagirmanov uttered confidentially, "You have asked me about our current problems, didn't you? I have to tell you, there is a problem, and a very serious one indeed: the headquarters team have not been paid anything up to now. My colleagues can confirm that."

"You have not been paid by your candidate?"

"No, we haven't. And it is a very disturbing situation."

"I am sorry. I really feel for you. Does your candidate have a programme?"

"What?"

"A programme."

"Mr Paizullaev has not presented any programme so far."

"But he will?"

"Very unlikely…"

"Then, how are you promoting him? What did you tell the people when collecting these 13,500 signatures?"

"Well, I personally explained everything to the campaigners. I have known Paizullaev for a long time. We said that he had initially worked at the market carrying various loads, and he is that type of a person…"

"And that was enough?"

"He is a folk poet."

I recalled one poet running for the presidency of Chechnya before – Zelimkhan Yandarbiev – the best proof of the poor compatibility of these roles.

"And how do you run the campaign? What campaign materials do you disseminate?"

"Materials?"

"Like posters, leaflets…"

"No, we just give people Paizullaev's portraits and the Constitution of the Chechen Republic."

After that, I was handed a green brochure entitled 'Draft Constitution of the Chechen Republic', which seemed to have been left over from the time of the unforgettable March referendum. Reverently holding the brochure, I decided to ask a delicate question, "If I am not mistaken, it was your candidate who initiated the withdrawal of Malik Saidullaev?"

A puzzled woman shielded her mouth with a hand:

"What, Malik was removed?"

"Yes, a week ago."

"But this is the first I've heard about it."

Other staff started exchanging opinions and asking questions. They learnt from me that the RF Supreme Court was in process of reviewing the case, and would make a decision soon...

The chief of the headquarters tried to take control of the situation, "We found out about that only afterwards. We did not know before. And our candidate himself did not know. He was told at the last moment, and he filed the complaint."

"And who told him?"

"Well, you know..."

"And what is your candidate going to do?"

"As the saying goes, 'The Moor has done his deed – it's time for the Moor to leave.'"

"Do you think he will quit, then?"

"We are telling you that our staff have not been paid a penny. And we haven't seen the candidate for a couple of weeks. We could not get his signature for some important documents for two whole weeks! You're telling me about the candidate! We were the ones who put him up this high, so we'll be the ones to bring him down..."

I noticed a sheet of paper on the table on front of Kagirmanov – the head of the headquarters. Under the heading 'Sociological Poll Questionnaire' there was a table with the names and brief personal data on the candidates and two simple questions for the voters, 'Who are you going to vote for?' and 'Why are you going to vote this way?' There were also columns to record some basic information on respondents.

"You've got a questionnaire. How many people did your survey cover? What are the outcomes?"

"We have not surveyed anyone. We do not know how to conduct surveys. And we have not been paid for two months..."

"And why is the questionnaire here, then?"

"Somebody brought it and asked us to conduct the survey. But we are not doing anything. I just use the questionnaire to mark the withdrawn candidates. I put a 'minus' next to Aslakhanov's name. Yesterday Tsuev left, so I put a 'minus' next to his name too. And a very little 'minus' sign next to Saidullaev's, because it is not certain yet..."

At this dramatic moment I got up and left. Either I had gone mad, or the world had turned into bedlam. This theatre of the absurd would have been funny if there had been no real living people within it; people worn out by the war and reading in the newspapers today that *'Chechnya's presidential election will lead to the unification of Chechnya. This election is necessary and timely.'*

Two hours later I was talking to mothers of the 'disappeared' crowded on the doorstep of the local administration building in Shali. The women kept repeating, "How can we speak of an election when we do not even know where our sons are or whether they are alive or dead?" These words, and the grief the expressed, put into perspective the ridiculous scene in Paizullaev's headquarters, turning it from farce into tragedy.

Chronicle of Events: 17 September to 25 September

On 17 September Deputy Military Commandant of Chechnya Said-Selim Tsuev withdrew from the race.
Strana.Ru

On 17 September the Supreme Court of the Chechen Republic considered the application filed by Chechen Republic presidential candidate Shamil Buraev who, referring to a number of violations, asked to cancel Akhmat Kadyrov's registration as a candidate. The rationale presented by Buraev concluded that the meeting between Kadyrov and president Putin had been election propaganda supported by administrative resources. But the Court rejected this case. The Court also considered the meeting, also shown on TV, on the issue of compensation payments to those who had lost housing as a result of combat activities. The court also ruled that complaints against the government of Chechnya to the effect that it had been holding its meetings in various districts of the republic in order to campaign for local leaders in favour of Kadyrov were unsubstantiated.
Strana.Ru

On 19 September the State Duma adopted a resolution 'On Sending to the Chechen Republic a Group of the State Duma Deputies to observe voting on 5 October 2003 at the Election of the First president of the Chechen Republic. The delegation included represen-

tatives of all nine deputies' associations of the Duma. The commission was headed by Frants Klintsevich, Deputy Duma Leader of the 'Unity – United Russia' faction.
Strana.Ru

20 September 2003. In the village of Elistanzhi, Vedeno district, local residents report that Russian military captured and took the Yunusovs, father and the son, to an unknown destination. According to relatives, Samrail Yunusov and his aged father Said Selim were kidnapped by men from the 45th regiment of the Defence Ministry of the Russian Federation. This paratroop unit, often accused by the residents of Vedeno district of arbitrary violence against peaceful people, is located near the village of Khattuni. Relatives of the kidnapped persons tried in vain to establish the whereabouts of the Yunusovs and what happened to them.
Chechen Committee for National Salvation

20 September 2003. Military from the 45th special air-force landing troops, quartered near the village of Khatuny, arrived at the village of Elistandzhi, Vedeno district and undertook a special search operation. Military vehicles were moving through the village all night. The military seized and took away two brothers. They also took the passports and cars of several residents. The next day the brothers were set free. No local policeman were involved in the operation, although the special unit of the military commandment under Sulim Amadaev is based in the region.
Memorial Human Rights Centre

21 September 2003. A policeman from the Bashkir Republic was killed in the Urus-Martan district in a fight between the Chechen and Bashkir special police task force units. The incident took place at the checkpoint between Urus-Martan and the village of Gekhi. It was Sunday when people usually come to the fair in Urus-Martan. Men of the Bashkir special police task force who were on duty barred the way leaving enough space for only one car to pass. This made it easy for policemen to extort payment for passage through the checkpoint. This resulted in a queue of vehicles. A man from the Chechen special police task force, having left his car in the line, came up to the checkpoint and showing his police ID asked the patrol on duty to let him through. The man on duty responded with insulting language and a fight broke out. When the law enforcers were dragged apart, the Chechen policeman radioed for help, and when the help arrived, the fight continued on a massive scale. In the course of the fight one Bashkir policeman was shot while the others, abandoning their weapons, fled into the fields. Two Russian colleagues injured during the fight were pushed by the Chechen policemen into their car and taken away. It is believed that the Chechen policeman who wanted to be let through was a resident of the Shalazhi village of Urus-Martan district.
Russian-Chechen Friendship Society

On 21 September Ibragim Akhmatov, Ichkeria Parliament Deputy, stated that not a single Ichkeria deputy living in the territory of Chechnya and Ingushetia signed the impeachment of president Maskhadov.
kavkaz.memo.ru

22 September 2003. According to local citizens, collaborators of Russian and Chechen power groups kidnapped an officer of the Chechen Ministry of Internal Affairs, Zelymkhan Zakriev, in the village of Novie Aldy, Zavodsk district. As evidenced by relatives of the policeman, a group of masked Russian military broke in Zakriev's house around 4 am. The attackers woke up Zelymkhan, beat him with his rifle, took him out to the street, threw him in a car, and drove away. Zakriev's mother reported that one of the Russian military told her that she would never see her son again. The attempts of the kidnapped officer's relatives to establish his whereabouts and fate were unsuccessful. Zelymkhan Zakriev, abducted from his own house by collaborators of the groups is classified as missing.
Chechen Committee for National Salvation

On 22 September in the village of Gekhi of the Urus-Martan district of the Chechen Republic, school principals took school-bags from the students. This was done to make them bring their parents to school for a meeting. But the meeting had nothing to do with teaching. The principals stated that "the children of those who do not vote for Kadyrov would be expelled from schools". But Beslan Gantamirov, who had been deposed from his post as minister of the press and information of the Chechen Republic by the acting president of Chechnya stated that the villagers would not vote for Kadyrov. According to information received from teachers, the principals of the Gehki schools were acting under instructions given at the one of the regular meetings of the district department of education.
kavkaz.memo.ru

23 September. In the village of Sernovodsk of the Sunzha district, election headquarters to support Kadyrov was set up in the agricultural college that was being prepared to house forced migrants returning from Ingushetia. At first they occupied one room on the first floor, then two more on the same floor and three on the second. This was done with the consent of the head of administration of the Sunzha district Khizir Vitaev and agreed upon with the building superintendent Zarema Guchigova. During the night of 19 September the building of the agricultural college was fired at from assault rifles by unidentified gunmen. Luckily no one was hurt. At present forced migrants are greatly concerned and worried because of the headquarters and propaganda posters on the building facade. Posters are pasted on the buildings by teenagers who get paid in cash for each poster. Headquarters staff are paid $100 per month.
Memorial Human Rights Centre

23 September. Prior to the presidential campaign in Chechnya the Chechen Ministry of the Press had drawn lots for candidates to get free newspaper page space. Two weeks before

the election the mass media people stated that the newspaper space granted is not made full use of by the candidates. According to Hassan Gafuraev, deputy chief editor of the Vesti Respubliki newspaper, the least active in terms of paper campaigns are Nikolai Paizullaev and Avkhat Khanchukaev.
kavkaz.memo.ru

On 23 September the head of the Chechen Republic Ministry of Internal Affairs press service, Ruslan Atsaev, reported that in Chechnya republican police personnel had started a 24-hour guard duty at 20 local election commissions. According to Atsaev the order had come from the Minister of the Interior Alu Alkhanov. 'These measures are taken to prevent provocation and possible terrorist attacks on the eve of the presidential election scheduled to take place on 5 October,' stressed R.Atsaev. The local election commissions will be guarded by a combination of police patrols, departments of site protection and local police. Atsaev said that the police would soon start a 24-hour guard duty at all election commissions.
kavkaz.memo.ru

On 23 September an official representative of the regional operational headquarters on controlling counter-terrorist operation in the Northern Caucasus, Ilya Shabalkin, reported that the law enforcement agencies had received information that an international organisation 'Muslim Brothers' had allocated 3 billion US dollars to the leaders of armed detachments. The money was intended for use for disruption of the presidential election in Chechnya. The money was paid to the organisation's official Abu al-Valid who passed it on to Maskhadov, Basaev, Gelaev and leaders of armed formations. On 22 September in a Grozny store which was used as a rendezvous place, a money trafficker was detained. 360,000 forged dollars were found in his car. The messenger admitted that on 5 September 2003 he had received 280,000 genuine US dollars and, upon the instruction of Maskhadov himself, he purchased 1,127,000 forged dollars from criminals. "Thus, Arab mercenaries, as well as Maskhadov, Basaev and others were going to pay their rank-and-file fighters in forged dollars," stressed Shabalkin.
kavkaz.memo.ru

23 September. Alexander Veshnyakov, Chairman of the RF Central Election Commission said in an interview that CIS representatives will take part in the deliberations of a group of international observers who will monitor the presidential election in the Chechen Republic on 5 October. According to him, the CIS observer group will include up to ten members, and will be headed by CIS Executive Secretary Yuri Yarov. "A number of public and human rights organisations displayed their initiative. These organisations cooperate with the human rights commission and with the president of the Russian Federation," noted the RF Central Election Commission Chairman. He added that up to ten more observers from these organisations are willing to go to Chechnya. Veshnyakov also added that the State

Duma had made a decision to send to the republic a group of Duma observers. Veshnyakov said that official invitations to send observers to Chechnya had been forwarded to a number of international organisations. "So far we haven't receive replies from the Council of Europe, League of Arab States and Islamic Conference organisation," he said. The OSCE had replied that "they are not in a position to send their representatives to the republic."
kavkaz.memo.ru

23 September 2003. The residents of the Goi-Chu district (Komsomolskoe), of the Urus-Martan region, have made an official appeal to the Special Representative of the president of the Russian Federation on Human Rights in Chechnya, Sultygov. The appeal has been signed by 52 persons. The appeal text is cited here unaltered by the Memorial Human Rights Centre:

An unhealthy situation is developing around the preparatory work for compensation payments for loss of housing and property in the resolution of the crisis in the Chechen Republic. The tragic example of the destruction of the village of Komsomolskoe shows that these payments will not be carried out smoothly. First of all, many of us are not satisfied that 300 thousand roubles is adequate to build a two–three room house – even without taking into consideration re-establishing household stock, gates, fences, poultry, etc. Second, in summer of 2000, a region commission (OKS) drew up a report covering every farm, and approved of by every farm, giving a precise account of the level of damage to housing and other buildings. Third, before the referendum it was declared, that each family member should have 18 square metres living space, and that one square metre costs 8,400 roubles. The Chief of the State Building Ministry of the Russian Federation, N.Koshman, announced this sum in the TV programme 'The Hero of the Day.' But after the referendum it was decided to make all dwellings the same size.

At the end of the summer of 2001 representatives of the Danish Refugee Council came to the village with a programme for the creation of living conditions for everybody who would like to return to the village. Roof materials, windows, doors, floors, glass and cement were promised. People were assured, that this support would not affect compensation payments. Many people agreed to receive the humanitarian help. In October–November 2001, people received between 10 and 102 sheets of slate and roof building material. But the programme came to a halt because of the war in Afghanistan. Many recipients were not living in the village and most of the aid materials were stolen during the winter.

When our villages were destroyed, thousands of the residents, including babies and old people, were forced to live in the open outside the village for many days and nights in the cold weather at the beginning of March. The regional authority was not concerned about our situation. There were several visits by the aides of the region's Chief and by the mayor of Urus-Martan, but they failed to resolve anything. Thousand of hostages witnessed the destruction. They could see large military transporters removing property from private homes. For some reason, nobody speaks now about the moral outrage we felt.

Nobody in the region has ever shown willingness to care about management of the living conditions of refugees. Everything is just left to slide. Four months have passed since the charitable actions of the Danish Refugee Council. Many people have been taken off the lists of recipients, and others have received only half of their allocation. It seems to be believed that those years of wandering and living in strangers' houses increased our wealth.

Dear Mr Sultygov! In our lengthy appeal we must earnestly ask that you defend the rights that have been violated. Egalitarianism does not settle matters because it does not suit our needs. The announcement of the regional authority and the «flying commission» that they are not interested in how many families are living in the same house is astonishing. It means that only one family in a house has a chance to be included in the lists for receiving compensation payments. The other families will have wait for another ten years to reach their turn for restoration of their rights. In the unlucky case of receiving even one sheet of slate from the Danish Refugee Council, it seems the family has to forget the compensation for lost housing. At the end of the appeal we wish to state that nobody is taking serious account of the problems of our village. The main goal of the benefactor agencies is their own benefits and advantages. The interests of those who are suffering are not taken into account. We therefore request that you defend our legal rights and take control the situation in the village.
Memorial Human Rights Centre

23 September 2003. For the whole day the gas supply of the city of Grozny was interrupted. According to reports, the gas supply was shut off because of a strike of workers from Grozneftegaz company. The strike was triggered by the killing by the Russian military of one of the workers from that industrial plant. The day before, a group of workers from Grozneftegaz travelled to the Shali district of the Chechen Republic to repair the gas pipe line around the district Chiri-Yurt. During the night, a worker went outside to manage his own business and was killed by Russian soldiers. Such arbitrariness outraged the workers of Grozneftegaz, who called a strike and demanded that the killers of their colleague should be found and punished.
Chechen Committee for National Salvation

On 24 September, there was an explosion in the basement of the school No 10 building in Kavkaz district, located within the limits of the town of Shali of the Chechen Republic. The basement houses election office No 284. The explosion partially destroyed the basement walls, smashed window panes and frames in some rooms. Nobody was hurt.
Russian-Chechen Friendship Society

On 24 September Akhmat Kadyrov arrived in New York as part of the Russian delegation headed by Putin. On 27 September they arrived in Washington. E.Khorishko, representing

the Russian Embassy in the USA, commented that it was not clear to Russia why the United States had met Chechen insurgents and terrorists but not asked for a meeting with Kadyrov. The Russian-American summit was accompanied by massive criticism in the US mass media and numerous protests on the part of human rights activists.
kavkaz.memo.ru

24 September. The Prefecture of the Central administrative district of Moscow refused to accept the notification of radicals about the organisation of a demonstration on 3 October in Teatralnaya Square [centre of Moscow] with the slogan 'Chechnya: Provisional administration of UN Rather than Election Imitation.' The reason given for the refusal was that police forces of the city of Moscow on that day would be deployed to ensure public order on the 10th anniversary of the October coup attempt in 1993. Therefore, the demonstration of the Transnational Radical Party and the Cathedral Club-Association for Liberal Reforms will be held in Teatralnaya Square near the monument to Karl Marx on Sunday, 5 October at 1 pm on the same day as the so-called 'presidential election' in Chechnya.
kavkaz.memo.ru

24 September. Observers from Georgia will take part in the presidential election monitoring in Chechnya on 5 October. As was reported by the State Office of Georgia the idea of such election monitoring had originated with the Russian president Vladimir Putin. He came up with the proposal at the meeting with Eduard Shevardnadze at the Yalta summit of CIS heads of state (18–19 September). Shevardnadze accepted the proposal but it is still not known how many observers from Georgia will go to Chechnya.
kavkaz.memo.ru

On 24 September the RF Central Election Commission Chairman Alexander Veshnyakov said at a news conference in Moscow that OSCE "for organisational reasons" had refused to send its observers to the presidential election in Chechnya, scheduled for 5 October. Other international organisations – namely the Council of Europe, Organisation of Islamic Conference and the League of the Arab States had not replied to the invitation of the Russian Central Election Commission. According to Veshnyakov, the presidential election in Chechnya will be observed by representatives of about ten CIS countries.
kavkaz.memo.ru

On 24 September the print shop in Nalchik printed ballot papers for the forthcoming presidential election in the Chechen Republic. Ballots were printed on orders from the Chechnya Election Commission. According to the print shop employees all 580,000 ballot papers were ready the previous week. They contain names of the seven candidates for presidency of the Chechen Republic: Akhmat Kadyrov, head of the current administration of Chechnya; Khussein Biybulatov, former vice-premier of the republic's government during Maskhadov's times; Shamil Buraev, ex-head of Achkhoi-Martan district; Nikolai Paizullaev, employee of the press service of the current administration of the republic; Abdulla

Bugaev, unemployed;, Avkhat Khanchukaev, professor at Chechen State University, and Kudus Saduev, Deputy General Manager of the Grozneftegaz joint stock company.
kavkaz.memo.ru

24 September. On the basis of information received from members of the local population the law enforcement personnel discovered and confiscated a flame-thrower RPO-A 'Shmel' from Isa Ramzaev, born in 1978, resident of Nozhai-Yurt district. The regional operational headquarters for control of counter-terrorist operations in the Northern Caucasus, reported that one of the leaders of insurgents had instructed Ramzaev to set fire to the polling station in Nozhai-Yurt.
kavkaz.memo.ru

On 24 September Ludmila Alexeeva, Chair of the Moscow Helsinki Group, said at the news conference that Russian human rights activists would not observe the presidential election in Chechnya. The decision was made because three 'real candidates' – Malik Saidullaev, Aslambek Aslakhanov and Khussein Dzhabrailov had been kicked out of the race. They were candidates who could compete with the acting head of the republic. MHG also decided against inviting foreign observers to Chechnya since their presence could lend legal status to the election.
kavkaz.memo.ru

24 September. Ilyas Akhmatov, Minister of Foreign Affairs of the Maskhadov government called upon the United States to promote provisional international rule on Chechnya in order to resolve the conflict which had assumed the magnitude of genocide. In his address circulated on September 24, Ilyas Akhmatov maintained that over the past 10 years at least a quarter of Chechens had been killed as a result of hostilities, hundreds of thousands had left the republic, and those who stayed faced the threat of torture, illegal arrests, kidnappings and looting. Ilyas Akhmatov urged the United States president to turn to Vladimir Putin with a proposal to withdraw federal forces from Chechnya, allow the involvement of international forces and commence a genuine political dialogue with elected president Aslan Maskhadov.
kavkaz.memo.ru

24 September. The Minister of the Interior posted guards at the building of the Chechen State TV and radio company (branch of VGTRK) and the Grozny Broadcasting Company (a structural division of the Chechen Ministry on National Policy, Information and Foreign Relations) for the presidential election period. This was reported by Akhmed Dovletukaev, director of the State Radio of Chechnya.
kavkaz.memo.ru

24 September 2003. Around 5 am in the Cossack village of Novoshchedrinskaya, Shelkovsky district, unidentified people, allegedly members of Russian law enforcement agen-

cies, kidnapped Ruslan Uvaysovich Merzaev, born in 1974. In the words of his relatives speaking with representatives of the Memorial Human Rights Centre, unknown people entered the house and, without letting the hosts turn on the lights, started pointing a flashlight at their faces. The visitors spoke in Russian without any accent. Seeing Ruslan, they immediately took him out of the house and led him away in an unknown destination. According to his relatives, he was first taken to the local commandant's office. His relatives believe that the kidnapping came as a result of an incident on 8 September 2003. On that day Mersaev went fishing and happened to witness the blowing-up of the bridge over the river. Ruslan got scared and ran away but was stopped by the military that were present at the explosion. They came to his house, checked his documents and let him go.

On 28 September the villagers blocked the road to Kyzlyar. On 1 October, F.Klintsevich, Russian State Duma deputy, and H.Yamadaev, representative of the United Russia party in Chechnya, visited the improvised roadblock and promised to find the kidnapped person. However, the protesters did not unblock the road. Later that day the head of the district administration also promised he would show up together with Merzaev, but he did not keep this promise.
Memorial Human Rights Centre

As of 25 September 425 polling stations have been set up and start functioning. From today on they will be guarded 24 hours a day. At some of the stations (in a number of villages in the mountains in Chechnya) the communications issue is still unresolved, "but it will be resolved" an employee of the Chechnya Election Commission told the Caucasus Times correspondent. The ballot papers printed last week at a print shop in Kabardino-Balkaria are known to have been delivered. Meanwhile election commission employees express concern about possible terrorist attacks during the election.
kavkaz.memo.ru

As of 25 September the Chechnya Election Commission had not received official documents related to the ruling of the Supreme Court of Russia confirming the legitimacy of registration cancellation of Malik Saidullaev who is running for president of Chechnya. This cancellation was reported in mass media and the election headquarters of Saidullaev in Grozny has been closed down and the personnel have been disbanded.
kavkaz.memo.ru

On 25 September the Supreme Court of the Russian Federation confirmed the legitimacy of the cancellation of Saidullaev's registration. By so doing the Supreme Court turned down the appeal of his representative Hasa Djantaev against the ruling of the Chechen Supreme Court which had cancelled Saidullaev's registration. Over 13,580 signatures had been submitted in support of Saidullaev to the Chechen Election Commission. After 2,179 signatures were checked only 2% or so were deemed invalid and thus Saidullaev was registered on 27 August 2003 as a candidate running for president of Chechnya.

After that another candidate, Nikolai Paizullaev turned to the Supreme Court of Chechnya with a claim to cancel the Election Commission decision of 27 August arguing that the signatures submitted for Saidullaev were invalid. To consider this claim the Supreme Court of Chechnya requested the signature lists from the Election Commission and deemed 89.9% of signatures invalid (1960 signatures). The grounds were that there had been many serious violations in the process of signature collection (such as absence of the name of the subject of the Federation, voter age, address of collector's signature). On these grounds the Supreme Court of Chechnya complied with Paizullaev's request and cancelled the Election Commission resolution on Saidullaev's registration. The election deposit in the amount of 4.5 billion roubles submitted by Saidullaev on 18 August 2003 was not taken into account because the registration had been done on the basis of signature lists.
kavkaz.memo.ru

On 25 September businessman Malik Saidullaev stated that since the very beginning of the election race he had been receiving proposals to withdraw from the race following the examples of Aslambek Aslakhanov and Khussein Dzhabrailov. "They could have removed me in a different way, by starting a criminal case, but they decided to go to court," said Saidullaev. According to him he made up his mind to nominate himself not to become rich or win some lucrative position. "I decided to run because I wanted to rid Chechnya of such criminal characters as Kadyrov and his retinue," said Saidullaev. He noted that if we are to have order we must have a fair election in the republic. But today anyone can see that "instead of an election we have a farce."
kavkaz.memo.ru

Statement by Mukhamed Arsanukaev, head of Saidullayev's campaign. 25 September

Today, on 25 September 2003, the Supreme Court of Russia put the last touch to the argument about whether the Chechen people have the right to elect the president of the Chechen Republic. The Court decided that the Chechen people have no such right.

Our opponents, enemies of the Chechen people realized that even unlimited use of administrative powers cannot help them win the election. So they also resorted to dirty methods. They threatened business interests, the health and life of the candidates, they resorted to bribery, beatings, kidnappings and murder of members of other election teams, unjust court proceedings, even the authority of the Russian president. Everything was used to pave the way for the Kremlin's candidate.

Somebody believes that the many thousands of Chechens who died during the jihad declared by Kadyrov in his time are not sufficient. It is not enough that tens of thousands of peaceful Chechens died because of irresponsible decisions of the Moscow politicians and their Chechen lieutenants. Kadyrov headed the Republic for three years and during all this time many people disappeared without trace, others have been brutally tortured or executed without any court proceedings. It is obvious that this situation is suited to those who did not want to allow the Chechen people to conduct their own election. That is why they are doing their best and stop at nothing to prolong the life Kadyrov's bloody regime in the Chechen Republic.

I am not surprised because I have never been enamoured with president Putin and his methods of solving the Chechen crisis. The political history and the past of Putin influence everything his hand touches. The presidential in the Chechen Republic are conducted as a thoroughly planned operation of the special task force.

Light seemed to be appearing at the end of the tunnel of the Chechen tragedy. But now it has disappeared again. The darkness will not dissolve until, not only the Kremlin, but also we ourselves realize one simple truth. Nobody can change the tragic fate of the nation watching indifferently desperate attempts of just a few of its sons to change it. It was not enough to be ready to vote on the day of election. Our people needed resolution to fight for its right to choose. But today our people are tired of fighting and nobody can blame them for that.

Until the time we can make a choice, my comrades and I will be proud that Malik Saidullaev was our candidate for the post of the president, that he did not give up when he faced threats, that he was not seduced by numerous promises, that in his disinterested desire to serve the cause of the Chechen people he went on till the very end! He has no reason to blame himself for political cowardice and inconsistency, Malik Saidullaev revealed himself as a mature, persevering and resolute politician who is capable of conducting dialogue with all the sides of the Chechen crisis, of consolidating the Chechen nation and leading it to a better future.

We believe that the Chechen road will see its celebration! And it is not far away.

We know that this celebration will be organized by Malik Saidullaev, the president of the Chechen Republic!

Mukhamed Arsanukaev – former head of M.Saidullaev's election campaign.

8 THE STORY OF SAIDULLAEV'S REMOVAL

Tanya Lokshina, Moscow Helsinki Group/Centre 'Demos'

On 17 September, in Grozny, I visited the main election headquarters of Malik Saidullaev, a former presidential candidate. I unexpectedly came across two people I knew from Moscow, a journalist and a public relations consultant. Both had joined the Grozny headquarters to work on Malik's campaign. The timing of my visit was not auspicious. A decision of the Supreme Court of the Chechen Republic of 11 September had suspended Saidullaev's campaign that had only started on the fifth of the month and had never really got a chance to develop. By the time I met Saidullaev, both Muscovites and his local staff had been stuck in limbo for a week.

At that time there was still a glimmer of hope in the headquarters as well as in Chechnya because the Supreme Court of the Russian Federation was in the process of reviewing Saidullaev's appeal. There was hope in Chechnya that the Russian Supreme Court would prove to be more independent and less politicized than the Chechen Court. But to an outside observer, particularly one from the capital, that idea seemed illusory. There had been a clear sign 'from above' on that same ill-starred day of 11 September; the acting president of Chechnya Akhmat Kadyrov received a widely publicised audience with president Putin. Everything looked set.

It is natural for people living at the epicentre of events to hope for a miracle. Without hope there is no way to survive. My acquaintances taught computer skills to their colleagues to kill time while we waited for the miracle. With no opportunity to deliver election propaganda, they developed a public relations campaign. They promoted the Vozvrashcheni (Homecoming) Fund, timely and appropriately founded by Saidullaev in August. The aims of Vozvrashcheni are highly relevant to the needs of Chechen society – searching for the 'disappeared' and preparing the ground for the activities of a special plenipotentiary commission on the 'disappeared'. The aims were worthy; the possibilities of realisation unclear. But the creation of such a commission was part of Saidullaev's presidential programme.

We enjoyed our meeting, parted not without regret and agreed to keep in touch one way or another. There was a phone in the headquarters – an incredible advance – and even access to e-mail, something virtually unknown in Grozny.

On 25 September, the RF Supreme Court predictably declined Saidullaev's appeal. I sent a letter of sympathy to my friends, but did not imagine that the headquarters would be immediately closed down. Malik's brother Milan Saidullaev, established in the patriarchal residence in Alkhan-Yurt, and Mukhamed Arsanukaev, the leader of the election campaign, had sounded very convincing while explaining that in the case of a negative decision of the court, their headquarters would campaign for people to vote against all candidates. Both Milan Saidullaev and Arsanukaev were eloquent and persuasive. Though generally distrustful and sceptical, I almost believed them. Big mistake. The bubble burst immediately.

Already on 26 September my worried calls to the headquarters were met by long miserable beepings. Arsanukaev's cell phone was 'out of coverage' and unreachable. The situation was clear. But the future of Saidullaev's staff and guards raised serious concerns. Kadyrov's people dislike any opposition, and those who were on Saidullaev's side could be in danger. I was particularly worried about my Moscow friends. How are they? Where are they? How are they going to get out? And where should I look for them if there is no number to call? The headquarters phone was almost the only working number in Grozny that I knew of. I know many people in the city – but telephones are an other-worldly luxury there. If you find it difficult to digest the fact that one of the subject states of the Russian Federation has no phone connection in the 21st century, just make a trip to Grozny.

My fears proved unfounded. On 27 September both of 'Saidullaev's men of Russian origin' burst into the office of the Moscow Helsinki Group safe and sound. Yura, a 25-year-old public relations consultant, offered to tell the story of the premature end of their HQ activities and share his impressions about pre-election Chechnya. Our conversation lasted about two hours; I will refer just to the part concerning the election.

Yura got into Saidullaev's headquarters through his friend Kheda, a Chechen journalist. Kheda is well-known in the region: she writes, works for TV and has even made reports for the BBC. At the outset of the election campaign, she got many tempting offers; virtually all candidates including Kadyrov tried to enlist her support. However, she backed Saidullaev as the optimal choice. For the past two years, Malik had been giving humanitarian support, had became politically active and had won the support of many Chechens. He had the image of a smart, thrifty and peaceful man taking care of his people. Khussein Dzhabrailov, another Moscow businessman, projected the same kind of image, but only got his act together quite close to the election. Yura, who actually advised Kheda to support Saidullaev, promptly followed her to Grozny to become a member of Saidullaev's team.

Having settled down in Saidullaev's headquarters, they were curious to find out how their main rivals from Kadyrov's headquarters were faring. Kheda made a call to the press service of the acting president of Chechnya. She had been approached by them earlier, so she pretended to accept that offer. However, she was told that Kadyrov's headquarters no longer needed her professional services or, in fact, any public relations support. But if she wanted to make some money, then she should get some fighters for Kadyrov, 'and the more, the better!'

Kadyrov's election campaign was thus revealed. He staked all on force, and needed mercenaries for his notorious 'security service,' preferably Islamic extremists. This 'security service' intimidates not only the local people but also federal servicemen. At least 10% of the gang are plain criminals.

Saidullaev set up 26 district offices within a short time. The central office contained the most loyal staff and functioned on a semi-military principle. There were odd-ball characters in the district headquarters. Reliable members and relatives composed the backbone of the teams. The rest of the applicants were initially supposed to be subject to careful screening. They tried to avoid those who had been originally in favour of Ichkeria and went around chanting, 'Freedom or death' – and subsequently came to Saidullaev's headquarters in a suit with a document case singing his praises. Chechen etiquette did not allow a blunt refusal, even if they hampered the work. With Saidullaev's deregistration, all those people vanished into thin air. About two-thirds of the headquarters staff were 'tested' people who knew that if Malik became president they would get certain power positions. And the remaining third came just for the money.

Saidullaev's election campaign was simple. No creativity was required because of the burning hatred of voters toward Kadyrov, the popularity of Saidullaev, Dzhabrailov's early desertion and the passivity and further withdrawal of Aslakhanov. The main campaign materials for Saidullaev were posters (handsome Malik in a handsome sheep hat and another one – an equally handsome Malik not in sheep hat but in a suit – with a background of Mecca and slogans on fences ('Malik is our president!' 'Vote for Malik!' etc.). Sympathetic voters helped with the slogans – they also tore off many Kadyrov's posters and attacked Kadyrov's slogans. In the standard 'Kadyrov – our president!' slogan, the last word would be effaced and an eloquent curse 'goat' would be written over it. In some places, skilled craftsmen even nailed freshly cut off ram's balls to the photogenic forehead of the acting president. There wasn't a need to encourage people in these activities – things ran pretty much of their own accord, initiated by the blatant love of the electorate for Kadyrov with his 'pure intentions and strong power.'

All Saidullaev's 26 offices worked with the electors – collecting their signatures in support of the candidate and distributing his campaign materials. The Grozny headquarters prepared a media campaign. Two TV spots were made; one called '*I am a Chechen*' focused on Malik himself, another on his family and his humanitarian initiatives. They managed to start the campaigning activity they had expected to use in the last two weeks prior to election day. But on 11 September Saidullaev was withdrawn – putting an end to open campaigning by his team. However some materials prepared earlier were published by newspapers that ignored the formal prohibition and did not want to lose money.

In the context of Saidullaev's de-registration, it is only the story of the deposit that remains unclear to this day. The candidate himself (in his interview to the respectable weekly Ezhenedelny Zhurnal and other news media) claimed that he had been prevented from paying a deposit. But the deposit was paid on 26 August with a letter signed by the candidate himself and Mukhamed Arsanukaev, the head of the campaign. The letter was sent to the Chechnya Election Commission with a request for Saidullaev's registration as a candidate in the presidential election on the basis of the deposit. And the money was duly transferred to the appropriate account.

Then the signatures of Saidullaev's supporters were also submitted to the Election Commission. They were recognized as satisfactory to the fullest and the original deposit was returned to the candidate. The question is still open: why did the candidate or his team members take this money back, why did they not secure themselves with the deposit in case of de-validation of the electors' signatures? The staff of the main headquarter had given me some very vague answers to this pertinent question before, and even Yura could not clarify the matter. I suspect that it was human error on the part of the candidate's team.

It is interesting to note Paizullaev's claim that led to Saidullaev's withdrawal was a little irregular. (Paizullaev is an established Chechen poet who used to recite odes praising Malik when drunk, but succumbed to Kadyrov's aforementioned 'intentions' and 'power'.). Paizullaev's claim was dated 1 August but containing references to 27 August. That means that even the form was not quite in order. But, as Yura has emphasized, the complaint was not limited to signatures. Three more complaints were registered against Saidullaev – concerning violations in campaign materials, bribery of voters and on possession of undeclared property. So, the matter of signatures might not have been crucial.

From 11 to 25 of September, Saidullaev's headquarters were not active in campaigning or in organizing meetings. The candidate did not want to spoil his relations with Moscow; he tried to solve the issue informally. In general – meetings in Chechnya are a dangerous activity. Since 1991 people hold meetings and shoot, frequently combining these two activities. Large-scale meetings traditionally end with shooting.

Saidullaev regularly called to his Grozny headquarters from Moscow to support the fighting spirit of his team, "You just wait, guys, the deal will be settled in our favour and we will get to work – just wait a bit more!" Those who were there just for the money chose not to wait and pulled out almost right away. But the majority remained. It was rumoured that the whole story of the withdrawal from registration was just a brilliant manoeuvre within the election campaign. The scandal would boost Malik"s rating sky-high and the Supreme Court would then take a just decision enabling Saidullaev to mount to the Presidency on a crest of glory without further effort. The rumour spread at an unbelievable speed and was taken for granted by many. But as we know now that rumour was just wishful thinking.

Saidullaev's withdrawal was confirmed by the Russian Supreme Court. The earlier affirmation that, if there was confirmation of Saidullaev's de-registration, his followers would stand firmly against Kadyrov and call upon the people to vote against all candidates, dissolved into thin air like a soap bubble. Whether due to the lack of human (read – military) resources or fear of spoiling the relationship with Moscow, not a single Saidullaev office remained from 26 headquarters. And Malik Saidullaev temporarily left for Europe.

Tomorrow, 5 October, the 'all-nation election for the president of Chechen Republic' will be held. And the turn-out will certainly be high. And Akhmat Kadyrov, who all this time 'was with his people in the very place where, unfortunately, his people ended up,' will be elected without a shadow of a doubt.

One can hope for nothing. Or, to think about it, the only hope remaining is that the election will not be followed by a lot of shooting. Let us hope for that – that would also be a miracle.

Chronicle of Events: 26 September to 30 September

On 23–27 September the public opinion polling service 'Validata' conducted a poll in 86 localities in the 15 districts of the republic. The poll showed that 66% of the Chechnya population were ready to take part in the election. According to the poll, up to 60% of those willing to vote would possibly be voting for Akhmat Kadyrov.
kavkaz.memo.ru

On 26 September Kadyrov acting president of Chechnya joined the Russian delegation to the US with president Putin.
Newsru.com

On 26 September people who coming out of the mosque in Achkhoi-Martan after Friday prayers were surprised to find representatives of the local administration waiting for them. The officials were handing out free ration packs – a packet of tea and a kilo of sugar. Some said that they hadn't seen such generosity on the part of local authorities since sheik Mansur's sermon and the time Chechens became Muslims. It was explained by talkative benefactors, that the packs were gifts from Kadyrov acting president.
Russian-Chechen Friendship Society

On 26 September the Chairman of the Chechnya Election Commission Abdul-Kerim Arsakhanov stated that on election day 425 polling stations would be open where about 545,000 voters could vote, including some 30,000 servicemen stationed in Chechnya permanently. 580,000 ballot forms had been printed for the election.
kavkaz.memo.ru

On 26 September in Brussels the statement of Italy, Chairman of the EU, on the Chechnya election was published on behalf of the European Union. The document states that the EU had noted intimidation of candidates and counterfeit votes. The EU asks that in the meantime that the election should be recognized as legitimate by all the Chechens including those residing outside Chechnya. This EU statement is more strongly worded than usual and calls on Russia to provide answers to accusations related to the violation of human rights in Chechnya. Moscow is urged to guarantee that the Chechens who had found refuge in other republics of the Northern Caucasus will not be forcefully returned to Chechnya. The EU draws the attention of Russia to the fact that independent mass media play a fundamental role in organizing and conducting free elections. The statement also points out that since 1999 the EU has sent 110 billion Euro worth of humanitarian aid to the Northern Caucasus, thus being the largest donor for the region.
kavkaz.memo.ru

On 26 September at a closed door meeting of the Bureau of the Parliamentary Assembly of the Council of Europe resolved not to send observers to the forthcoming presidential election in Chechnya.
kavkaz.memo.ru

26 September 2003. In broad daylight, Russian soldiers kidnapped Elina Gakayeva, a 19-year-old female student in the Faculty of Physics and Mathematics, from the Chechen State University (CSU) campus in Grozny. According to witnesses, the military came in an APC with mud-covered number plates, seized the girl who was standing at the entrance to the university building, forced her into the APC and drove off in an unknown destination. On 30 September 2003, many people, including CSU students, relatives, neighbours, and friends of the kidnapped girl, gathered in the city centre in front of the Government House. They urged the authorities to take all necessary steps to find and release Elina Gakayeva. According to unconfirmed information, in the evening of the same day the girl was released and returned home.
Chechen Committee for National Salvation

27 September 2003. According to residents of the village of Chechen-Aul in the Grozny rural district, at around 4 am armed people in masks and military uniforms killed two old men and their sons in their own homes. The names of the victims are being ascertained. According to the villagers, the victims were in no way related to the military operations in the Chechen Republic and were not engaged in any blameworthy activity. There is no clue as to the reason for their murder or the identities of the killers.
Chechen Committee for National Salvation

During the night of 27 September in the village of Alleroi of the Kurchaloi district some unidentified persons threw around leaflets entitled 'File.' They contained extracts from the interview by Ramzan Kadyrov, son of the acting president and head of his personal security army, given on Chechen TV on 1 August 2003, and an extract from Chechen field commander Doku Umarov's appeal to 'Kadyrov supporters'. The leaflet also included words of Kadyrov himself who said after the end of the 1994–96 war, that "if a Muslim shakes hands with a Christian he is taking a risk of becoming a Christian himself." These words are accompanied with a illustration of Kadyrov hugging president Putin.
kavkaz.memo.ru

On 27 September Buvai-Sari Arsakhanov, Deputy Chairman of the Chechnya Election Commission stated that the republic is ready for the presidential election. "The preparation for the election have been carried out in a calm atmosphere. There have been no serious incidents reported that indicated attempted terrorist attacks on buildings accommodating polling stations."
kavkaz.memo.ru

28 September 2003. At night, armed people in masks and military uniforms kidnapped Musa Ganayev (about 30 years of age) in the village of Roshni-Chu in the Achkhoi-Martan district. According to his relatives, the kidnappers were agents of Russian law enforcement agencies. They dragged Musa out of bed, took him out on the street and drove off in an unknown destination. All efforts to ascertain his whereabouts were in vain. Agents of the district law enforcement authorities (military commandant's office, police, etc.) refuse to acknowledge Musa Ganayev's detention. The reason for his kidnapping is still unknown.
Chechen Committee for National Salvation

In the evening in the Staropromyslovsky district of Grozny unknown people opened fire at an UAZ car with four police officers inside. Three policemen were killed and one was wounded. The attackers escaped in an unknown destination. Steps taken by the Russian law enforcement authorities under the 'Perekhvat' (Interception) plan produced no results.
Russian-Chechen Friendship Society

On 28 September in Nozhai-Yurt, polling station No 84 was fired at with assault rifles by unidentified gunmen. A guard was killed and the building was slightly damaged.
kavkaz.memo.ru

On 28 September a diplomatic scandal arose over the inclusion of Kadyrov in the Russian delegation for the Russian-American summit. The US side made it clear that Kadyrov's presence in Washington and Camp David is highly undesirable. A White House spokesman in his interview for the Los Angeles Times categorically stated, "He (Kadyrov) is not going to Camp David."
kavkaz.memo.ru

During the night of 28-29 September unidentified persons posted leaflets on the walls of the school and village administration buildings in Belgatoi, Shali district. The leaflets urge people not to vote at the presidential election in Chechnya.
kavkaz.memo.ru

On 29 September the President Hotel in Moscow hosted a meeting between Kadyrov and leaders of Russian communities who had left Chechnya. There were representatives from Stavropol, Voronezh, Rostov and the Karelia region. At the meeting one of the top priority issues was compensation payment for lost property and shelter which that was due to be paid from 25 September 2003. The meeting also discussed the return to Chechnya of the Russian speaking population.
kavkaz.memo.ru

On 29 September an arson attempt on a school-based polling station was prevented by local people in Urdyukhoi village in the Shatoi district.
kavkaz.memo.ru

On 29 September unidentified gunmen in the town of Aiti-Mokh of the Nozhai-Yurt district opened automatic fire at the police patrol guarding polling station No 232. Aha Ahmatukaev was killed in the exchange. The attackers managed to get hold of two Kalashnikov assault rifles and a Makarov pistol.
kavkaz.memo.ru

On 29 September unprecedented security measures were prepared for the administrative border between Ingushetia and Chechnya for the forthcoming presidential election in Chechnya. Additional interior forces and Ingushetia police patrols with armoured vehicle appeared on the border. Reinforced guard units patrolled the tented camps for temporary relocated persons and blocked footpaths between Chechnya and Ingushetia.
kavkaz.memo.ru

On 29 September officials started to issue application forms for voting at the presidential election the tent camps and other areas with Chechen refugees on the territory of Ingushetia,. The constitution pre-referendum situation of 23 March 2003 is evident again. At that time and now there are occurrences when officials at various levels threaten refugees that if they refuse to participate in the election they will be removed from the humanitarian aid lists and will lose the opportunity to get compensation payment for the housing and property they had lost.
kavkaz.memo.ru

On 30 September in connection with the coming presidential election in Chechnya all units of Dagestan police are on heightened alert. Dagestan police believe that opponents of the election may penetrate into Chechnya.
kavkaz.memo.ru

29 September 2003. A powerful explosion killed two Russian deminers during a mine clearance operation on the Argun-Belgatoy highway in the Shali district. After the explosion the highway to Belgatoy was blocked by federal forces for several hours.
Russian-Chechen Friendship Society

30 September 2003. In the morning all points of entry to Grozny were blocked by federal forces. According to a female resident of the capital who tried to enter the city, the bus from Sleptsovskaya (Ingushetia) and several following cars came under fire from the checkpoint near the village of Chernoreche. No casualties were reported.
Russian-Chechen Friendship Society

On 30 September. In North Ossetia police chief, K.Dzantiev, ordered that personnel of the force assume heightened alert. Special investigation operational groups and mobile patrols have been established in North Ossetia. Local newspapers published telephone numbers for rapid response investigation teams. Passport and visa control, as well as vehicle in

spection became more strict. Public places where a lot of people congregate, such as marketplaces, train stations and major stores are permanently under surveillance.
kavkaz.memo.ru

30 September. Representatives from the League of Arab States and the Organisation of Islamic Conference will observe the presidential election in Chechnya. Some other international organisations will also send observers. Earlier the Parliamentary Assembly of the Council of Europe had refused to send representatives as election observers.
kavkaz.memo.ru

30 September. Minister of Justice of the Russian Federation, Yu.Chaika, called the PACE refusal to send observers to Chechnya presidential election a mistake. The Minister stated that the invitation implies that the safety of observers is guaranteed. He added that Ministry of Justice special task units earlier provided reliable security for all delegations.
kavkaz.memo.ru

On 30 September a statement by 25 deputies of the parliament of the unrecognized Chechen Republic of Ichkeria was published. The statement says that 'There can be no election on 5 October on the territory of sovereign, democratic, independent, law-based state Chechen Republic Ichkeria because of the 'military occupation'. The Ichkeria deputies urge the international community to support this position which in their opinion 'meets moral norms and conforms with current international law.'' They call upon international organisations – UN, OSCE, PACE and the Euro parliament – to boycott the presidential election in Chechnya. The statement resolutely rejects the impeachment of the Ichkeria president Maskhadov as reported by Russian mass media on 12 September 2003. The statement expresses hope that the international community will take the side of the Parliament and the president of the Chechen Republic of Ichkeria.
kavkaz.memo.ru

On 30 September an attempt to blow up the polling station building in Samashki village of Achkhoi-Martan district was prevented. Federal forces personnel, engaged in engineering reconnaissance, discovered a black bag some 30 metres from the polling station containing a powerful home-made explosive device. A search of neighbouring buildings revealed a hideout and an assault rifle and a grenade launcher .
kavkaz.memo.ru

On 30 September federal servicemen started to guard all 425 polling stations in Chechnya prior to the presidential election scheduled for 5 October.
kavkaz.memo.ru

The All-Russian survey conducted in late September by ROMIR polling centre revealed that the majority of Russian citizens (59%) believe that the situation in Chechnya after the presidential election will not change. 21% of respondents are of the opinion that the situation will change for the better, and 13% are sure that it will deteriorate. The survey shows that 51% of respondents in Russia do not support the policy pursued by the Russian authorities towards the Chechen Republic. At the same time 43% of Russian citizens have some kind of a positive attitude to federal actions towards Chechnya. The survey was based upon a representative sample of 1,500 respondents.

kavkaz.memo.ru

9 FROM THE LIFE OF ELECTION HEADQUARTERS: INSIDE INFORMATION

Alexander Mnatsakanyan, freelance journalist

Half a year ago, I could not have imagined even in my dreams that I, a journalist, would be serving the interests of a politician eager to become the president of Chechnya. But my Chechen friends suggested a meeting with Mr Candidate and I complied — mainly out of curiosity. He turned out to be a charming individual who behaved very properly. When he offered me cooperation I said something about the ethics of journalism. The candidate looked at me seriously and said, "Do you like Kadyrov so much? I know you don't. You care about the Chechens, including those in guerrilla formations? I think so. Do you want peace? I'm sure you do. Then why don't you take this opportunity?"

The Candidate also gave me his word that should I sense any unfair play, it would be easy for me to quit working in his campaign HQ. In fact there wasn't a single occasion throughout the whole campaign when I had the slightest reason to suspect the Candidate of anything underhand. The Candidate stuck to the spirit of his words.

Chechnya. The HQ is making defence preparations. In a joint effort, the HQ staff and security personnel are filling sacks with sand and then piling them up to build parapet structures — not forgetting to leave portholes. The next day, a truck full of concrete blocks arrives and they put up something resembling a checkpoint at the entrance to the building.

In the backyard of the building, I can see a group of elderly people who are quietly discussing a seemingly very important question. Noticing a bright-coloured rucksack on my back and thus guessing that I am a stranger, a grey-haired bony man leaves the group and approaches me asking surreptitiously, "Are you from Moscow? So, what do you think?" Later on this same man being a very nice person became my daily nightmare. Every day he would approach me, sometimes several times a day, and would ask the same or a similar question. He would speak under his breath, apparently showing off in front of his buddies, trying to display that he was privy to secrets far beyond their competence. He would never listen to what I had to say in reply but would consistently waste up to half an hour of my time by telling me the news (as a rule, two-weeks old) or sharing with me his ideas (as a rule, quite logical but awfully boring).

It's my third day here and I still don't have a clue as to what my responsibilities are. The person who is officially my boss is an old friend of mine, a well-known person in Chechnya, who has worked with practically all pro-Russian forces in the republic. However, he has not shown up at the office even once. Everybody is waiting for the Candidate to come and assign everyone his task. The reason for the impasse is that there are at least two groups in the HQ that are hostile to each other and they do not tolerate the other group taking the upper hand. Moreover the HQ seems to pursue at least two strategies. One amounts to not doing anything at all because the final choice would be made in the Kremlin anyway – and it is not possible to jump over your head. The other strategy stems from the need to do at least something because the final choice would be made in the Kremlin – and we can't just sit on our hands. The biggest secret is our plan of action for Election Day. But it looks like it's an open secret since everyone is bragging about how much he knows.

On the fourth day, I learn that the Candidate has hired a cool and very expensive Moscow-based public relations group. They are not coming to Chechnya because the final choice would be made in the Kremlin anyway.

I'm getting on friendly terms with the most advanced group in the HQ. These people have worked in Russia a lot, they are reasonably well educated, they have elaborated a plan of action, but are handicapped because the campaign funds are in the hands of the other group. We sleep over at the HQ because of a) security, b) communications, c) electricity, water and gas, d) and it would be too costly to rent other facilities. I play a spy visiting various pro-Kadyrov events. I always feel on leaving these events that I should ask for a rise for working in a hazardous environment.

One week later, I almost lose my sanity and head off for Moscow to brief the cool public relations guys about what's going on in Chechnya. Upon my arrival I'm subjected to a third degree type of interrogation because nobody thought about notifying the Moscow office that I was coming and that I'm working for the Candidate's campaign. Having had them establish my identity (10 minutes on the phone), I give them a briefing on the political situation.

In the meantime, my new friends are feverishly trying to make me tell them how much I'm paid. After they realize that its way less than they charge, they relax and become very nice. They have to work almost in secret, because they have not informed their public relations agencies that they are working for the Candidate. I already know many of them by name so once I'm at home I get on the internet and soon find out everything I need to know about their places of permanent employment.

The Candidate whose whereabouts have remained unknown for a long time turns up in Moscow. He calls a staff meeting and we are told that the election will be held in a month but we have neither the strategy nor the tactics. It becomes apparent that there is serious friction between the Moscow and the Chechnya teams as to who was in charge. Finally, we agree that the campaign strategy will be developed in Moscow, while tactical decisions will be taken in Chechnya. My responsibility is to write summaries of the Chechen mass media reports twice a week and forward them to Moscow. I ask the Candidate to give me an assistant in Chechnya who would in my absence collate the newspapers.

Upon my return to Chechnya, I find out that the group I was getting friendly with has been defeated and expelled. Nobody intends to be accountable to Moscow because "they have no understanding of what's going on down here." It's hard to disagree; one of the ideas of the top-level public relations guys was to hold primaries in Chechnya! On the other hand, it's also hard to agree because the leading Chechen group comes up with the idea of forgetting about the law altogether and handing out posters with the Candidate's photos that haven't been paid for from the Candidate's campaign fund. My attempt to explain that it may be disastrous for the Candidate is countered by the airtight and unquestionable argument that it doesn't matter because "the final choice would be made in the Kremlin anyway".

One of the staff brings a videotape with a campaign ad of our Candidate for our review. The Candidate looks nice and cool. Everybody is excited. Then, the same staff person says that he is going to take the tape to the TV station to be broadcast immediately. With great difficulty I manage to convince him that if he does so, the Candidate will not only be removed from the race but might also be immediately jailed.

We have new security guards. The previous intelligent and quiet guys have been replaced by people apparently recruited at random. It's not that they are inferior in any way; they simply have a different attitude. Their main enjoyment is showing off with an automatic rifle. One of the guards is an oversized kid. Having seen a 'Shrek' animation, he acted it out for several successive days. Another was so impressed by a movie about werewolves that he went out at night and started shooting stray dogs in the street. A third one was persistently trying to find out the difference between fax, copier and scanner. There are two more guys with obviously criminal backgrounds and manners.

The large majority of them are from urban localities rather than from rural areas. It's hard not to pity them. They are 20–25 years old. Half of their life has coincided with the war. The most incredible thing about them is an almost total absence of life experience. One told me, a total stranger from Russia, that he has been trained with Khattab. Sounds like he is telling the truth. "Aren't you afraid I'm going to report on you?" I ask and get in reply. "No, you won't – you are a good man!"

The Candidate arrives. He immediately draws a crowd of people who want to get access to his ear to secure for themselves money and positions in the future. The Candidate delivers a speech. He promises that everything will be fine. At the same time, we learn from the audience that the Candidate's representatives in the districts face a lot of problems. But none has contacted the main HQ hoping that they would be able to cope with the problems by themselves. I get an assignment from the Candidate through my immediate superior (who has finally materialized!) to collect all such stories and turn them into articles. It's hard to do this because those who have had problems are not willing to identify themselves. Their argument is convincing, "I have a family to think of!"

The Candidate starts having problems with the Kremlin. The problems are serious; that means we are bound to lose the election. The only remaining question is whether we shall give up on fair terms or whether we shall simply be withdrawn from the race. The female staff are in tears. The male staff are mad with frustration. A couple of people have a heart attack or develop acute gastritis. I feel again ashamed for the country where I have had the luck to be born. On the surface only two or three of the most reasonable people manage to remain calm. On the third day of our ordeal we get a command to stay in place and not to leave because everything may still change. The final choice will be made in the Kremlin anyway.

My journalist colleagues from Moscow start arriving in Chechnya. While making their round of different candidate HQs, they suddenly run into me. I learn from them the details about our competitors. At one place, the campaign staff doesn't even know the whereabouts of their candidate, at another place they are not aware of the statements made by their boss. That sounds comforting. We also get most of the information *post factum* but try to put on an appearance that we know everything. At the very start of our work, the Candidate recorded a couple of hours of interviews on various topics. We can now cut and paste that material ready to make it public in any suitable way.

We have two weeks to go till election day. All local TV stations broadcast the energetic face of Kadyrov. The whole republic has been covered by his portraits. A youth movement pops up called 'For a Clean City.' The boys are instructed to paint over all campaign slogans not praising Kadyrov. After the tea party in Sochi with Mr Putin no one has any doubts as to the choice of the Kremlin. Chechnya is brooding in anticipation of property loss compensation being available only against a considerable kickback. Against that background, our public relations activities (and anyone else's for that matter) fail to catch any attention. The election is as good as lost. But the Candidate has no intention of formally giving up the fight. We've been wandering around the office joking about a retreat march into the mountains.

The contenders for the Chechen crown drop out one after another. A couple of them have withdrawn their names from the slate; one was deprived of his registration by a court order. Some of the candidates have decided to make peace with the Kremlin. Our Candidate is also in the group of the dropouts. It hurts but there's nothing one can do about it. It was clear from the very beginning that the final choice would be made in the Kremlin anyway. The HQ wraps up its activities. I'm very sorry for the guards, who, as I suspect, will be vulnerable to attacks by Kadyrov's supporters for having worked for an opponent. The guards also seem to be edgy. They believe the office will be attacked any minute now. At the same time, they earnestly discuss who shall take home what from the office equipment "so it won't get damaged during the forthcoming attack".

We are leaving. We take photos for keepsakes. We amuse ourselves with the thought that Kadyrov won't last for long. So till next time when the Kremlin will be doing all the decision making. But that time will be without me, if you please. I quit.

Chronicle of Events: 1 October to 2 October

1 October 2003. At 5 pm, on their way home by car, Musa Dakaev, the head of administration of Shali, born 1948, and his son Said-Selim Dakaev, born 1972, were killed by unidentified persons. As they passed the cemetery a white Zhiguli drew up alongside. Masked men in the Zhiguli opened fire with machine-guns. Musa and his son Said-Selim died from their wounds. Witnesses stated that the perpetrators were not known to them, and that after the killing they drove in the direction of the village of Serzhen-Yurt. The car used by the attackers was later found burned out close to the city.
Memorial Human Rights Centre

On 1 October in Grozny a house on Saikhanov Street in the Oktyabrsky district where Kadyrov's election headquarters was located was burnt down.
KMNews.Ru

On 1 October A.Politkovskaya, the Novaya Gazeta observer, talking on the Echo of Moscow radio stated that "the Russian authorities are playing against themselves for political reasons and not providing precise and complete information about the developments in Chechnya – including the situation of the poisoned chairman of the government, Anatoli Popov." "The reality is that everything unpleasant related to Chechnya, even a military criminal trial, is not being made public until 5 October." Politkovskaya noted. According to her, "it means that authorities are panicking with fear that their plans will be upset. The plans are for presidential election in Chechnya on 5 October."
kavkaz.memo.ru

On 1 October the Ministry for Foreign Affairs of Russia responded to concerns expressed by the European Union represented by the Ambassador of Italy, G.Fakko Bonetti; Ambassador of Ireland, G.Harmam; and by the head of the European Commission's mission Richard Wright. Deputy Foreign Minister, V.Chizhov, presented a political assessment of the statements made by the EU about presidential election preparations in Chechnya. He described the position of the Russian federal authorities on the issues under consideration.
kavkaz.memo.ru

On 2 October the Association of Belgian Chechens called upon all Chechens of Europe on 3 October to take part in a protest rally in Brussels and in Luxembourg Square, opposite the European Parliament building "against the attempt of the Russian government to hold a presidential election in occupied Chechnya". "The action will be carried out throughout Europe. Each Chechen can join in by having a banner near their house or by hoisting the Chechen flag at 3 pm sharp, Brussels time."
kavkaz.memo.ru

On 2 October Abdul-Kerim Arsakhanov, Chair of the Chechnya Election Commission, stated that "Chechnya is 100% ready for the election." According to him all 425 polling stations are fully equipped technically and are supplied with required numbers of ballot forms. "561,000 people in Chechnya are entitled to vote including about 30,000 servicemen of the units permanently stationed in Chechnya" said Arsakhanov. "The system of security in the republic allows us to say that the election will not be frustrated, but we cannot rule out isolated incidents". Besides that, Arsakhanov stressed that Chechen migrants who now live in Ingushetia will be able to take part in the election. They will be taken by coach to polling stations located in Sernovodsk and Assinovskaya in Chechnya. "We expect that 1.5–2 thousand internally displaced persons (IDPs) will also take part in the election" he added.
kavkaz.memo.ru.

2 October 2003. Three bodies, found in the suburbs of Mesker-Yurt village (Shali district), not far from the federal road 'Kavkaz', opposite the sovkhoz (state farm) 'Neftianik' and close to sulphur springs, were transported to the village by lorry in the evening. The bodies were not identified and were lying for several days in the local mosque. According to in-

formation from local people, the bodies were dropped from a helicopter the day they were found. They were found on a busy place, where they could not lie unnoticed for long. On 6 October they were buried in the local cemetery (after photos had been taken). The region of sulphur springs was already infamous as a place for dropping the bodies of people who had been killed after being detained by Russian soldiers. On 10 February of this year the remains of Seda Khurikova were found (with hands and head blown off by an explosion). She had been abducted by Russian soldiers from her home at night on 28 January 2003 to Urus-Martan. One or two weeks earlier the blown-up bodies of four young people who could not be identified were found at the same place. On 22 June 2003 the dead bodies of two women were found at the same place: Olga Sanaeva, born 1977, and her mother, Nina Zindrina, 55 years old, who had been abducted in the early morning of 22 June in Grozny by armed people in masks. Bodies were also found and identified at the same place in 2001 and 2002.
Memorial Human Rights Centre

On 2 October the border protection department of Georgia made a decision to open additional border checkpoints on the Russian-Georgian border and to increase the strength of the border guard contingent. The aim is to counter attempts to cross the border during the presidential election. Similar measures are being taken by the Russian Federal Border Guard Service. Activities to reinforce the border are coordinated on both sides. At present the situation on the Russian-Georgian border remains stable, no movements of armed formations have been reported.
kavkaz.memo.ru

For the period of 2–6 October restrictions are imposed on truck traffic by the Chechen Ministry of Internal Affairs. These measures are taken to prevent possible terrorist attacks on the eve of and during the presidential election in Chechnya. Owners of trucks are recommended not to use the highways during the election, and traffic police have instructions to inspect all trucks thoroughly.
kavkaz.memo.ru

On 2 October The RF Minister for Chechnya, S.Ilyasov, stated that Chechen refugees staying in the Georgian territory will not take part in the presidential election on 5 October because 'Georgian legislation does not provide for opening polling stations for refugees.' According to Ilyasov, there are about 2,000 Chechen refugees in the territory of Georgia, but not a single Chechen family living in Georgia wants to return to their motherland with the Russian delegation which had been visiting the Pankisi Gorge.
kavkaz.memo.ru

As of 2 October many candidates running for the presidency had not fully used the free TV and radio time granted. The statistics are as follows: Chechen State TV and Grozny TV – free time used by all candidates; paid time – only A.Kadyrov. Free radio broadcast time is

used 100% only by Sh.Buraev. A.Bugaev and Kh.Biybulatov used only 40% of the allotted free radio time. K.Saduev used only 30%. Not a single candidate paid for radio time.
kavkaz.memo.ru

2 October. In connection with the 5 October presidential election in Chechnya students of the Chechen schools will have additional holidays. Nearly 90% of the 425 polling stations are located in school buildings. For the sake of security the decision was taken to suspend classes until 7 October. All rooms used as polling stations have been heavily guarded 24 hours a day since 27 September. The Chechen Ministry of Internal Affairs allocated 16,000 men to ensure security during the election.
kavkaz.memo.ru

10 CHAIR OF THE ELECTION COMMISSION ABDUL-KERIM ARSAKHANOV (BEFORE THE ELECTION)

Interviewed by Ruslan Umarov, kavkaz.memo.ru

Abdul-Kerim, what is your assessment of the candidates' campaigns for the presidency of the Chechen Republic? Do they meet the necessary requirements?

On the whole everything is happening within the law. But there are complaints from individual candidates, from sections of the population and from journalists. There are complaints about inequality in the use of election materials – in particular in street posters.

But there were no restrictions. All the candidates opened accounts. Private persons and organisations, but not the state, paid money into these accounts. Everything depends upon the financial position of the candidate. Kadyrov, for instance, has 29 million roubles in his account. The limit is 30 million. Kadyrov has spent only about 3-4 million so far. There is no way candidates can exceed the limit. We control that.

We cast lots to determine the time allocated to each candidate for his televised speeches and newspaper articles – both paid and free time. But some candidates did not take full advantage of the free time offered.

Remind our readers, how many candidates are taking part?

There are seven candidates left. As you know, Malik Saidullaev sent an appeal to the Supreme Court. If the court decides to restore his registration, his campaign will be continued.

Abdul-Kerim, why does nobody mention the deposit Saidullaev paid. Isn't that sufficient ground for registration?

The collection of signatures of voters is the primary ground for registering a candidate. The deposit does not secure anything.

Does the deposit replace collecting signatures?

The deposit does not substitute for anything. If we had had any doubts or worries concerning signatures provided by M.Saidullaev, we would have registered him on the basis of his deposit. From our point of view the signatures he collected contained no essential omissions or faults. We think that it is sufficient to give information about the person who gave a signature so that we could contact him or her if we need to. But the Court found faults with the subscription lists.

He did pay the deposit, didn't he?

Yes, he did. But he or his agent indicated that he wanted to be registered on the basis of the deposit.

So, these are two different ways?

Yes. They are different. And they are specified on the day when the registration documents are considered.

Please, list the people who are still in the presidential race.

They are Akhmat Kadyrov, Khusein Biybulatov, Abdula Bugaev, Shamil Buraev, Kudus Saduev, Nikolai Paizullaev, and Avkhat Khanchukaev. By the way, Avkhat Khanchukaev makes very good use of the free time. His behaviour is very correct. He does not denounce anybody, and he speaks only of himself and his presidential programme.

Abdul-Kerim, have you had any complaints from candidates or their agents? There are rumours that the authorities have not allowed certain candidates to open offices in some districts.

I can only assess the situation for statements or complaints that made to the Election Commission. We have received nothing yet. If we received any complaint we would immediately react. I use every meeting with the heads of district administrations to remind them that it is inadmissible to infringe the rights of any candidate. They all have equal rights. But, to my surprise, some candidates are passive in claiming their rights. Perhaps they are not confident that they will be able to attract the necessary number of votes?

Or perhaps they are over-confident?

That is possible, too.

Have there been any lawless or subversive acts in the election system?

There have been attempts at arson and explosions, but that is not surprising in Chechnya. We have something of that sort almost every day.

Who is guarding polling stations of the Chechen Election Commission – federal or local forces?

The Ministry of the Internal Affairs military commandant's office, and the Prosecutor's Office of the Chechen Republic made a plan of work for security at polling stations and for the population. From 25 September all the polling stations will be guarded 24 hours a day. Mainly local forces will be used, but federal agencies will also be involved.

How did you tackle the problems of communication and transport?

A lot of work has been undertaken. Each of the 425 polling stations of the republic will be provided with means of communication. At some highland locations radio communication and land transport will be used. We are 90% ready for the election today. We still have to make signs for the polling stations, but we have time to do that. The required number of ballot-papers has been printed and together with office equipment, they are already in place. The stations have full financial support. We provided all the money based on our estimates – 57 million roubles. Everything is going in complete accordance to schedule.

Does the Election Commission feel any pressure from anybody?

This is a question journalists often ask...

That's our job.

Yes. We feel pressure, but not serious enough to hinder our work or limit our activities. There were attempts to bribe members of the Election Commission but, to the credit of the Commission, members did not succumb. You must have heard that there was a scuffle here, in the Election Commission. If people fight, it means they are engaged. I have already spoken to a newspaper about it. I pointed our that this scuffle means that in this respect we are at last equal to economically developed countries, such as America, Japan, and Italy! And the State Duma of the Russian Federation seems to have a fight every day.

You are not lagging behind the times?

We made the two sides of the fight sign a truce and shake hands.

Abdul-Kerim, I'd like to hear your comments concerning the unexpected withdrawal of competitive candidates from the presidential race. Evil tongues claim that they were neutralized by the Kremlin to pave the way for its lieutenant.

I cannot say that they withdrew their candidacies against their will. I have no facts to support that. I admit that the Kremlin unwittingly campaigned for Kadyrov, but that was connected with his work. Life cannot stop because of elections. The leader of the republic, even during his election campaign, cannot avoid governmental business and pre-arranged meetings. That has led to the accusation of unfair use of administrative resources. Nobody is going to take from Kadyrov's shoulders the responsibility for all that is going on in the republic – such as arranging for payment of damages to those who suffered from the war.

It is obvious, Abdul-Kerim, that the result of this election is predetermined by the objective reality we have in the Chechen Republic, and it will hardly be influenced by irregularities in the election campaign. What can you say about elections that are scheduled later, and about the elections for the State Duma?

Yes, the second wave of elections is already on us. Some citizens have already offered themselves as candidates. Their documents and lists of signatures are reaching us. Already we are working towards the elections which are scheduled for 7 December of this year. And then we are going to elect the president of the Russian Federation in March 2004.

Obviously, the next year will see the election of the Chechen Parliament. The State Council of the Chechen Republic is just a step towards a fully-fledged legislative body or Parliament.

Yes, we shall at last have legitimate power with its extensions in the Republic. I believe that the parliamentary elections of the Chechen Republic should take place before the election of the Russian president. The quicker we form the organs of government, the quicker we'll revive our republic.

So let it be. Thank you for the interview, Abdul-Kerim.

24 September 2003

(Note: It was already known that the elections for the Chechen Parliament would be held in mid-March 2004, on the same day as the election of the president of the Russian Federation.)

Chronicle of Events 3 October to 4 October

3 October 2003. Two people were killed in daytime in the centre of Grozny. One, a driver for international journalists, was shot by people in plain clothes in Rosa Luxemburg Street in the centre of Grozny.
kavkaz.memo.ru

3 October 2003. In the afternoon a young girl was shot by Russian soldiers at a checkpoint. Allegedly, soldiers checked her documents and allowed her to go, but then shot her in the back.
kavkaz.memo.ru

On 3 October in Baitarki village of Nozhai-Yurt fighters from M.Khambiev's group tried to set fire to the polling station, but local people managed to put the fire out.
kavkaz.memo.ru

On 3 October vigilance of the local population helped disable an explosive device in the vicinity of Gerzel-Aul village, Gudermes district. A time-bomb type device was fixed to a propaganda poster about two metres above ground level.
kavkaz.memo.ru

On 3 October the Republican Boxing Federation of Chechnya announced over the local radio that, "Each boy born on 5 October in Chechnya will get a special prize – 10,000 roubles. In case of twins the prize will double."
kavkaz.memo.ru

On 3 October, commenting on the refusal of OSCE and PACE to send their observers to the election in Chechnya, A.Veshnyakov, Chairman of the RF Central Election Commission stressed that the election of the head of republic are not federal elections, thus the position OSCE and PACE "could be understood."
kavkaz.memo.ru

4 October 2003. Strict traffic restrictions in the Chechen Republic have been in force for several days. In Grozny they also extend to pedestrians. Police reinforcements and soldiers have been located on all main roads in built-up areas. Military patrols are in the streets of cities and villages. Checkpoints are also reinforced by armoured troops. The locals are indignant about what is happening. A traffic toll was raised from 10 to 50 roubles by the soldiers on duty on checkpoints, who claimed that this measure was a 'reinforcement of the security measures'. In the locals' opinion, the Russian soldiers deliberately created kilometres of traffic jams to increase the 'tribute'.
Russian-Chechen Friendship Society

On 4 October in the Sernovodsk village of the Sunzha district of Chechnya, at polling stations located on the premises of schools No 2 and No 4 two bombs were disabled. (The devices were plastic containers filled with explosive equipped with detonators with wires and a remote control). Both schools were taken over by Chechen special task police (stationed in Sernovodsk village for the election period). At the school No 2, a bomb had been planted behind the school building, and another in a flower bed right in front of the school building. Human rights monitors managed to find out from a special task policemen that the bomb locations had been discovered from interrogation of Bekhan Nakaev, who had been arrested a day earlier. He said during the interrogation that the bombs had been planted two weeks earlier and he pinpointed the places.
Memorial Human Rights Centre

On 4 October in Serzhen-Yurt bombs were planted in three polling stations despite the fact that polling station are heavily guarded 24 hours a day, and some by APCs and armoured infantry vehicles.
kavkaz.memo.ru

According to the Chechen Ministry of Internal Affairs official spokesman Ruslan Atsaev, on the evening of 4 October a man was detained in Sernovodsk village of the Sunzha district. He was trying to plant a bomb with 5 kg of hexogen near a polling station.
Strana.Ru

As of 4 October more than 120 representatives of leading foreign mass media outlets were accredited to cover the election in Chechnya.
kavkaz.memo.ru

On 4 October all polling stations started to be heavily guarded. No trucks are allowed on the roads. The police control long-distance trains heading for Grozny, and commuter trains from Grozny to Gudermes. Mass media election propaganda is banned, as well as public meeting of candidates with voters.
kavkaz.memo.ru

On 4 October the International Federation for Human Rights called the forthcoming presidential election in Chechnya a 'masquerade' with continuous human rights violations as a background. Human rights activists underscore that after the March 23 referendum which had set the stage for the presidential election, Chechnya began to witness increased crime against civilians, especially cases of kidnapping and taking hostages.
kavkaz.memo.ru

On 4 October an additional polling station was set up for forced migrants living in Ingushetia in the village of Assinovskaya.
kavkaz.memo.ru

On 4 October in Istanbul at Eresin Hotel a conference was held to discuss the presidential election in Chechnya. Over 100 people took part in the work of the conference, including MPs from Turkey, Maskhadov's official representatives, spokesmen from Human Rights Watch, as well as journalists from Turkish TV agencies, broadcasting companies, newspapers, and Chechen journalists. The conference was organized by the Turkish IHH humanitarian organisation. All the speakers unambiguously stated that the 5 October election was not legitimate. General representative of the Chechen Republic of Ichkeria abroad, Minister of Health of Ichkeria Umar Khanbiev, stated in his presentation that despite manipulations by Moscow in occupied Chechnya, Kadyrov would never be "president of Chechnya, but would for ever remain Moscow's chief of the station." A representative of Human Rights Watch maintained that in Chechnya Russian troops commit military crimes against civilian population. In such a situation elections are illegal and invalid.
kavkaz.memo.ru

11 THE EVE OF THE ELECTION

Tanya Lokshina, Moscow Helsinki Group/Centre 'Demos'

As I set off for the airport, my husband shrugged his shoulders, humming the opening to one of our favourite songs, 'Moses has stepped into the Jordan river and nothing can stop him now.' He was more or less right.

My friends tried to dissuade me from going to the Chechen election, "It is dangerous, they are fighting there, there are the feds, Kadyrov's men and rebels. It is a foolish and worthless risk". Their arguments were spirited at first, but then they wearied. Finally, they also shrugged their shoulders.

'Risk' was not the strongest of their arguments; the most powerful word was 'worthless.' Why go to these this election, when there is no election to see? Why bother to see Akhmat-Hadji Kadyrov, elected by the Kremlin on behalf of the Chechen people, become a fully-fledged president of the Republic? Why be a voluntary spectator of this grotesque show?

What is the answer to these questions?

Probably, the following:

Responsibility for this senseless charade lies with all of us – we are involved in it regardless of our will. Your feeling of belonging to whatever takes place in your own country and in your own backyard should not allow you to close your eyes or turn your back on this shameful performance in Chechnya. Our team was single-minded. We must watch all of THIS and tell others about it.

The opportunity to witness the 5 October events in Chechnya will not make us feel less ashamed of what is happening. But, we will do whatever we can. We will watch the election in all its false attire of democracy. Maybe our reports will make it more difficult for others to gullibly accept official propaganda. Maybe our reports will make it more difficult for others to ignore what is happening.

On 4 October we left Nazran in Ingushetia for Grozny. Six human rights people from different regions of Russia are going to Chechnya for the election. I am in charge of this tiny group. We want to go to different places, so as to establish as full a picture of the situation as possible. Two members of our team have already reached the Shali district. Another two will spend the entire voting day in Grozny talking to voters and aiming to visit all the polling stations in the city. A third group of two, including me, plan to spend the night in Grozny and then go to a range of localities in the republic.

To our surprise the nearly 100 km journey to Grozny took us only a little over an hour. The Rostov-Baku highway was completely deserted. No military transport, no civil vehicles. Just two weeks previously, travelling along the same route, I had been surprised at the volume of traffic. There were many military conveys, with heavy APCs taking the middle of the road and forcing tiny cars into the gutter. Today – silence, emptiness, calm. This graveyard serenity seemed eerie and ominous.

We enter Grozny. My feeling of concern became undisguised anxiety. Two weeks earlier life had been bursting forth in the ruined city. The streets were crowded, cars honked round the market square, cafes were packed with people, and groups of youngsters wandered the streets. Now Grozny was a desert, lit by unexpectedly bright October sunlight. We stopped at the square with its fountain. The square is always crowded, which is why our local colleagues suggested we meet there. If any group gets delayed, the others will not be too obvious in the promenading crowd. But there is no crowd today. There is no one else in the square but us. And we still have an hour to wait, the journey having been unexpectedly short.

We seize the opportunity to take a walk in the streets. They are quiet and empty. Nothing but sun and dust. Our intention was to talk to passers-by, to ask what they thought about the election of the next day, and then vanish into thin air. But there are no passers-by. No one to talk to. We walk in silence. The walls are all covered in election posters. Compared with my visit two weeks ago, some progress is evident – one can see not only Kadyrov's portraits, although his are naturally, predominant, and most impressive with their excellent print quality. The unintelligible Khanchukaev, who never uttered a meaningful phrase during the entire campaign, stares at us from small portraits on black and white leaflets. Saduev and Biybulatov look down on us with winners' gleams in their eyes. Occasionally I see Buraev and Bugaev whose faces are already familiar from my previous visit, but their posters are rare.

I remember what a friend from Grozny visiting Moscow on business said laughingly when she came by to see me just before I left for the Caucasus. She said that the Election Commission of the Republic had started to prepare the capital for the arrival of hordes of Western journalists and Moscow bosses. The very day she had set out for Moscow portraits of other candidates had appeared alongside Kadyrov's colourful posters.

It is hot. My colleagues are dying for coffee. We come by a tiny summer café. A blue tent provides an escape from the sun. Synthetic velvet and white chairs. The woman behind the counter is visibly happy to have us – business is poor today. There are only two other customers besides us. We ask why it's so empty, why the town is deserted.

"What's happened?"

"Well, you know, elections…"

The woman brings thin sweet coffee with milk and ice cream with chocolate sprinkling in a misty thick glass. In the background – a small yard, spared by the war, looking very much like many a Moscow yard. Dusty, not yet yellow leaves on tallish trees. A simple children's swing. Two old women chatting animatedly at the threshold. It seems you are back in your childhood again – suddenly your heart grows warm and peaceful.

It only takes a glance to the left, however, to brush away the fleeting feeling of serenity. A huge hole gapes in the shattered wall of the neighbouring building. You remember where you are, who you are and why you came here.

We chat with the woman in the café about how she is not planning to vote and how nobody is planning to vote, because everything has been decided beforehand and "whatever we do, they'll count the votes without us, in any way they want". Then, we get going, heading to the central market square in the hope of finding some more people to talk to. But the market is also deserted. Most stands are empty. Behind the others sit subdued traders, a few customers pass them by, and then they just wait.

"Where are the people?" I ask an elderly woman.

"What are you talking about – what people? Everybody has gone. It's election time. You know yourself. They are afraid of terrorist acts. There were so many rumours, and they talked about it on TV and in the newspapers – it will be bad on 5 October. It is terrifying. I myself am leaving for Ingushetia first thing in the morning."

"So you are not coming to the market tomorrow?"

"What are you talking about? There is no market tomorrow! They ordered it closed, to avoid anything happening here."

"What about the voting?"

"Why should I vote? Everything is clear, anyway. The president is elected already. But it was not us who elected him. Moscow elected him."

We move along the stalls. Everywhere, traders say the same. "People chose to leave." "There is no sense in voting." "What elections are we talking about, when there is nobody to choose between?" "This election will not bring peace, either. There is nothing to hope for."

In the late afternoon we take the car again to get to where we expect to spend the night in the suburbs. On the way there, we stop at a small street market to buy something to eat – for us and our hosts. This is the only way to thank them for taking us in. We talk to the people there. We hear again everything we were told in the town centre. Our driver is getting nervous.

"Its seven already. We must get going. We won't be there before dark. Hurry up, hurry up!"

We grab our bags and jump into the car.

A middle-aged woman meets us at the door and smiles in welcome. "Come in, come in!" But she avoids meeting our eyes. We rush to apologize for the trouble – we are so many and the place is not big. The hostess responds with the standard "guests are always a blessing!" and instantly plunges into a hasty discussion in Chechen with our driver – a relative of hers. The tone of voice indicates that something is not OK. We are not welcome here. But it is already dark outside and it would be sheer madness to drive to the other end of the town, where there is another place, where we could possibly stay. I look questioningly at our driver, then at the woman. She puts her hand on my shoulder and says in a hurried whisper:

"It's dangerous here, very dangerous. You were seen in the street. What happens if they arrive suddenly to take you during the night? They come to take our own people, let alone strangers. Not to mention journalists. You are journalists, aren't you? I'll give you something to eat. Then I'll take you to the Refugee Centre – its right opposite us. There are guards there and everything. I'll arrange for you to have a room. My nephew works as a guard there. There will be only one room for all of you, but you will be taken good care of. Otherwise I don't know what we would do if anything happens. Please, excuse me, but it's been very restless here the past month. Even yesterday they were shooting throughout the night... And there are all those people walking around..."

I go to my companions, who are smoking outside, and explain the situation. We have no choice. We had better go to the Centre, although the prospect of having the guards 'take good care' of us is not exactly alluring. We cross the yard, walk a short distance and there we are at the Centre. A new block of dormitory-type residences. An outhouse and several wash basins are positioned outside – a few yards away from the entrance. Nearby – a couple of kiosks for bread, Coke, cigarettes, chocolates. On the horizon – the highlights of a burning sunset. Bats dive around; looking like tiny swallows from a distance. Our almost hostess hugs a youngish guard and pointing at us, tells him how things stand. My companions light cigarettes anew. I look around sheepishly and take a drag myself, carefully covering the cigarette with my hand. Women are not supposed to smoke here, especially in the street...

The guard approaches us. A handsome young man in a black uniform and bullet-proof vest. Waving his rifle as normally as he would wave his hand he says hurriedly and softly:

"Please, excuse me. She vouched for you. So I'll trust you. But you need to show me some documents – I need to take down the information. Otherwise the others will not let you in. Everybody is afraid here. Such are the times. Security is tight throughout the republic. For a whole month now we have been receiving indications and intelligence that there are plans for terrorist attacks. A couple of days ago eight people arrived at the neighbouring hostel, in uniforms, with guns. Said they were a patrol. The guards – two guys I know, opened the door and the group beat them up, almost killed them. They took the guns and said they'll be back and that next time they'll burn down the dormitory."

"And who were they? – asks my colleague.

"If we knew, they would not be coming again!" the guard retorts. "Please hurry up. I'll take down some details from your documents and get you in the room. After 9 pm no one is allowed in or out. So – toilet, washing – you know..."

"What? A curfew at the dormitory? So early?"

"It's only for now. This week. Before, the doors stayed opened until 10 -11 pm. But in the current situation..."

We climb the stairs to the third floor. We can hear voices, but there are few people in the halls, and seemingly, the dormitory is quite empty.

"Is the Centre under-occupied?" We ask the guard.

"Why under-occupied?" He seems offended. "Some 700 people live here. All the rooms are taken."

"It doesn't look like it."

"Of course it doesn't! What do you expect? There are about 150 people here now. No more than that."

"Where are the others?"

"What do you mean – where? They left, went to stay with relatives. Those who could go to Ingushetia did so, others went to the villages – to wait for the election to pass."

We settle in for the night. There are four bunks in our room and a small balcony. We go out there. Everyone is tired and somehow in low spirits. We stay there for a couple of hours or so, watching the black star-studded southern sky. Besides intermittent gunfire and artillery only barking dogs break the silence. My colleagues, experienced in such matters, discuss with interest the source and whereabouts of the shooting.

We arrived to watch the Chechen election. But the locals have chosen to leave, rather than stay for their own election. There is no doubt whatever that the election will take place without them. This is so strange, ladies and gentlemen. Perhaps it should not be like that in this best of all possible worlds? Or do you think it should?

12 ONLY GOOD NEWS ON TV

Tanya Lokshina. Moscow Helsinki Group/Centre 'Demos'

Most of the reports about the election campaign appeared on central TV channels whose preference for Kadyrov the Kremlin's nominee was predictable. So on the eve of the presidential election, on 4 October, I decided to watch Chechen TV news. I hoped to learn something related to the election – but was swiftly disappointed.

The nature of the Chechen news broadcast on the eve of the election led me to enquire of my more experienced friends whether the local news programmes had always been like that. From their answers it seems that TV life in Chechnya in the past was more entertaining – and perhaps better in other ways.

Prior to the 1997 elections the local TV was a battlefield. Candidates denounced each other on all three channels at the same time. Movladi Udugov promised an 'Islamic Order', but that did not prevent him from drinking and eating after his TV appearances despite the Islamic Uraza fast. TV campaigning continued until the last day before the election. But the influence of TV was uncertain. The winner Maskhadov kept a comparatively low TV profile.

TV continued to be a battleground after the 1997 elections. Sometimes it was even accompanied by real shooting. In June 1998 Lechi Khultygov, head of Maskhadov's security department, was killed on the staircase of one of the TV stations. Just before the assassination he had announced the discovery of a Wahhabist plot. He said that Wahhabis were not real Muslims but agents of the world of Zionism who had discredited proud Ichkeria in the eyes of the world community. Khultygov was murdered not by Wahhabis or Zionists but by the people of Salman Raduev who controlled the TV channel. Sometimes Raduev also made sensational denunciations on TV.

In September 1999 when the second war started the local TV tower became a key target and was soon put out of action. Chechnya could only watch central channels. For lack of anything else children watched cartoons and adults watched news programmes. But these programmes had nothing to do with local or regional culture and information. Later local TV resumed and on the eve of the 2003 election Moscow experts came to restore local TV.

It appears that Chechnya had all the necessary prerequisites. During the years of dominance by official outpourings from Moscow and Grozny TV, scores of local rural TV stations were also transmitting. Many villages had their own cable networks to add local interest. Volunteer-run studios run relayed channels selected by local media barons rather than by the main federal-level ORT or RTR.

They telecast local news, non-political of course, like, 'Vakha X. lost his cow, one horn is crooked, the other missing.' That's the news the whole village was discussing. Senior citizens denied this was news – guerrilla scouts were looking for the same cow in the German retreat as far back as 1942!

Local cultural programmes sometimes left a lot to be desired. It was not easy for local DJs to get away from the familiar pattern of playing listeners' requests. But even this genre might have added a modicum of local excitement. After all the rural community is nearly as important 'a cell of society' as the family in Chechnya. The whole village hears a song performed upon the request of a grateful Akhmet Montekki for Madina Kapuletti. Relatives of Juliet are chasing Romeo all over the village to ask what the girl had done to make him so appreciative. The village wits were smiling. You don't sing serenades for nothing!

Sometimes this idyll is interrupted by war. Insurgents occupy the village. One detachment takes over the TV station and substitutes a video with a speech by Maskhadov for 'Titanic' or 'Star Wars'. Another detachment patrols the village streets telling the people to go home and listen to their dear president. The third takes control of the transformer unit in case someone attempts to switch off the electricity.

Sometimes more serious incidents occurred. This happened in the village of Avtury, the village where the people of the late Adam Deniev had sheltered journalist Andrei Babitsky when it was assumed he had been handed over to the military. Adam Deniev was generally loyal to the Russian authorities and especially loyal to the special services. He was full of energy but managed to develop bad relationships with many his countrymen – with separatists, because he worked for the federal special services, with others because he wanted to be their boss. Deniev, mistakenly, felt safe in his native village of Avtury. One day he decided to make a televised appeal to his fellow countrymen – but was killed by an explosion which demolished not just him but also the TV station. Who did it – his opponents or competitors – remains an enigma. But we can see that in Chechnya it is a very short step from an information war to a real one.

On the eve of the presidential election in Chechnya I watched the news on the Chechen State TV, Radio Company. It was the 7.30 pm prime time news. I locked myself to the screen hoping to see some of the latest news related to the next day's election. But I found only Soviet-type 'good-news-only'. I decided to take notes of the patriotic reports of achievements in the restoration of a peaceful life. Federal news channels haven't quite reached this 'good-news-only' level – but there is a feeling that we don't have to wait long... It is usually comforting to be aware of what you might face tomorrow.

News item No 1. In Nozhai-Yurt district a bridge across the Yamansu river has been restored. The road to Yalkhoi-Mohk, Benoi and Vedeno villages passes across this bridge. This is a tremendous achievement in Chechnya rebuilding, a great contribution to developments in the republic. The picture shows a brand new bridge and a crowd of happy people.

News item No 2. Another café for youth is open in Grozny – café Stolichny – that meets European standards. This was confirmed by the Mayor of the city, Sup'yan Mokhchaev, who attended the official opening. The Mayor appreciated both the ample menu and the friendly atmosphere. His favourite cake was missing from the selection. But the Stolichny owners promised they would bake the favoured cake for the Mayor on his next visit. Why not cater for a cherished guest? The picture showed the entrance of the café, the red ribbon being cut with shining scissors, the hall, freshly-washed floor, brand new tables and a blow-up of the Mayor's smiling face, happy young people, and a tray full of pastry... Isn't that a sight for sore eyes!

News item No 3. Rosselhoz-Bank opened its savings bank branch in Grozny. Naturally it was the Mayor of the city who inaugurated the branch. Besides that, the city administration convened a special meeting to discuss the issue of equipping polling stations. It should be noted that in the entire news programme that was the only mention of the next day's election – hardly a direct call to focus attention or stir citizens!

News item No 4. A gas pipeline has been laid in the villages of Alkhazurovo and Varandy. Soon they will have a water supply pipeline. The picture shows village inhabitants dancing with joy and thanking the generous authorities. What comes to mind is a commercial endlessly played by Russian TV. The Villariba village is celebrating use of a new washing-up liquid while in Villabaggio nobody is washing the dishes because there is no water. But, God willing, the water will come relatively soon...

The reality in Alkhazurovo is more complicated. As far back as 2000, Alkhazurovo inhabitants pooled money to buy pipes. I suspect the pipes were brought from destroyed Grozny refineries. The villagers hired a team of welders who started to lay the pipeline from Chiri-Yurt to a cement factory, now destroyed, and to the village. The welders were working for a long time. After a year a motorized rifle brigade passing the pipeline arrested the welders to 'filter' them. (The brigade has the number 205. People call it 'two hundred and drunk' – the sound for 'five' and 'drunk is somewhat similar in Russian. The courageous members of this unit were indeed drunk most of the time.)

Perhaps the welders were spies: there was a war going on and they just pretended to be working. Perhaps the welders were convincing in their interrogation, or perhaps the villagers pooled money again – but in any event work soon resumed. The main problem was that it was not clear that any gas would be pumped into the pipeline when it is ready. Chiri-Yurt lacked a compressor to pump the gas. Apparently the villagers again trumped up with the money and two years later the gas reached Alkhazurovo. It was a pity that the news report overlooked this history. (In January 2004, one of my Moscow colleagues who travelled to Chechnya took the trouble to find out whether the gas had actually reached Alkhazurovo. The answer was negative.)

News item No 5. Inhabitants of the Oktyabrsky district of the city of Grozny rebuilt their mosque. Construction materials were supplied free of charge by the Chechengasprom company. The picture was showing some unrecognizable construction site.

News item No 6. A notable event in the life of 122-year-old Pasikhat Dzholaeva. At the police station of the Lenin district of Grozny she receives a new Russian passport to replace her old Soviet passport. A very old babushka wearing a white kerchief signing papers with her shaky hand, and happy faces of passport department employees. There was a blow-up frame showing a relative, probably a grand-daughter. She was a sturdy not-so-young woman, who was smiling shyly and saying that grandma was still doing well – she would go out for a walk and talk to people, But age has had its impact – she had become a bit short-tempered.

News item No 7. Five senior citizens in the Staropromyslovsky district of Grozny were given awards – for assistance in organizing and conducting the March referendum on the Constitution of the Chechen Republic. The picture showed handshakes with proud-looking senior citizens. The hint was clear – we expect help from you at elections and in return you will get what you deserve from the master's table. There is nothing to add to this – indeed its fine work...

News item No 8. The Republic hosted the forum 'Equal Rights and Equal Opportunities for the Disabled!' The picture showed dancers in traditional costumes. The crowded theatre was applauding the performance of the dancing company Daimokh at the closing ceremony,

News item No 9. *Vainakh* magazine published a series of essays – forty biographies of Chechen writers of the XIX and early XX centuries. It is a very important event in the cultural life of Chechnya.

News item No 9 happened to be the last item and was followed by sports news. The news programme abided by the law and did not mention the presidential election directly, but, according to official information that we received later on, 87% of the Republic's population fulfilled their civic duty. Apparently 'polling station preparation' was carried out at the top level.

13 ELECTION DAY

Tanya Lokshina, Moscow Helsinki Group/Centre 'Demos'

Early in the morning of 5 October we are back in the centre of Grozny. There are still no people in the streets. Everything is again deserted, quiet and anxious. Two people from our group take the car that is to drive them around the polling stations in Grozny.

A colleague and I set out for a long trip – Grozny – Samashki – Achkhoj-Martan – Valeric – Gekhi – Urus-Martan – Argun – Tolstoi-Yurt – Grozny. But we have managed without great effort and felt no major discomfort except heat and dust. We left the capital at 9.30 in the morning and returned by 6.30 pm. We passed checkpoints with incredible ease.

We move from one place to the other. We walk along the streets, try to talk to the occasional passers-by, but they answer in mono-syllables, "Yes, I have voted," and hasten away. We visit polling stations. Everywhere the picture is the same. The rooms are impeccable. All the documents that are supposed to be displayed hang neatly on whitewashed walls. No campaign posters for any of the candidates. The heads of local election commissions – smiling women in colourful headgear, the idols of Soviet films of the 50s – welcome us courteously. We are shown everything, we are told everything. The polling booths are properly furnished. The voters' lists look impeccable.

We do encounter minor violations from time to time. Sometimes two or three people go together into the booth. Or one person brings five passports for his whole family and tries to vote for all of them. But this is nothing serious. What's striking is that voters are NOT numerous. No more than a couple of people at a polling station, whereas preliminary turnout figures are very high.

"How come – you report that 29% of voters had already cast their vote by 1.30 pm, yet we see no activity at the polling station?"

"What do you mean? You just came at the wrong time. Had you been here an hour ago, you would have seen lots of people! We were working hard to cope. Now everyone has gone home. People have chores waiting for them –

the field, the vegetable gardens. In three hours or so, there will be crowds again. It's just that you picked a wrong time for your visit."

We met seemingly hearty welcomes at all the polling stations. We felt a sense of nausea from the farce that the election for the president of the Chechen Republic had become, from the boredom of the lifeless streets to the cheerleader-like chirping of meaningless speeches by awfully similar officials. From time to time we yielded to bouts of irrepressible hilarity in connection with this or that incident which obviously stood beyond good and evil. I cannot but share some of those stories with my readers. Please enjoy the carnival of the Chechen election.

In the village Gekhi, which we reached around 1 pm., our attention was attracted by a bus, next to a freshly painted fence. An APC was parked near the bus together with some other military cars. "Look, it seems we came across the Yastrzhembsky tour. Let's go and see what kind of a show they managed to put together for the foreign press!" – says my colleague.

The 'Yastrzhembsky tour' (called after Sergei Yastrzhembsky, president Putin's aide) is organized especially for foreign journalists. They are carried throughout Chechnya on buses in a convoy, making stops in places chosen in advance. There, they are 'released' (stepping away from the group is a nono) to enjoy the events and decorations arranged especially for them. Then they are pushed back into the bus. And on they move to another picturesque location. That's how they get to spend the whole day.

We approached the gates and heard sounds of cheerful music coming from the other side of the fence. After presenting our press-passes, we entered a spacious clean-swept yard swarming with journalists and security officers. It was difficult to say which of the two groups was more numerous. Locals dressed in colourful costumes were playing traditional music, dancing and clapping. The action was being filmed by journalists. I took out my own camera – am I any worse than foreign correspondents?

"Take some pictures, this entertainment is worth recording" approved my colleague a professional journalist, as he started moving through the crowd looking for old friends among the press representatives. But suddenly security officers began to surround us. Strictly speaking, not us, but me. My colleague was of no interest to them. I became a bit flustered, as I could not understand the increased attention being given to my humble person.

"Your documents!'" – roared a burly man. Seemed he was in charge.

Politely smiling I hold out to him my journalist accreditation issued by the same office of Yastrzhembsky. It's worked faultlessly so far. I was let in everywhere. Evidently respect for Mr Yastrzhembsky in the Chechen Republic is very high. The chief of security twirled my magic accreditation in his hands for a long time and asked suspiciously:

"You are a journalist? Came on the tour?"

"No, we are journalists, but came on our own," my colleague joined in the conversation.

"How?"

"What do you mean 'how'? We have our own transport."

"This is not allowed! "– authoritatively stated Mr Chief

"What does it mean 'not allowed'?"

"If you are journalists, please join the tour. And you'll travel with security."

"What for? We do not need any special security arrangements. We'll manage somehow by ourselves."

"Its not allowed."

The ring of guards tightened. I completely lost all understanding of what was happening.

"Stay here. I'll be back,"- the chief left, looking back twice over his shoulder.

"What's the problem?" – flabbergasted, I asked all of them and nobody in particular.

And suddenly a guard in camouflage bent down to me and sympathetically whispered:

"Hey, take off your headscarf."

"Say that again?" My colleague and I repeated in unison.

"Look, you came in here dressed in black, your hair covered with a shawl, so we thought you are a suicide-bomber. Big resemblance."

Our hilarity was endless. In fact, I do look like a local. In Chechnya – a Chechen. In Ingushetia – an Ingush. In the streets, I am addressed in the local language. I make good use of this resemblance. Put on a long skirt and blend with the landscape. But a suicide-bomber – now, this was for the first time ever.

"A suicide-bomber with a photo camera? Great! No luck here, guys. But if you fret so, we'd better go."

To the silent approval of the guards, we made off fast before the chief returned. We got into the car and drove further, relishing the details of this incident. The funniest thing was that our small adventure attracted the attention of two foreign TV journalists. Imagine a news story in some remote country being broadcast with a comment, "At the election for president of the Chechen Republic, security officers identified a potential terrorist in a crowd of rejoicing Chechen villagers".

We reached Urus-Martan fairly quickly, asked an unidentified person in unidentifiable uniform how we could find the nearest polling station and, following his wise instructions we came directly to the Urus-Martan district election commission instead of the sought-for polling station. Once there we decided to explore. Finding out that we were Moscow correspondents, the commission's members became quite excited. We asked them to take us to their boss and without delay we were led to an impressive office. There were two desks forming a letter T, and an imposing man in a white shirt, with dashing moustache, was sitting in an armchair as if presiding over the room. One of the staff of the commission respectfully bent down to him and whispered in his ear. He stood up with a look of authority, shook our hands, and invited us to sit down. The office began to fill with men. Some were wearing name-tags – 'observer for Akhmat-Hadji Kadyrov.' Who the others were remained a mystery. The imposing man did not introduce himself, and we simply assumed that he was the head of the Urus-Martan election commission – after all, when we asked for a meeting with the boss we were brought directly to him.

The commission head took the floor and made a speech about the good timing and the necessity of the presidential election in Chechnya. That after the election, competent local authorities would eventually come to control the situation and effectively cope with terrorism, extremism, and 'international Wahhabism' (the last impressive term could not but raise admiration). And as soon as a new president takes office, as soon as civil authorities are established and the situation is controlled by the local law enforcement bodies, everything in the republic will go right. The war is over, but some secret Russian and foreign forces are still sowing discord and do not allow Chechen society to consolidate. And becoming more specific, he shared his secrets with us. Apparently, as a historian by education, he knows that there exist two major forces, namely the Slavophiles and the Westerners. The Westerners wanted to follow the way of Western countries. And the Slavophiles – the way of Russia. The Westerners brought criminal privatization and started the Chechen war to destroy Russia.

The excursion into conspiracy theory was so lengthy and predictable that at some point I just stopped listening to the monologue and started thinking about something different. But my thoughts were interrupted by an exclamation uttered with a special pathos, "The new president will solve all these problems. I look forward to the pleasure of consolidation in the Chechen Republic with Kadyrov and only Kadyrov."

Now, this head of the Urus-Martan district election commission is actually campaigning for Kadyrov even to the press!

"Do you mean that you personally support Kadyrov and want him to become president?"

"Sure I do. I am his deputy-chief!"

"Sorry?"

"I am a head of Kadyrov's headquarter in the Urus-Martan district."

The local reality is so absurd that surprises are not rare. But this situation was outside our wildest imaginings. To come to a territorial election commission, ask for a meeting with the head and be brought to see the head of Kadyrov's headquarters, comfortably occupying the office of the commission's head and acting like a boss. We were torn between hilarity and despair. We had seen more than we wanted to see. We did our best to wrap up the conversation. We had heard the conspiracy theories before. On leaving, we asked our *vis-à-vis* to give us his name. Otherwise how could we publish the interview with such a high placed person? Suddenly he looked suspicious. He probably understood that something was wrong.

"My name is Wakhid. But please do not get the wrong idea. It is not that I spend all my time here in the territorial election commission. I just passed by to see how they are doing."

Sure, my man without a surname! You simply stopped by. And we were brought to you by chance. "How curious! How bizarre! What a coincidence!"

For an hour or so, I talked with the head of the election commission No 7 in Argun, Tamara Khalidova. She told me with some regret about the excellent attendance of the referendum – 96%, and 50% of electors had voted by 1.30 pm.- but today at 1.30 pm the turnout was only 29%. That means that attendance won't be as high as at the referendum.

"And why do you think the attendance is lower compared with the referendum?" – I asked curiously.

"Well, people are more afraid. Now, things are uneasy."

"So, in March it was quieter than now, in October?"

"Oh, no! Now it is quieter than back then."

"And why then are people more afraid now?"

"Well… bad rumours… And we all went united to the referendum. We all voted for ONE thing. But now there are seven candidates. For some people it is difficult to make a decision. They do not understand."

So, that's the reason. Seven candidates – this is too much for an ordinary voter. Optimally, only one is needed. That one could not by chance be mistaken, or manipulated.

However, most probably, nobody will be mistaken in any case. And if a few people make a wrong choice through sheer stupidity or delusion, someone will certainly correct the unfortunate blunder and put things right.

The last stop on our way was Tolstoi-Yurt, where Abdulla Bugaev, a candidate for president, was born and raised. In Tolstoy-Yurt people were celebrating a wedding. And so they came to the polling station No 58. A real wedding! Bride and groom, relatives, a crowd of guests, music. The 18-years old bride wanted to celebrate simultaneously her wedding and her first vote.

A rather sordid government advertisement involuntarily came to mind. The one which called upon young people to participate in the Russian federal elections in 1995: a boy and a girl in bed under the slogan, 'You'll never forget the first time!'

But the festive invasion of the polling station was not limited to the married couple and their ceremonial escort. They were quickly joined by Mr Dokamaldaev, head of Groznensky district, Mr Anasov, a representative of the Chechen government, and several journalists. To the accompaniment of exultant cheers from the crowd, the government officials ceremonially handed over an envelope with some banknotes to the newlyweds – a present from the acting president of the republic. (Let us recall that not long before the election Kadyrov had promised presents of money to couples wed on 5 October, as well as to the parents of babies born on that glorious day.)

Strangers at these awesome festivities, Mr Bugaev's watch dogs complained about this obvious violation to the head of the polling station, Bela Tsybaeva, a teacher at the school, in which the polling station No 58 was placed. But Ms Tsybaeva saw nothing wrong in what happened. She explained to us very convincingly that she did not know what was in the envelope. Generally speaking, there were so many people and it was so noisy that she could not see what was going on. "And a wedding, you understand, is a wedding! So many guests. And journalists filming the event. The bride is 18 years old. By the way – a former pupil of ours, now getting married and casting her vote for the first time. Two happy occasions on one day. Such a big day for her. We could not spoil it!"

You are probably thinking – this absurdity has nothing to do with us? A lot of things happen in Chechnya – and everything is wrong. That's Chechnya for you. But we do not have and could not have the same level of ludicrousness anywhere else.

Wrong answer! At the press conference in Grozny on 6 October, Seibshakh Shabiev, the representative of the RF Central Election Commission, stated that the election was conducted "in full accordance with the principles of rule of law and publicity" and added that "this election can set an example to candidates in other regions of the Russian Federation." The significance of this comment is more than clear. And we, by the way, will have all-federal parliamentary elections in December. And in March we will have the honour of electing the president of the Russian Federation. So, be ready, Ladies and Gentlemen. The stage is well set.

We drove on till evening. We did not find weddings at other polling stations, but every stop was made at the 'wrong time.' Everywhere the voters had just gone and the next batch had not turned up yet.

Our two colleagues who stayed in Grozny travelled throughout the city and did not miss out a single polling station. They had a similar experience. Frustrated, they both stayed waiting at one of the polling stations for half an hour and counted all the voters that came. The count came up to FIVE people. Somehow, not convincing. Probably their timing was wrong ....

When my companion and I returned to Grozny in the evening, after driving about the whole day, we were hardly in the best of spirits. All seemed clear about the much proclaimed turnout. No doubts whatever. But how were we to prove it? Our less than cheerful thoughts hung in the car like a dark impenetrable cloud. To break the oppressive silence I suggested to my sparring partner a bet on the turnout figures and election results.

"Well, what would be your figures?" he joined in without enthusiasm.

"86% turnout and 82% for Kadyrov," was my shot in the dark. Next day, it turns out to be a bull's eye.

At the official press conference the Chairman of the Election Commission, Abdul-Kerim Arsakhanov proudly announced that according to preliminary estimates (at 3 pm data was processed from 77% of the polling stations) the turnout figure stood at 85% and the uncontested leader in the election was Akhmat-Hadji Kadyrov, for whom 81.6% of voters cast their vote.

This is the performance put up by the Grozny stage managers. In such cases, the famous Stanislavski used to say, 'I don't believe it.' I can only repeat after the great man, 'I don't believe it.' Do you?

Chronicle of Events: 5 October to 6 October

5 October 2003 witnessed voting at the presidential election in Chechnya. According to official information of the Chechnya Election Commission, 561,817 people are eligible to vote. This number includes nearly 30,000 servicemen permanently stationed in the republic. Memorial Human rights organisation, Civic Assistance, and Moscow Helsinki Group estimates show that the adult population of Chechnya is less than 300,000 people. 426 polling stations were open for voting. According to Chechnya police chief of staff on election security, deputy head of the republican Ministry of Internal Affairs Akhmed Dakaev, election security was ensured by 15,000 policemen and military. On 2 October in Chechnya restrictions were introduced on truck traffic. Limitations on civilian trucking were imposed for the period of 2–6 October.
Strana.Ru

According to the chief of staff for election security, deputy head of the Chechen Ministry of Internal Affairs Akhmed Dakaev, during the voting on 5 October an inhabitant of Assinovskaya village tried to enter polling station No 343 carrying a grenade launcher. He refused to obey the order of the police guarding the station and the guards had to use their rifles. The wounded Chechen was detained and his Kalashnikov rifle and a Mukha grenade launcher were confiscated.
Lenta.Ru; Gazeta.Ru; INTERFAX

During the night of 5 October polling stations No 398 and No 400 in the Oktyabrsky district of the city of Grozny were fired at. The shooting at the vocational school building that housed the polling stations started at about 11 am. The attackers use automatic assault rifles and grenade launchers. As a result of the shooting, the building was damaged and window panes smashed. The room of the polling station also suffered. A polling station in the town of Alkhan-Kala was also attacked.
kavkaz.memo.ru

During the night of 4-5 October unidentified gunmen fired at two polling stations in the village of Assinovskaya of the Sunzha district using automatic weapons. But there were no casualties.
kavkaz.memo.ru

5 October. International observers, Central Election Commission representatives, State Duma deputies and a large group of journalists arrived in Chechnya to observe the presidential election. According to Alexander Veshnyakov, Chairman of the RF Central Election Commission, 15 international observers had been accredited to monitor the election. The delegation of the Council of Mufti of Russia headed by Ismagil Shangareev, Mufti of the Orenburg region, represented Russian Muslim observers. The delegation also included Zaur Radjabov, expert of the Islamic Human Rights Centre, Farid Farisov, and Chairman of the Trusteeship Council of the Spiritual department of the Muslims of the European Part of Russia.
kavkaz.memo.ru

On 5 October staff members of the public organisation Echo of War visited several polling stations in the Staropromyslovsky district of Grozny. According to them, the picture was always the same – no voters and commission members putting packs of ballots into the ballot boxes. Eyewitnesses state that the polling station located in the building of school No 26 of the Staropromyslovsky district of the city of Grozny was visited by some 7–8 people between 10 am and 12 pm.
Chechen Committee for National Salvation

On 5 October. Russian armed forces established checkpoints at all crossroads and main thoroughfares of the town of Argun. Each checkpoint was reinforced with two or three APCs. In the afternoon the military had a dispute with a group of Kadyrov supporters. After that the feds closed several streets barring people from moving along the streets. It is not clear how people living on the blocked streets could vote.
kavkaz.memo.ru

On 5 October each person who voted in the village of Khanbi-Irze of the Achkhoi-Martan district was given a present at the exit from the polling station by Russian servicemen. The gift included two packets of tea, two packets of sugar, and two packets of biscuits. Everybody was getting a present for taking part in the election.
kavkaz.memo.ru

On 5 October activists of the Transnational Radical Party and the Cathedral Club held an hour-long rally under the slogans: 'Chechnya: Provisional administration of the UN, Rather Than Election Imitation,' 'International Protectorate For Chechnya,' 'Save the Chechen People,' 'Stop Genocide In Chechnya,' 'For Peace And Democracy In Chechnya and Russia,' 'Europe, Wake Up,' 'Against Terrorism – Individual and State,' 'Presidential Election in Chechnya – Mockery Over Democracy.' The demonstration involved 15 persons and it went without incidents. The picket managed to collect about a score of signatures of passers-by to support the peace plan 'For UN Provisional administration in Chechnya.' Some pedestrians displayed aggression towards the protesters; however the police resolutely curbed this activity.
kavkaz.memo.ru

5 October. Observers from CIS countries staying in Grozny noted that the presidential election is being held in accordance with generally accepted democratic rules and regulations. Yuri Yarov, executive secretary of CIS, who heads the CIS observer group, stated on Sunday they had visited several districts of Chechnya and made sure that voters could freely express their will.
kavkaz.memo.ru

On 5 October, 2 pm local time, Chair of the Chechen Central Election Commission A.K.Arsakhanov announced the presidential election in Chechnya had taken place because 240,000 people had already voted. This number corresponds to 42.66% of the number of voters. The turnout in Nadterechny district and in the third largest town of Argun exceeded 50%.
kavkaz.memo.ru

5 October 2003. In Goity, Urus-Martan district, special task police detained Roman Tausovich Khaidukayev, born 1984, living in Pushkin Street. He was arrested in his home at approximately 2 pm. Representatives of law enforcement agencies broke into the Khaidukayevs' house and without explanation pushed Roman outside and took him away. According to Khaidukayev's fellow residents the police officers (approximately 10, wearing masks, and armed with automatic weapons) had arrived in a UAZ-452 vehicle. Relatives of the detainee followed the police vehicle in which Roman had been taken away. The vehicle headed towards Grozny. On the first day they did not manage to establish the location of the detainee. Roman Khaidukayev was released on 6 October 2003. According to his relatives he was kept for 24 hours in Kadyrov's personal security service base in the vicinity of the old airport of Grozny.
Memorial Human Rights Centre

At 8 pm on 5 October 2003 polling stations in Chechnya were closed. According to Chechnya Election Commission the turnout as of the closing time was 81.4%. Under the law 'On the Election of president of the Chechen Republic' elections are to be recognized to have taken place if 30% of the registered voters participated in the voting.
Strana.Ru

On 6 October Boris Gryzlov, RF Minister of Internal Affairs, reported to president Putin that 13 bombs had been deactivated on the eve of the election. "We received information that some people wanted to carry out terrorist attacks, but all had been prevented." said the Minister at a meeting of the president with the members of the government.
Izvestia.Ru, Regions.Ru, RIA Novosti

On 6 October head of administration of the Akhmetsky district in Georgia, Nukri Alavidze, stated that no polling stations had been set up in the Pankisi Gorge and that the Chechen refugees who live there refused to participate in the presidential election which had been conducted in Chechnya on 5 October.
kavkaz.memo.ru

On 6 October Chairman of the Chechnya Election Commission, Abdul-Kerim Arsakhanov, reported that Akhmat Kadyrov can be considered elected as president. According to preliminary results after half of the votes had been counted, Kadyrov received over 82% of votes. The other six candidates together accounted for a little over 5% of votes.
kavkaz.memo.ru

On 6 October a spokesman of the Information department of the RF president Igor Botnikov said that about 120 representatives of foreign mass media and nearly 100 Russian journalists had covered the presidential election in Chechnya. Leading world mass media representatives had visited all polling stations on the territory of the republic, except for a few high in the mountains where the population is sparse.
kavkaz.memo.ru

On 6 October the press service of the Minister of Foreign Affairs of the Chechen Republic-Ichkeria circulated a statement which resolutely condemned 'the so-called presidential election'. The statement maintains that the election was a complete failure because there had been no voters. "Only Russian punitive units and several thousand Russian occupation forces have taken part in this theatrical performance. The Chechen nation, despite intimidation and violence on the part of Russian special forces and Kadyrov's criminal gangs, refused to play a role in the farce. The Chechen people have turned away the hand of Russian genocide and have shown that Chechnya could not be enslaved".
kavkaz.memo.ru

On 6 October the US State Department press secretary Richard Baucher said that the presidential election conducted in Chechnya did not meet international standards. "Unfortunately," he maintained, "the election and the political process that had led to it, did not bring about a positive democratic result." According to Baucher "the absence of real contenders for Kadyrov and pro-Kadyrov forces' control over the mass media makes us conclude that this election did not conform to international standards for the free expression of people's will." Baucher expressed doubt that the election "will be sufficiently legitimate to win the confidence of the Chechens, or to promote a settlement process."
kavkaz.memo.ru

On 6 October, during a news conference of the Chechnya Election Commission in Grozny, the Al-Djazira correspondent asked official to comment on the Kadyrov portrait on the wall of the local election room although the law stated that all election propaganda materials

should be removed on the election day. The Commission Chairmen Arsakhanov replied: ' If the posters were lying around then it would be a violation, but when it is on the wall… there are lots of different things hanging on the walls.'
kavkaz.memo.ru

On 6 October the UK Ministry of Foreign Affairs made a statement that London supports the Kremlin's wish to stop the conflict in Chechnya. The statement emphasised that the situation in the republic cannot be resolved by military means. Bill Rammel, Foreign Office spokesman, noted that the presidential election in the republic would be an important step to continue the political process started with the referendum on the constitution. "But we do have a serious concern regarding the conditions under which the election has been conducted … That is why it is very important for the successful candidate to show his readiness to work on restoring accord. It is essential for a genuinely open political process to emerge and for human rights to be observed."
kavkaz.memo.ru

14 REPORTS ON VIOLATIONS ON ELECTION DAY

Received by the MHG editorial office by telephone from candidates and their representatives.

From Abdulla Bugaev, presidential candidate

I express my doubts about the validity of the polls. My observers made an excursion on the East-West route. They were denied access in a number of districts: Shali, Gudermes, Urus-Martan, and Nadterechny. In Shali polling booths were closed down 20–30 minutes before 8 pm. Ballot boxes were transported for counting in security vehicles and observers were not allowed to see the count.

Our observers did not get access in the district of Urus-Martan. We have good reason to believe that the heads of the local election commissions gave instructions to deny access.

In my native Nadterechnyj district I received 350 votes. My main opponent – 27,000 votes; the other candidates – 5–10 votes. We have polling stations with 100% turnout and 100% voting for Kadyrov. In No 66 polling station [Bekart-Yurtovsk precinct election commission] of 1,016 votes 1,016 are for Kadyrov. In the No 95 polling station of 1,371 votes 1,371 are for Kadyrov.

From Sharip Fatuev, observer in the Achkhoi-Martan district and authorized representative of the presidential candidate Shamil Buraev,

There have been many violations. Observers could not see ballot papers being put into boxes. There have been violations everywhere. It was difficult to find any place where proper procedures without violations could have been followed. Observers did not have proper working conditions. We could not regularise the situation. The chairs of local election commissions did not support our role.

From Sergei Shimovolos, Nizhnii Novgorod Society for Human Rights

In the territory of the Shali district, 27 polling stations were set up, two specifically for servicemen.

On 4–5 October 2003 access to polling stations were blocked, including polling station No 284 situated in school No 9. In the Avtury village entrances to three polling stations were blocked with concrete blocks and logs. The head guard ordered all unknown people to stop. On the night of the 5th at 1.40 am, shelling set on fire polling station No 281 located in the school No 6 in Shali. At 3.00 am polling station No 279 located in school No 4 in the town of Shali was similarly treated.

There were posters campaigning for Akhmat Kadyrov on the walls of polling station No 280 situated in school No 5 of Shali and in the polling station situated in the administration office in Avtury village. Kadyrov propaganda posters were also displayed on the walls of the administration building of the Shali district, where the regional election commission was located.

In No 284 polling station located in the school No 3 of the Shali town a voter could get hold of several ballot papers. Additional ballots were given to voters when they showed the passport of their relatives or neighbours who had not come to the polls themselves. Seventeen ballot papers were handed out in this way between 10 and 11 am. The same practice was observed in the polling station No 278 in Shali and in the polling stations situated in schools No 1 and 2 of Avtury. Several signatures in the same hand on the ballot paper confirmed the handing out of several ballot papers to one person.

For security reasons some polling stations in Shali town were closed down several hours before the officially stipulated time. At 5.30 pm in Duba-Yurt and Chiri-Yurt. At 6.30 pm the Ashty district polling station was shut down (a mine was discovered on the road). At 6.40 pm in the Germentchuk district voters. At 7.30 pm (polling station No 279). By this time other polling stations in Shali were closed ahead of schedule.

The ballot papers from the polling stations that closed earlier than the official time were transported under the supervision of the Ministry of Internal Affairs to the Shali district electoral commission that shares premises with the Shali district administration, and were delivered to representatives of the local election commission – Chair, Deputy Chair and Secretary. After discussion with the representatives of the election commissions I found out about the rules covering the activities of the local election commissions of the Shali district. Between 9 pm and midnight, representatives of the election commissions were located in a separate wing of the administration building. It was impossible to communicate with them because security was provided by 200 armed guards. Representatives of the commissions in consultation with the Chair of the Shali district commission and the head of the Shali district administration prepared reports, filled in forms and adjusted column numbers. Observers were not present at the count. Only a few of the local election commissioners attended.

It can be assumed that the signatures of commission members on the district commission reports were made earlier. In the Shali district commission I saw signed reports for individual candidates without voting figures.

From the Memorial Human Rights Centre

(On the conduct of the election in the village of Mesker-Yurt, Shali District)

Local residents reported that activity was low. Most people decided to stay at home and did not go to the polling stations situated in the buildings of the two local schools.

The first people who came to the polling station on that day were given a packet of tea and 100 roubles. Other people who came early received 20 roubles. Some residents were motivated by money and went to the polls but the allocation of money presents stopped early.

From the Memorial Human Rights Centre

(On the conduct of the election in the Kurchaloi district)

Village administration heads received new VAZ-2106 cars two or three days before the election. The September pension was given out in the Kurchaloi district on October 3–5. That timing is unprecedented in Chechnya in the last ten years and is not expected to be repeated in the future.

The election on 5 October 2003 in the village of Kurchaloi was held with a very low voter turnout. There are three electoral districts in the village: Nos 147, 148, and 149. A record turnout number for the whole day – 105 people – came to election centre No 147 between 10.45 and 11.45 am – a time that coincided with a visit of Grozny TV journalists. A third of the 105 people were family members and relatives of district administration deputy head Shuaipov, including Mr Shuaipov himself. Thirty-three people came to the same election precinct between 2:15 and 3:15 pm. Later the voters' activity was still lower.

Ruslan, a local villager, said that his father, who had died 5 years ago, was on the voter lists. One man was allowed to vote for his relatives as well. Observers of the presidential contender Shamil Buraev and a member of the human rights organisation Consolidation were at the polling station. They sat silently and did not interfere in anything.

Twenty eight people came to the polling station No 148 between 12.05 and 1.05 pm. Even fewer voters came to the centre later. The situation at the election precinct No 149 was the same. Almost no people came to any of the three polling stations after 5 pm.

Here are the official statistics for the number of people who voted in the Kurchaloi district. Kurchaloi: No 147 – 1,300 people (62% of all voters); No 148 – 2,170 people (75%); No 149 – 1,880 people (60%). The average voter turnout in Kurchaloi is reported as 66%. Geldagana: 5.200 – 93%; Tsotsin-Yurt: 4080 – 85%; Tsentoroi: 2735 – 100%; Bachi-Yurt: 5,800 – turnout 100% at one polling station and 98% at the other two; Alleroi: 4,400 – 98%; mountain villages: average turnout 90%.

Chronicle of Events: 7 October to 8 October

On 7 October the information centre of the Council of NGOs of Chechnya reported that only 40% of refugees in tented camps and temporary locations in Ingushetia agreed to take part in the presidential election in Chechnya. Special coaches were allocated to take forced migrants to Assinovskaya, Sunzha district, where a polling station had been set up for them. However, only the migrants from Bart camp in Karabulak displayed some degree of understanding. Not a single person from refugee camps located on the outskirts of the village Sleptsovskaya, Sunzha district, went to vote.
kavkaz.memo.ru

On 7 October Chairman of the Chechen Election Commission Abdul-Kerim Arsakhanov made public the preliminary results of the voting for the presidential candidates: Akhmat Kadyrov – 82.5%, Abdula Bugaev – 5.6%, Shamil Buraev – 3.4%, Khussein Biybulatov – 1.6%, Kudus Saduev – 1.3%, Nikolai Paizullaev and Avkhat Khanchukaev – 0.8% each. The total turnout was over 462,000 people.
kavkaz.memo.ru

On 7 October former presidential candidate businessman Malik Saidullaev announced his decision to end his business in Russia. The explanation was absence of safeguards for his business and personal rights. According to him, business in Russia cannot be separated from politics. In order to be engaged in business "one has to be welcomed in the Kremlin." Saidullaev's decision was also influenced by the deprivation of his registration as a candidate for the presidency of Chechnya. This was done under "a far-fetched pretext, with gross violations of Russian legislation." "I was treated in an unfair filthy way in this country. I cannot see any reason to stay here, provocation against me will continue in the future," he added. He also said that, according to the data he had, only 17% of voters voted. At the same time, Saidullaev congratulated Kadyrov on his victory in the election. "Confrontation is counterproductive to the interests of the Chechen people" ... "It would be wrong to oppose each other when our people suffer. We have one Motherland. I will support all of your initiatives that could increase the well-being and prosperity of Chechnya."
kavkaz.memo.ru, Strana.Ru, Newsru.com

On 7 October the European Commission expressed doubt that the presidential election in Chechnya had been free or fair. Diego de Ojera, the Commission spokesman, emphasised that we could call the election successful if a decision was reached that met the aspirations of the majority of the Chechen people. OSCE chairman, future NATO Secretary General Jap de Hoop Shefer, stated that the voters had no choice.
kavkaz.memo.ru

On 7 October the US State Department criticized the 5 October presidential election in Chechnya. "The election in Chechnya and the political process leading to the election did not bring about a positive democratic result." said Richard Baucher, US State Department official spokesman. "We are disappointed that the opportunity has been lost. Taking into account all the problems it is not clear that the election can be considered legitimate or the result will win the confidence of the Chechen people," said Baucher. "Nevertheless we still believe that the Chechen conflict can be resolved by peaceful means, and we continue to insist that there is no military solution".

kavkaz.memo.ru

7 October 2003. From early morning Russian troops checked documents and luggage of everyone, including women, passing through the mobile checkpoint in Tevzan, Vedeno district. At noon the neighbouring Makhkety near the Khatun district was closed off by a detachment of troops of the 45th parachute regiment, and was unblocked only when night fell. Aina Deniyeva of Krasnopartizansky, on the western outskirts of the Alkhan-Yurt, petitioned the Urus-Martan office of the Memorial Human Rights Centre. She complained that on 16 March 2000 her son, Uvais Khusseinovich Deniyev, born 1975 (without a right hand) who lived with her, was arrested by federal forces and then disappeared.

Memorial Human Rights Centre

On 7 October former special representatives of the Ichkeria president Maskhadov, Salambek Maigov, said that the election would not change the situation in Chechnya. "It takes the Kremlin's political will to change anything in Chechnya, said Maigov. So far I cannot see any real steps made by Moscow towards a political settlement." In Maigov's opinion without peace talks between belligerent parties there is no ground to speak about any breakthrough in the situation or establishing normal life in the republic.

kavkaz.memo.ru

7 October 2003. At 9.40 am Ibragim Zelimkhanovich Zairkhanov, 24 years old, was abducted by enforcement agencies of the Russian Federation. A group of about fifteen armed persons in military uniform arrived in two UAZ vehicles and a Zhiguli (ninth model). The vehicles had no identification signs. Threatening with their guns, they pushed Zairkhanov into one of the cars in Sheripov Street, the main street of the village, and drove off in an unknown destination. The abduction was witnessed by a number of people gathered at the village water tower.

The relatives of the kidnapped man turned to the police department of the Shali district and the district office of the military commandant. They were informed that the neither the police nor the military had arrested Zairkhanov. Both offices stated that they had not been notified of the incident. The statement was questioned by the inhabitants of the village. Both entries to Serzhen-Yurt are controlled by checkpoints patrolled by the staff of the commandant's office and policemen on duty. There are no other ways out of the village.

Serzhen-Yurt, stretches along the mouth of Vedeno gorge and is bordered by steep woody mountains on one side and by the Khulkhulau river on the other. Therefore, the motorcade of abductors could not but pass through one of the checkpoints of the federal forces. According to the statements of the villagers and the elders, Zairkhanov did not participate in armed resistance to the Russian troops.

House-to-house searches had been conducted that very day, apparently by the same group of armed men. The siloviki visited the houses of the Sadayevs and the Basuyevs located in Dagestanskaya Street, but the occupants were not at home. The siloviki broke into the Suleymanovs' house, which was also empty at that moment. They broke the entrance door and some windows. The neighbours asked for the reasons for such actions, but received threats and advice not to interfere as replies. On their way out of the village, the siloviki arrested another villager whose name is being currently ascertained.

Imran Ezheev, the chair of the regional office of the Russian-Chechen Friendship Society, who is currently in Moscow, commented on the events in Serzhen-Yurt. He reported that Ibragim Zairkhanov was carrying out commissions as an active member of the Russian-Chechen Friendship Society. This is already the second case of abduction of members of this organisation: on 2 April Arthur Akhtamanov was abducted and nothing has been heard of him since then.
Russian-Chechen Friendship Society

On 8 October Daid al-Barami, head of the representative office of the League of Arab States in Russia, stated that the election of the president of Chechnya had been "legitimate, free and democratic."
Strana.Ru

On 8 October Anatoly Popov, head of the government of Chechnya, accepted Kadyrov's offer to head the Cabinet of Ministers again. The basic composition of the government of the republic will not be drastically changed.
kavkaz.memo.ru

On 8 October the European Union noted that the presidential election in Chechnya had taken place. It stressed some negative aspects of the process and expressed hope that the political settlement in the republic would continue. The statement was circulated by Italy in the capacity of the EU Chair. "The EU has been keenly watching the election process in Chechnya," the document says. "The EU has already identified negative aspects, *inter alia*, lack of real pluralism of candidates running for president, and absence of independent mass media. Bearing this in mind, the EU expresses serious concern regarding the conditions under which the election was conducted." The statement underscores that "the EU expresses hope that the process of political settlement will continue in Chechnya."
kavkaz.memo.ru

8 October 2003. In the morning the Makhkety district of Vedeno was blocked by a large number of military vehicles including tanks. At noon artillery shelling of the outskirts of the district began. The shelling was conducted from the territory of the 45th parachute regiment based near the Khatun district. At 2 pm the vehicles pulled out of the district and returned to their military base.

On the night of 8 October in Bugaroy district of Itum-Kalinsky the chairman of the council of the district's patriarchs, Khumid Visaitov, aged 82, was murdered in his own home. Khumid Visaitov had been temporarily staying with his family in the district of Prigorodnoye. He had been making repairs to his house in Ushkaloi to which he had intended to return. In the evening he arrived in Ushkaloi and stayed for the night in his own house. Apparently aware of that, the perpetrators made their way into his courtyard and shot Visaitov through the window of the room in which he was sleeping. His neighbours found out about what had happened only in the morning when they came to see him. Visaitov's murderers had left a note on the site in which they threatened to kill all active supporters of the current regime.

In 1995 Khumid's brother, Arbi Vitargov, and his wife were killed by shelling from from a helicopter. His son, Khavazh Khumidovich Visaitov, aged 25, disappeared in 2000.
Memorial Human Rights Centre

15 DID THE REFUGEES VOTE?

Tanya Lokshina, Moscow Helsinki Group/Centre 'Demos'.

From the beginning of the second Chechen war in 1999 tens of thousands of refugees fled to the neighbouring Republic of Ingushetia. Beginning in 2001 federal and regional Chechen authorities tried to implement strategies to compel the refugees to return to their areas of permanent residence. On the one side were promises to help in Chechnya, and on the other threats to cease support in Ingushetia. But many of the refugees did not to take steps to return for fear of their own safety and that of their family. Despite the appalling conditions of their life in the tent camps, it was much safer in Ingushetia. Many refugees participated in the March Referendum. They voted in favour of the new Constitution of Chechnya and the laws on election of the president and the Parliament of the Chechen Republic in the hope that the creation of a new government would lay the ground for a return home.

During my trip to Chechnya and Ingushetia in September 2003, I spoke with several dozen Chechen refugees about the forthcoming election, about their attitudes to candidates running for the presidency and about the course of the pre-election campaign.

On 16 September I visited two refugee camps in Ingushetia – officially Temporary Accommodation Centres (TACs) – known as Bart and Bella. We discussed many things, including the election due in three weeks time. No refugee I spoke to expressed the wish to participate in the vote or put any trust in the election. They all said that they had initially intended to go to the election and cast a vote for one of three candidates – A.Aslakhanov, Kh.Dzhabrailov or M.Saidullaev. Saidullaev seems to have enjoyed the greatest popularity according to frequency of mention, but any of these candidates would have been acceptable. At that time, after Aslakhanov's and Dzhabrailov's 'renunciation' ("they were pressured to pull out from the race" people repeated) and Saidullaev's deprivation of registration, only Kadyrov remained. The refugees expressed a refusal to vote for Kadyrov.

I can illustrate this response with a few quotes:

"With Saidullaev or the other two (Dzhabrailov, Aslakhanov)], we would have returned to Chechnya. If Kadyrov stays in power there will be no peace. There is nowhere to come back to" (Satsita, 38 years old).

"I wanted to vote for Malik (Saidullaev) – his hands are not bloodied. But now we will not go to the election. There is no point." (Sveta, 41 years old).

"No refugee will vote for him (Kadyrov). All this time, neither he nor any of his representatives came to see us. They say that after the election, under Kadyrov`s regime, all the camps will be closed down. And people will have to return on their own. There will be no support. We are being told that we should return now while we can get some assistance. But it is scary to go home. And especially with Kadyrov – we will return to vote only under the threat of the barrel of a machine-gun." Having noticed me taking notes, the woman stopped suddenly, "Do not write these words about Kadyrov. They will come and kill me." Finally she agreed to being cited after my assurance that neither last names nor tent numbers would be disclosed in the article. She also asked me not to give her first name to be on the safe side. So I will give only her age – 39 years.

Everyone said the same thing, with more or less the same wording, so there is not point in giving other quotations; they would be just variations of the same theme. And I was speaking with tens of persons. I have never come across such striking unanimity amongst such totally different people.

It is worth mentioning that the large majority of my respondents participated in the March Referendum. And they voted 'pro'. They put trust in the referendum. They believed that it might end the war, stabilize the situation, and that a president would be elected, maybe this candidate, maybe another, but not Kadyrov. They were waiting for something. And now, "What election? This is not an election. It is a fraud. Nobody to elect. Nothing to hope for."

Usam Baisaev, Memorial Human Rights Centre

To be honest I had doubts that the refugees would vote even as I made my way to the camps in Eastern Ingushetia. A painful question was constantly on my mind. 'These people are tired of uncertainty. Their hopes have been dashed by many disappointments over many years. Why should they buy the empty promises of the officially approved candidate?'

Then I thought that when people feel trapped they can come to believe in the supernatural. Unconsciously they come to believe that there could be a miracle. Like a reflex, a miracle does not require rational thought. Is there anything in pre-election Chechnya that calls for rational thought? The attitude might be 'After all Kadyrov is a Chechen like us, maybe...'. That could be the way some potential voters were thinking. Few people would count on Kadyrov's moral, political or personal qualities. Kadyrov was involved with the four long years (even the Great Patriotic war was shorter!) of unashamed bloodletting into which the republic was plunged. Kadyrov didn't even try to stop the bloodshed. All that was left to hope for was that after inauguration as president he would remember that he is part of his people and he would come to feel ashamed of the crimes perpetrated against his fellow citizens. Some people might be prepared to clutch at this shadow of a straw...

The Memorial Human Rights Centre officially distanced itself from all matters related to the election of the first president of the Chechen Republic. The Centre even decided against routine monitoring because it could be easily labelled by the authorities as an attempt to supervise. So it was solely on my own initiative that I went back to the tent camps. I wondered what my fellow citizens would do in a situation when other candidates, perhaps less unpopular than Kadyrov and with a real chance of being elected, had been brazenly removed from the race. To put it simply – would the refugees show up at the voting places?

My collaborator Ruslan Badalov, head of the public organization Chechen Committee for National Salvation, made the camp called Bart in Karabulak our first destination. Bart is the largest and best maintained camp in the vicinity. Of all the refugees, inhabitants of Bart are the best cared for – by both the local Ingush and Federal authorities. It is a show camp – the place shown to Lord Judd, and other international and national officials, whose positions call for demonstration of how well people in the camps are looked after.

Murat Zyazikov, the president of Ingushetia, was among those who had visited the camp – usually in an attempt to persuade the refugees to go back home. These attempts usually triggered waves of indignation from the human rights and international community. Arriving at the camp, Zyazikov would utter stock phrases into TV cameras about the inadmissibility of violence and of attempts at coercion of those who had lost their home and property. Then turning to the people gathered around he would ask, "Is anyone forcing you to leave Ingushetia?" Their answer was obvious. Federal TV channels would show this clip to counteract criticism of Russia.

Refugees, pawns in this propaganda game, learned to take advantage of the performance and played up to the bureaucrats. At Bart, unlike at other camps, the migration authorities issue humanitarian aid regularly, and until recently, no attempt had been made to move refugees by force. If any Russian authorities lose sleep at night worrying about poor and humble displaced people they can switch their mind to the positive image presented by Bart. If any Chechen refugees have ever stated that their life in Ingushetia is good, you can be sure those refugees are part of the performance at the Bart Karabulak camp.

Ruslan Badalov and I arrived there at 10.30 am. There was a grey UAZ jeep without license plates on the road leading to the camp. The passengers of the jeep – solidly built servicemen, masked and clad in camouflage uniforms complete with military paraphernalia were wandering about. We could see parked cars on the other side of the lowered bar of the camp entry checkpoint, but only pedestrians were allowed in. We left our car at the checkpoint and produced our IDs that were thoroughly scrutinized. Then we proceeded to the tents.

A red Mercedes coach parked by administrative building stood out in the gloomy greyish atmosphere of camp. The coach gave the impression that it had just left a Hollywood film set, but the C 317 MA license plate showed registration in Ingushetia. The windshield sticker featured the large letters UDM MVD Ch (Migration department of the Ministry of Internal Affairs of the Chechen Republic). The expectation was that the coach would be used to allow refugees to fulfill their civic duty. The polling station was in the Chechen village of Assinovskaya, not far from the administrative border between Chechnya and Ingushetia. There was very little activity near the coach – only a few people in military and police uniforms.

We looked into the coach to count the passengers. There were nine – six women and three men. More people were standing nearby waiting for the coach to depart. I spoke to a boy of about seventeen and a man from the village of Sernovodsk where they wanted to visit their relatives. "You are going in the Mercedes?" I asked them. "Yes" answered the man. "The coach is going to Assinovskaya. We shall get off at the bend and walk to our village. It is only three kilometres. We'll make it alright." "We won't be voting, well I don't think we will" joined in the teenager, "I was not planning to go home but they sent the coach. It'll take me almost to my house. I don't have to pay. It's good to be in a Mercedes and be able to get through all the checkpoints without producing an ID".

Four more people came up to the coach. A mother with a teenage son, almost eligible to vote, had decided to "mix with the crowd" and visit their family home in Assinovskaya. A perfect arrangement. The woman, her name was Rumisa, planned to use the same coach to get back to the camp. "They say that the polling station is in the school close to my father's home," she said. "While people are voting we shall take some food to my parents and show them their grandson. They haven't seen the boy for ages. And then we'll come back to the camp." At 11.00 am the Mercedes left the camp and was heading towards Chechnya carrying twenty-four people. Passengers or voters? I don't think the terminology is of importance.

From Bart we proceeded to the village of Ordzhenikidzevskaya without stopping at any of the smaller tent camps. On the outskirts of Ordzhenikidzevskaya, very close to the Chechen border, there are more large camps: Satsita, Sputnik, and the remnants of Alina. A major camp, Bella, had been liquidated by the joint effort of Federal, Chechen and Ingush authorities on the eve of the election. The Ingush police blocked the only road to these camps. But our timing was fortuitous. Just as we arrived three large coaches pulled up on the opposite side of the checkpoint and we were overlooked. The coaches stopped, the drivers got out and were approached by several men in plain clothes and policemen from the checkpoint. They all then entered the service building.

Passing by the abandoned post we could see vehicles (two Ikarus coaches, model 256, C 399 BO and C 932 EE, and a LiAZ C 675 AT), their windshields showing the same letters, UDM MVD ChR, we had seen at Bart – indicating that they belonged to the Migration Service of the Chechen Ministry of Internal Affairs. The first two coaches were empty. We couldn't see how many passengers were in the third because the curtains were drawn on all the windows. If there had been anyone inside they would surely have opened curtains of at least one window.

When we reached the Sputnik camp whose refugees the coach was supposed to be taking to the polling station we found confirmation of our supposition. The refugees we interviewed all stated that not a single person from their camp went to vote. The LiAZ coach had left the camp empty of passengers. No one from other camps expressed any desire to go to Assinovskaya to vote, neither refugees, nor administration personnel, nor the police who were numerous at and around the camps. On the contrary, many of those we talked to found our interest in the election rather strange. Some asked the rhetorical question: "Why should we go to vote – abandoning our private business and risking our lives at checkpoints? Our business might not be very important but it is our own. The outcome of the election was clear before it started. Why should we vote?"

Ruslan Badalov did manage to find one person who was surprised by the lack of active involvement with the election. This person was a police major on a business trip from Dagestan – that is symbolic in itself. But when Ruslan asked him to imagine that he was one of the people who had lost all their property as a result of war, and that the authorities were now trying to drive him out of the tents provided by international organizations, the major after a moment's pause said, "If it were me, I wouldn't have gone… anywhere." Had this major been an ethnic Russian I think we would have heard more colourful language.

The three coaches, from Satsita, Alina and Sputnik, were parked near the administrative building until 11.45 am. When it was realized that no one was eager to fulfil their civic duty, the coaches were sent to the checkpoint to park near the police and the offices of the migration authorities of Chechnya and Ingushetia authorities responsible for refugee voting. It was these three coaches we had seen when we arrived at the first checkpoint. After our departure the coaches returned to the camps. It appears that they were standing by in case journalists and observers showed up.

It is easy to imagine an official saying "You see, people are still prepared to go to vote for the first president of the Chechen Republic, and the authorities are prepared to take them to the polling stations". At Bart another fifteen people expressed their wish to go to the polling station. But the coaches at Satsita, Alina and Sputnik waited in vain until dark at 5.30 pm. The authorities were expecting too much. Perhaps they should have sent Mercedes? But it has to be admitted that even sending Mercedes probably wouldn't have worked at Alina, Satsita or Sputnik.

In summary the total number of persons carried to Chechnya was 39, all from Bart, and including those who used the opportunity to go home in comfort and safety in a Mercedes. We have to admit that this was a result, and not the worst possible. But there is another result – the official one.

According to official information, 1,241 forced migrants residing in Ingushetia cast their votes in the 5 October election. Where and how those additional 1202 people voted remains an enigma to me and to Ruslan Badalov. They must have voted in a different and better world.

16 BOOK OF NUMBERS: BOOK OF THE LOST

Alexander Cherkasov, Memorial Human Rights Centre

In 1999, when the second Chechen war started, the federal centre estimated the population of the Chechen Republic as 350 thousand. In November 1999 Igor Shabdurasulov, at that time deputy head of the Chechen presidential administration, stated "Today more than 750 thousand Chechens are living in Russia outside the republic. According to various estimates 150 to 200 thousand people are left in Chechnya and those we call forced migrants are some 100 to 150 thousand". Shabdurasulov thus provided support for the 350 thousand federal estimate,.

But the estimates of turnout in the three votes of 2003 – the 26 March referendum, the presidential election of 5 October, and the Duma elections of 7 December – were based on the results of the census of population conducted by the federal authorities in 2002. In October 2002 it was officially declared that the population of the Chechen Republic amounted to a little over a million – to be more exact 1,088 thousand people.

How can these two very different sets of figures be reconciled? How could the population of Chechnya triple in the three years between 1999 and 2002? Did all the refugees of the second Chechen war and nearly all the republic's diaspora return – just in time for the 2002 census?

To try to unravel this puzzle we need to try to deal with three kinds of question. 1) What was the population of the republic at different times, how many people actually lived in the territory of Chechnya? 2) What was the scale of migration from the republic, how many refugees were living outside Chechen borders at different times? And 3) How many Chechen residents perished in the course of the armed conflicts of recent years?

To obtain consistency between answers to these questions and to relate our answers to the 2003 election we need to look critically at the way the results of the census were produced and identify the extent to which census statistics were used, and misused, in presenting the election results. This poses two more questions. What was the population of Chechnya at the time of the 2002 census? And 5) How were figures for the size of the electorate in 2003 obtained?

This chapter attempts to answer each of these questions in turn.

1) What was the population of the republic at different times, how many people actually lived in the territory of Chechnya?

The preceding census was conducted by the USSR in 1989. The census counted 1,276 thousand people as the *de facto* population, and 1,270 thousand normally resident in what was then called the Checheno-Ingush Autonomous Soviet Socialist Republic (CIASSR). No separate data were published for Chechnya and Ingushetia but we can estimate that the numbers were a little more than 1,100 and 170 thousand respectively.[1] Out of the CIASSR total of 1,270 thousand permanent residents, 735 thousand were Chechen, 164 thousand Ingush, 294 thousand Russian, with about 40 thousand of other nationalities.

There are no exact data about the ethnic composition of the population of Chechnya proper as of 1989, but we can estimate that out of 1,084 thousand permanent residents about 715 thousand were Chechen, 25 thousand were Ingush, and 269 thousand were Russian. The highest reasonable estimate of the Vainakh population, i.e. Chechen and Ingush, at that time would be 755–760 thousand.[2]

According to the census, the number of Vainakhs in the USSR increased in the 1979–1989 decade by 27% – corresponding to an annual growth rate of

---

[1] The border between the two republics had not been demarcated. Extrapolation of the State Committee for Statistics figures gives the population permanently living in Chechen districts as 1,084 thousand, and in Ingushetia districts as 186 thousand. The State Committee assigned all the Sunzha district to Ingushetia, but a substantial part of Sunzha, including Sernovodsk and Assinovskaya, with 8 and 6.9 thousand inhabitants as of 1989, belonged to Chechnya.

[2] In 1989, besides Vainakhs, several thousand representatives of other Muslim nations resided in Chechnya: 23 thousand Kumyks, Nogaitsi and Avartsi, countryside residents mostly, and 5.1 thousand Tartars, mainly urban residents.

2.42%. The socio-economic situation in the 1990s was not as favourable to population growth as in the 1980s. But the table below extrapolates this 2.42% rate of growth to make an estimate of the maximum possible Chechen population of the Checheno-Ingush Republic at the start of the new century.

Maximum likely Chechen population of Chechnya and Ingushetia 1989–2003 extrapolated from the period 1979–1989

Year	Population in thousands
1989	734.5
1999	932.8
2000	955.4
2001	978.5
2002	1002.2
2003	1026.4

Had that rate of growth been maintained, we can estimate that the number of Chechens in Chechnya could have been more than a million in 2002. But official estimates do not show any sustained population growth in the 1990s. The Russian Statistics Annual Report gives the following figures for Chechnya and Ingushetia.

Population of Chechnya and Ingushetia (as at 1 January of year – thousands)

Year	Chechnya	Ingushetia
1989		1275
1990		1290
1991		1307
1992		1308
1993		1307
1994	1079	211
1995	974	280
1996	921	300
1997	813	309
1998	797	313

Estimating the size of the population of Ingushetia is difficult because of the scale of migration. In the course of the Ossetian-Ingush conflict of 1992 many thousands of Ingushs were driven from the Prigorodny District of North Ossetia: Ingush authorities tell of 70 thousand, Ossetian authorities speak of 17 thousand. In the first Chechen war of 1994-96 the number of forced migrants from Chechnya arriving in Ingushetia made up 150 thousand. According to the information provided by the Federal Migration Service 35 thousand were registered in Ingushetia of 1 January 1999. In 1989 41 thousand Ingush lived in the USSR outside the Checheno-Ingush Republic and North Ossetia, later some of them returned to their motherland. There was substantial outbound migration in the republic during 1990s because it was one of the poorest regions of the federation. In spite of this movement the second column of this table that is less doubtful than the first.

The Annual Report also gives information on the sex and age composition of the Chechnya's population.

Distribution of permanent residents of Chechnya by sex and age as at 1 January 1988 (thousands)

Male	362
Female	430
Under working age	266
Working age	418
Above working age	109
Total	**792**

Such a sex and age structure of Chechnya's population is credible. The obvious deficit in the male population of about 70 thousand can be attributed to Chechen males working in other regions of Russia rather than casualties of war. We should also note that, according to this table, the population of working age or above, i.e. the number of voters, was a little under 527 thousand.

The main factor affecting the level of population of Chechnya in recent years has been outward migration. The Russian media have reported mainly on the exodus of the Russian-speaking population, or non-Vainakh to be more exact, but that does not cover all emigration. The number of Eastern Slavs (Russians and Ukrainians) in the Checheno-Ingush Republic was falling as early as the 1970s and 1980s. According to the census this number fell from 380 thousand in 1970 to 306 thousand in 1989. This decline could not have been connected with the establishment of Ichkeria – or what were later described as the 'criminal regimes' of Dudayev and Maskhadov'.

There was also emigration from other ethnic territories in the Caucasus.[3] This is explicable in terms of relative overpopulation and insufficient land, tensions between ethnic groups (even during the Soviet 'friendship of nations' era), and the more tightly-knit character of the Caucasian nations in comparison to the Russian. These factors were particularly important in Chechnya where there was more unemployment[4]. The stability of traditional social institutions gave a measure of community protection to Vainakhs. But members of non-Vainakh ethnic groups were subjected to a variety of pressures including criminal pressures.

The weakening of governmental structure and law enforcement agencies during the 1991–1994 period accelerated the emigration of Russian-speaking residents, though Grozny remained a half-Russian city during the first Chechen war. The situation changed in the 1996–1999 inter-war period. Disintegration of the government, the collusion of the authorities with openly criminal agencies, and the fact that central authorities did nothing to protect human rights, led to the exodus of most of the non-Vainakh population from the republic. Chechens also

---

[3] In the 1990s both in the autonomous republics which became simple republics and in the autonomous districts 'Russian-speaking' people holding influential posts or just well-paid jobs were replaced with 'ethnic' representatives. Except in Chechnya national movements did not even think of independence from Russia. There were struggles between different elites for the control of resources and inevitable appeals to the federal centre to act as an arbiter.

[4] After the return of Chechens from exile in 1957 there were no vacant jobs in industry. It was impossible to return to a half of Chechnya because of difficulty in restoring mountain villages where there had been no life for 13 years – and the authorities did not want to have resistance resumed in the mountains. Highlanders were mainly settled in two districts to the north of the Terek, Naursky and Shelkovskoi, that were joined to Chechnya, but that provided only a partial solution. High unemployment was partially compensated by the agricultural subsistence economy and by seasonal work in other regions of the USSR, and labour emigration to work in the 'North'. Not only Slavs left the Checheno-Ingush Republic in 1970-80s, Vainakhs also went away, the total emigration of the latter reached 50 thousand in 1979-1989 according to the census. During the same period the number of Chechens permanently residing in the Stavropol territory went up 3.4 times, in the Astrakhan region – 5.5 times, in the Rostov region – 6.8 times, in Volgograd region – 13.7 times, in the Tyumen region – 33.7 times. The sum total of Chechen permanent residents of these five regions increased six times from 9.3 to 55.8 thousand. In the mid 1980s the opportunity to earn money went down due to the economic collapse of the USSR and resulting cuts of subsidies for construction in the agricultural sector.

fled. Up to 1500 local residents were kidnapped for ransom in this period. Most were Chechens. It became apparent that the traditional public institutions were in decay. The second Chechen war that started in 1999 completed the ethnic purge. Everybody fled from the fighting, but almost nobody but Chechens returned. Even the Grozny Ingush were not eager to come back and most settled in Ingushetia.

What was the size of these waves of refugees? In autumn 1999 Vladimir Putin, then Chairman of the Russian government, spoke of the Chechen diaspora. "We are ready for political cooperation with those citizens of Chechnya who moved from the territory of the Chechen Republic in recent years and, I must remind you, there are 220 thousand Russians and 550 thousand Chechens among them." The context makes it obvious that he spoke only of the war emigration prior to the second Chechen war.

One might agree with this estimate of Russian/Slavic migration, but the figure for the number of Chechens is quite inconsistent with the migration statistics from the Federal Migration Service (FMS). The FMS recorded less than thirty thousand Chechens among the hundreds of thousands forced migrants from Chechnya.[5] In the second half of the 1990s one circumstance preventing Chechens from leaving the territory of Chechnya for other regions of Russia, was that the authorities, and sometimes the local population as well, regarded them as foreigners, and hostile foreigners into the bargain.

The statistics promulgated by Putin were taken into account by officials of lower levels but made their situation uncomfortable. When in autumn 1999 the number of registered refugees fleeing the republic reached its peak of 350 thousand, Vladimir Kalamanov, then head of the Federal Migration Service, declared "All Chechnya is on the move, it registers and migrates!" That drew attention to the contradiction in the statistics. In the light of the official estimates of the Chechnya population of 300,000 at the start of the conflict, it ap-

---

[5] There was no mass exodus. Only putting on record what had already happened over a long period. Human rights activists managed to make the authorities register migrants who had left earlier.

pears that federal forces were having a hard time fighting MINUS 50 thousands gunmen.

The sad conclusion to be drawn from this absurdity is that Putin's statements and the supporting official statistics were part of a propaganda war. The Chechen population at the beginning of the war was understated in order to reduce the apparent size of the conflict. A more realistic estimate could have complicated the planning of the military operation and even cast doubt on its justifiability. Production of a more realistic estimate would also have indicated the scale of the potential flow of refugees.

Nobody among the authorities appears to have been deterred by the fact that as a result of the understatement bombs were falling on densely populated areas. The areas where bombs were falling contained many times more people than all concerned with the conflict had been led to expect. The wave of refugees exceeded all expectations. Official statements contradicted reality, common sense, and each other. Official statements also retreated from what was represented by the figures – the human lives that were the subject matter of the statistics.

Is there any real information on the size of the population of Chechnya at the start of the second Chechen war that is not based on unsubstantiated estimates or extrapolations? Some sources mentioned the 'Maskhadov census' (earlier I regarded this census as apocryphal) but further investigation in 2003 revealed that this census was fairly well conducted as far as it went.[6] The census of the population of the Chechen Republic of Ichkeria was undertaken over several months from August till October 1998. The standard census form of 1989 was used with minor modifications. During the three months census

---

[6] Russian propaganda claimed that Maskhadov kept the census results secret because they testified to a disastrous reduction in the size of the Chechen population. This claim echoes the story of the Soviet census of 1937 which was labelled as sabotage because it showed a decline in population attributable to Stalin's purges. The very possibility of undertaking such a complicated measure in the situation when the government collapsed caused doubts. The author even allowed himself to call the 'Maskhadov census' in Ichkeria the 'Library of Ivan the Terrible'. But after speaking to many people involved in the census and many residents of the Chechen Republic, enquiring if census workers called on them, the author changed his view.

takers conducted house-to-house visits, perhaps not thoroughly everywhere, but several enumerators said that they visited some homes three times before they were able to find the people at home.

The information was not entered into any computer. The processing of census results was limited to counting census forms. With the involvement of workers from all sections of the department for Demographic Statistics this procedure lasted till February 1999. They counted about 800 thousand residents of Chechnya; close to the figure of 797 thousand given for January 1998 by the Russian Statistical Annual Report. These figures seem to be the best answer to the question about the size of population at the beginning of the second Chechen war, and can be compared with the official annual figures given for earlier years in the table at the beginning of this chapter.

The contrast between these figures from local sources of 800 thousand for 1998 with the federally approved figure of 300 thousand for 1999 gives an indication of the scale of falsification. A contrast that draws attention to the scale of forced migration.

2) What was the scale of migration from the republic, how many refugees were living outside Chechen borders at different times?

Vladimir Kalamanov, head of the Federal Migration Service, cited 350 thousand as the number of refugees in the autumn of 1999. This figure may be close to reality but was uncomfortable for the federal authorities. The scale of migration was incompatible with the official position claiming normalization of the situation in Chechnya. The governmental aim was to deny the existence of refugees – or least not to have TV pictures of the camps of forced migrants. The federal public relations departments claimed that Chechen gunmen drove away people to create the 'illusion of a humanitarian disaster'. A telegram of 25 September 1999 from General Shamanov banned departments of internal affairs from letting migrants from the Chechen Republic through administrative borders.

Apart from Ingushetia, headed by president Ruslan Aushev[7], the subject republics of the federation followed Shamanov's order. As a result most forced migrants from Chechnya found themselves in Ingushetia, and at some points of time the population of the republic was almost double the number of its permanent residents. But from the autumn of 1999 till the autumn of 2003 the number of forced migrants in Ingushetia was a persistent challenge to representatives of the federal and local Chechen authorities loyal to Moscow. Being unable to create the conditions that would encourage or force the return of refugees the authorities tried to deny their very existence.

In the course of six months of 2002 the recorded number of forced migrants fell to 150 thousand. It remained at this level till the second half of 2002 when active attempts were made to begin a voluntary return of refugees to Chechnya. However, even eighteen months later half of the refugees remained in Ingushetia. As of late 2003 Russian official representatives cited 4.2 thousand or 4.5 thousand forced migrants living in tented camps. The UN department on coordinating humanitarian issues estimated the number of people staying in camps as seven thousand. In addition there were 24 thousand staying in temporary settlements in adequate conditions, with 36 thousand staying in the private sector, making all-in-all 67 thousand forced migrants. The reduction of the number of refugees in Ingushetia was not solely attributable to those returning to Chechnya. Those who could afford it moved to other regions of the Russian Federation or even beyond its borders.

The information provided by international humanitarian organisations was consistently challenged by Russian official representatives[8]. But when departments of the Ministry of Internal Affairs counted forced migrants in sum-

---

[7] Aushev was held responsible for the problem of refugees for all of the Russian Federation. Had Aushev acted according to the order banning refugees, he would have had no problems either with refugees, or with generals. But the number of civilian casualties in Chechnya would have been several times, if not dozens of times, higher. Not to participate in war crimes is a worthy choice for a general and a president.

[8] The Danish Refugee Council is a leading humanitarian organisation working in Ingushetia and Chechnya. It regularly conducts house to house rounds to compile lists of people eligible to humanitarian aid. But their information on Ingushetia where every family is checked is substantially more accurate than that on Chechnya where it had to satisfy itself with the data provided by the heads of village administrations.

mer 2002 their doubts disappeared. There was at last cooperation between government departments and humanitarian organisations. The cooperation in Ingushetia characterized by mutual transparency and control and cross-checking of data from different sources worked well.

The rationale for earlier denials of estimates of the number of refugees reflects the nature of the operations carried out by 'law enforcers'. The label 'counter-terrorist', suggests selective actions. The implicit goal of counter-terrorism is to save people's lives. We might assume that the saving of lives might be given equal priority to the capture or extermination of terrorists. But the main instrument for the military component of the Chechen campaign was indiscriminate bombardments and shelling, and for the police component indiscriminate detention. There were no files of terrorists to be detained, no lists of objectives to attack. 'Pointed strikes', 'humanitarian corridors', and 'security zones' existed only in official propaganda.

People were fleeing Chechnya from 'pointed strikes,' i.e. from massive indiscriminate bombing and shelling in the autumn of 1999. Roads declared to be 'humanitarian corridors' could more accurately have been called 'corridors of death'. The number of people who died outside towns and villages was comparable to the number who died inside towns and villages.

Officials offer various explanations of why all attempts to bring the migrants back to their places of permanent residence failed. The main reason is the lack of security in Chechnya. In December 1999 the return of refugees (sometimes forced) to the territory of Chechnya started. There were transfers to the so-called 'security zones'. This resulted in further human losses. Hundreds of peaceful citizens who returned died in bombings and shootings, on 9 January in Shali and in the villages of Zakan-Yurt, Shaami-Yurt and Katyr-Yurt early in February 2000. The 'security zones' were not, of course agreed with an identifiable opponent. The federal forces themselves did not limit their operations to areas outside the security zones. Federal forces and their opponents operated as if they were in a desert without burdening themselves with care or consideration for those living in the area.

When active combat operations finished in spring 2000 mopping-up or cleansing operations started in towns and villages. Unable to achieve the goal of identifying the participants in armed resistance, cleansing operations took the form of indiscriminate violence. The robberies, torture, and beatings, 'disappearances' and killings aroused hatred against Russian law enforcement agencies and the Russian government. The cleansing operations fed the ranks of resistance and did not promote any desire among refugees to return home. Late in 2002 the number of cleansing operations fell but people were still disappearing in the course of 'addressed' measures with night-time visits by unidentifiable armed persons in camouflage and masks in armoured vehicles.

In such a situation appeals for 'voluntary return' of forced migrants from Ingushetia are hypocritical and criminal. But many such appeals have been heard since late 1999. Why? Because even the formal transfer of forced migrants to Chechnya would mean the transfer of the streams of humanitarian aid, of financial flow, of 'live' money creating an opportunity for public expenditures[9]. So there was a 'social demand' for migrants to return from Ingushetia to Chechnya, coming from the federal centre, from the military and from Akhmat Kadyrov's administration.

During the first months of the second Chechen war up to 350 thousand of the approximately 800 thousand residents of the Chechen Republic fled its administrative borders. What about the rest?

Most of them were involved in the process of internal migration. At first people fled from the northern and eastern districts, then from Grozny and from the mountains. All those who could afford to tried to leave the area of combat operations. Many left one or two family members behind to protect their property from marauders.[10] This internal migration was usually local, people going to

---

[9] In the course of two years, dozens of the heads of local administrations in Ingushetia were dismissed from their posts for abusing 'refugee' money. But this indicates effective control in Ingushetia. Nothing of this kind was heard in Chechnya because there was little control. The cost of settling one refugee in a camp (providing a tent, flooring, bedding, a stove, communication) was 700 roubles in Ingushetia, while in Chechnya the cost amounted to 3,700 roubles.

[10] Thus in Grozny in January 2000, after it had been stormed by the federal forces, less than 40 thousand residents remained.

neighbouring villages or districts hoping to return to their homes, although in some cases they fled the republic.

When combat operations were completed the distribution of population in Chechnya had changed by comparison to the pre-war period. The Grozny population fell to a small fraction of its prewar level and there was substantial depopulation of highland districts. In 2001, according to the Federal Migration Service, up to one-third of the population of the republic – 200 thousand – had become internal migrants.

War made Chechnya *de facto* ethnically homogeneous. Almost all the non-Vainakh population left the republic. Most of the Ingush, both those who were not able to return to the Prigorodny district in 1957 and settled in Grozny and those who fled to Grozny in 1992, also left[11].

3) How many people perished in the two Chechen wars?

One of the basic historical sources of the period of rule of Ivan the Terrible – the Oprichny Synodic – was compiled whenever the Tsar thought that he was going to die. That was a fairly regular occurrence. To repent, to pray for those he had killed, it was necessary to make a list. The crowned murderer was diligent and insisted that the compilers of the Synodic had to finish it with the following words, 'As for the rest, You, Our Lord, know them Yourself...'

The Russian government found itself in the same situation. The government did not make any attempt to count civilian casualties in the war of 1994–1996, nor after 1999. There are no lists of names, not even incomplete lists. Rational discussion of cited figures of up to more than a hundred thousand is impossible for the Russian authorities. Only the Lord knows the truth.

Thus, on 17 September 2002 Salambek Maigov declared to journalists that "eighty thousand peaceful residents perished in the 'second Chechen war,"[12] For some unknown reason he referred to Human Rights Watch and the Me-

---

[11] About 60 thousand stayed in Ingushetia and intended to remain there. It was proposed to allocate land for them in the Sunzha District on their return to Chechnya.

[12] Reported by NTV.RU on September 17, 2002, 11:42:20.

morial Human Rights Centre as the source of this statistic. In fact neither of these organisations reported anything of the kind. Abdul-Khakim Sultygov, special representative of the RF president for the Observance of the Rights and Freedoms of the Citizen and Human Being in the Chechen Republic, reacted to this figure on the following day[13]. He remarked that "all the figures which are cited by human rights organisations at present are nothing but subjective estimates that have nothing in common with the real situation".

So what estimates do share something with reality?

During the first Chechen war there was an attempt to estimate the casualties in Grozny during the fighting from December 1994 till March 1995. The members of the Observers' Mission of human rights public organisation acting under the auspices of the Memorial Human Rights Centre (widely known as Sergei Kovalyov's Group) surveyed more than a thousand refugees from Grozny asking about relatives and acquaintances who died during combat operations. The method, as used by Eduard Gelman at the Kurchatov Institute in 1995, is a standard method for making estimates of casualties in local conflicts. The survey took into account the structure of families and, to support corrections for possible double counting, the processing of the data takes into account various degrees of kinship in family relationship and variation in the extent of acquaintances. The conclusion reached was that 25–29 thousand peaceful residents perished in Grozny in that period.

In January 1996 in the course of the war Vladimir Rubanov, deputy secretary of the Security Council of the Russian Federation, declared to the Interfax Agency that there were no official figures, that there were only human rights activists' data estimating that 25–30 thousand civilians had been killed. In spring of 1997 when preparations for a treaty between Russia and Chechnya were under way and a sum of potential damages due to Chechnya for economic destruction and human loss was discussed, Boris Brui, the head of the department for Demographic Statistics of the State Committee for Statistics of the Russian Federation, asked the Memorial Centre questions about the number of civilian casualties. Earlier he had asked the International Red

---

[13] Report of NTV.RU on September 18, 2002, 08:15:00.

Cross Committee the same questions but the Committee sent him to 'Memorial.' As a result, using the same data, the State Committee for Statistics made its own estimates of 30–40 thousand casualties. The Memorial Centre taking account of the possible inaccuracy of such estimates, formulated it as 'less than 50 thousand'.

Using the same method for the second Chechen war, the best estimate of civilian casualties in the period of active combat operations was produced by Human Rights Watch (HRW). Having collected and analyzed detailed information about 1,300 people killed in the course of the first nine months of the conflict, HRW came to the conclusion that their sample covered between one eighth and one fifth of the total number of victims. The best estimate is that between 6.5 and 10.4 thousand civilians were killed in those nine months.[14] The number of residents of the Chechen Republic who perished in the following years of armed conflict can be estimated on the basis of the Chronicle of Violence which has been conducted by the Memorial Human Rights Centre since July 2000. The number of people whose death was reported in the Chronicle varies from 489 in the second half of 2000 to 559 throughout the whole of 2002 (both figures exclude gunmen and Chechen policemen). The results of this monitoring are incomplete. But the MHRC data can be compared with the official statistics of the Ministry of Internal Affairs of the Chechen Republic for 2002. It may be seen that the Chronicle data may be registering about a quarter of deaths, and certainly not more than a half.

Extrapolation of the Chronicle data makes it possible to conclude that from 5.3 to 10.7 thousand civilians were killed after the active phase of combat operations was completed. In addition, in the course of the second Chechen war about three thousand people disappeared after being detained by the federal law enforcement agencies. Some bodies of the disappeared were later found

---

[14] The second Chechen war was more brutal than the first one, but the number of casualties during the first months of it was 3-4 times lower. Fear can save people. In autumn 1999 people fled Chechnya from massive indiscriminate bombardments and shellings. Fleeing was dangerous. The roads which were declared to be 'humanitarian corridors' ought to have been called 'corridors of death'. The number of people who died outside villages and towns was comparable to the number of those who died inside them. But those who fled may nevertherless have increased their prospect of survival.

and identified; it seems unlikely that the overwhelming majority of the rest are alive. Thus the total number of civilians killed during the second Chechen war, including those who disappeared, adds up to between 14.8 to 24.1 thousand. This is a conservative estimate which does not take into account the missing '10–20 thousands' who were not counted by the federal authorities and whose fate is unknown.

So, where did the other, substantially higher, figures of casualties come from?

Already during the first Chechen war people were speaking of 80, 100, 120 thousand killed. These figures were generated by political debate rather than by any link with reality. In the winter of 1996, soon after the statement of Rubanov that was mentioned above, several politicians ranging from General Lebed to a public activist Valerya Novodvorskaya claimed that, if the government was speaking of 25–30 thousand killed, there would have been three times more in reality, i.e. 80–100 thousand.

Another estimate is a result of misinterpretation. Lechi Saligov, who worked for the pro-Russian Chechen administration during the first war, claimed that 120 thousand perished in the Grozny area alone. This figure was based on a house-to-house count that revealed a difference by comparison with pre-war figures. Saligov interpreted that difference as the number of casualties. But migration provides a more credible explanation.

While the declarations of politicians tended to exaggerate the number of civilian casualties, the military and the official propaganda reduced or denied them. Thus, in August 2001 General Valery Manilov claimed that less than one thousand civilians were killed during the second war. A year later, in August 2002, Kostyuchenko, prosecutor of the Chechen Republic, mentioned the same one thousand. That estimate is refuted not just by estimates and extrapolations, but also by administrative statistics based on the count of registered deaths.

At the same time, the military and their public relations staff regularly made declarations of success in annihilating Chechen fighters, with claims amounting to tens of thousands. These figures did not come out of thin air. They were produced by a bureaucratic machine, although there is no evidence that they had much to do with reality. Estimates of civilian casualties made public by the representatives of law enforcement agencies also have a political character with no necessary link to systematically collected information. But the figures which the military cite for the number of 'killed gunmen' do correlate with the number of civilian casualties as recorded by civil rights organisations.

Thus the total number of peaceful residents of the Chechen Republic who perished during the two wars may have reached 70 thousand. The accuracy of our estimates is not high. But there is no alternative source for the government to count the number of civilians who perished in the course of 'counter-terrorist operations' or 'establishing constitutional order'.

4) What was the population of Chechnya at the time of the 2002 census?

In August 2002, at Government House in Grozny, the Group for Cooperation with OSCE was told that about 600 thousand people were living in the Chechen Republic. This figure looked very much like the truth because out of the 800 thousand of the pre-war Chechen population about 150 thousand[15] were living as forced migrants in the neighbouring republic and a smaller but substantial number had dispersed into other parts of Russia and outside its borders.

One month later, in September 2002, when Lord Judd visited Chechnya, he was told at Government House that the return of refugees had been so successful that the population of the republic had reached 900 thousand. This figure exceeded any real or theoretically possible figure, but was intended to demonstrate that all the forced migrants who fled the republic in the second Chechen war had returned to their homes. The argument was that if people had come back, the situation in the republic must be stable and secure – otherwise the people would not have returned.

The federal authorities made estimates on the basis of the Russian census conducted in October 2002. On 14 October 2002 Stanislav Iliyasov, Russian Minister for Chechnya, reported that the census had been successfully con-

---

[15] 137 thousand are in Ingushetia, and 10 thousand are in Dagestan.

ducted, and that the population amounted to 1,088 thousand. According to Iliyasov, the census results exceeded all expectations. The census takers ran out of census forms and had to ask for more. The authorities had expected to find a total population of less than 800 thousand, and taking into account the inevitable spoiling of some forms, had asked for only 825 thousand forms. The 1,088 thousand figure was credible only if all the refugees who had fled in 1990s, including not only Chechens and Ingush, but also Russians, Armenians and other representatives of non-Vainakh nations, had returned. Or it had to be postulated that, despite the two wars and the collapse of the socio-economic sphere[16], there had been a substantial natural increase in the population.

A normal person could hardly believe in such a 'demographic miracle'.

Now, at last, dear reader, we can give some light relief to this sad story. There are at least three plausible explanations for this demographic miracle!

First. Up to one third of the population of the republic comprised internal migrants including local refugees. The census takers had stated earlier that the documents of the census are anonymous, and they would not be used for any other purpose. Few people in Chechnya believed that. It was difficult to convince people that local administrations would not use census results to ban 'uncounted' people from receiving humanitarian aid or from receiving the promised future compensation for housing that had been destroyed. It was impossible to ensure that law enforcement agencies and special forces would not check people detained during cleansing operations using census lists to separate 'peaceful residents' from 'visiting gunmen'. If an enforced migrant found a place to live in a village but frequently went to rebuild their destroyed house in

---

[16] According to the preliminary census results the population of Ingushetia was 468 thousand including temporarily displaced persons from Chechnya residing in refugee camps. Other migrants, those who did not reside in camps or fled the Prigorodny District in 1992 were not put in a separate category. We should note that in this way the permanent population of the republic, and, evidently, the future budget financing of this subsidized region was increased by one half. We should also note that the migrants who seemed to have been resettled in Chechnya were, as a matter of fact, counted in Ingushetia. The population of Ingushetia was 256 thousand women and 212 thousand men – the asymmetry resulting from high unemployment and departure of men to work in other regions of Russia.

a town, he or she had all the grounds to be 'counted' both in the town and in the village – not just from a spectral expectation of compensation but out of real fear for their safety.

Second. Officials of various levels made numerous declarations that the census would help to determine 'how many schools and hospitals were to be built', and, specifically as far as the Chechen Republic was concerned, the level of financing necessary to revive the socio-economic sphere, and the size of transfers necessary to pay various personal allowances. A lack of control by central authorities (what facts could they use to make control effective?) meant that it was impossible to check information. The temptation was high for local administration at all levels to use statistics derived from the presentation of the 1995, 1996, 2000 election results to boost statistics used for the allocation of resources.

Third and most important. Representatives of various federal agencies made numerous statements declaring that the situation in Chechnya was stable and secure, that the forced migrants had already returned or were shortly going to return, and that the census could not but confirm this reality. Thus local authorities could hope for a favourable attitude from the federal authorities if the census confirmed the federal perception of reality.

The united volition of federal and local authorities, and the active cooperation of the population of the Chechen Republic produced this 'demographic miracle'. The population of Chechnya could hope for a generous attitude on the part of local administrators in cases when surplus relatives were counted on the basis of the words of other people. The episode supports the widely recommended custom of a moratorium on censuses and elections in areas of armed conflict and emergency situations.

So how many people lived in Chechnya in reality? The most reliable source is the house-to-house survey by the Danish Refugee Council conducted in the winter of 2002 to help determine the needs for humanitarian aid in Chechnya. The Council counted about 600 thousand people and cited this figure to OSCE representatives as late as August 2002. But nothing depended upon OSCE. The report of Lord Judd was to provide the basis for the forthcoming PACE resolution.

In November 2002, a month after the census, the Danish Refugee Council conducted its next regular house-to-house survey. The survey estimated the population of Chechnya at about 700 thousands. We should note that the interest of village administrations in the distribution of humanitarian aid might have helped to augment the earlier estimate. The difference between what might be estimated as the true population of Chechnya in 2002, say 600—700 thousand, and the census results, say 400—500 thousand, came to constitute an 'electoral reserve' of dead souls for the referendum and elections of 2003.

5) How were figures for the size of the electorate in 2003 obtained?

How many people have voted in the Chechen Republic in the elections of the past decade? The federal authorities conducted elections in Chechnya between 14–17 December 1995 when people voted for the deputies of the State Duma and for the head of the Chechen republic Doka Zavgayev, and on 14–16 June and 2–3 July 1996 when they voted for the president of Russia and the deputies of the people's assembly. High turnouts were declared ranging from 60% to 74% of the electorate of 503 thousand.

These were official figures but the OSCE mission declared that those elections did not meet the conditions of free and fair elections. For this reason representatives of the OSCE left Chechnya on voting days. According to independent observers, in most villages and towns people just did not go to polling stations. The Central Election Commission recognized these elections. But we must repeat our view that in such situations of armed conflict and *de facto* emergency there ought to be a categorical ban on elections.

On 27 January 1997 after the first Chechen war elections were held for the president and the Parliament of Ichkeria. The number of registered voters – 514 thousand – was established by house-to-house examination. Aslan Maskhadov won the presidential election with 59% of the 408 thousand votes cast. The elections were observed by 72 OSCE representatives. Yet, when the second round of elections took place on 15 February 1997, the turnout was little more than 25%. There is no evidence of any falsification but the level of turnout did not bode well for future elections.

In September 1999 the second Chechen war started; the December 1999 Duma elections did not take place in Chechnya. But for the war December 1999 might have produced the cleanest elections of the decade. Instead the war led to a massive exodus of population. In all later elections the figures for the number of electors and for the numbers voting were inflated. The 2003 election results appeared plausible only in the penumbra created by the fictional census statistics that gave Chechnya a population of more than a million.

On 22 February 2000 Sergei Danilenko, a member of the Central Election Commission supervising the Chechen area, in an interview with the Echo of Moscow radio station, stated that about 400 thousand people lived in the territory of the Chechen Republic and that 200-250 thousand of them were voters – half the number at the time of the 1997 elections. But a month later Abdul-Kerim Arsakhanov, Chairman of the Election Commission of Chechnya, cited a figure for the electorate that was twice as large – 460 thousand – as if there had been no emigration.

On 26 March, the day of the election, the Election Commission reported that more than 70% of voters had attended polling stations in Chechnya, and claimed that in Grozny the turnout was 97%. On 20 August 2000, when the elections for the State Duma were conducted in Chechnya, the Central Election Commission cited the total number of voters as 495 thousand. This implied a total population of about 885 thousand. The reported results of the 2002 census encouraged the Central Election Commission to give a further boost to the size of Chechnya's electorate for the referendum of 23 March 2003 – to 540 thousand. The Central Election Commission reported that 89% of the 540 thousand electorate voted in the referendum and that 95.37% had voted 'yes.'

The authorities had honestly admitted to a 25% voter turnout in the second round of the 1997 election, but by 2003 they became stuck with an incredible turnout figure of more than 95% attached to an unrealistic population figure.

In 2003 I had the opportunity to check some matters at a district level. On 5 September 2003 the administration of the Shali district stated that the total population was 104 thousand. The administration cited the number of voters as 43 thousand, and the number of under-age persons as 33 thousand. Thus there appeared to be 28 thousand who were neither of age, nor under-age. When I asked about this I was told that these were people who had been counted in the census on the basis of documents or the word of their relatives. The district authority could be said to have admitted the existence of about 27% 'dead souls' among the 104 thousand population. Such dead souls could be counted as electors and as voters should the need arise.

According to the chairman of the Central Election Commission, Veshnyakov, 11% more people voted in the polling stations in Chechnya during the December 2003 Duma elections than there were voters in the republic! Even the State Committee for Statistics is not using the results of the census because, according to their data, 813 thousand persons (as opposed to over a million) were living in Chechnya in 2003. The census figure is unrealistically high, but because of its influence on the allocation of resources many regard it as a beneficial overstatement. Those who played with these figures became victims of their own game. The authorities do not appear to have been deterred by the thought that inflation of the number of electors makes the claims of high turnout more exaggerated and implausible than they might otherwise have seemed.

17 CHAIR OF THE ELECTION COMMISSION ABDUL-KERIM ARSAKHANOV

Roman Rostov, kavkaz.memo.ru

Abdul-Kerim, as far as we know, the election of the Chechen president has taken place. Can you give us the preliminary results?

First place is taken by the former acting president of the republic Akhmat Kadyrov who has 82.5% of votes – though I must stress that these are not final figures. Second comes Abdula Bugaev who has 5.6% of votes, he is followed by Shamil Buraev with 3.4%, Khusein Biybulatov 1.6%, Kudus Saduev 1.3%, Nikolai Paizullaev and Avkhat Khanchukaev come last, they have 0.8% each.

When the final results are expected?

By law we have five more days to count the votes, but I think that we can manage it in three.

When is the inauguration to be expected?

Ten days after the day the final results are declared.

How many people took part in voting?

More than 462 thousand residents of Chechnya.

Abdul-Kerim, could you tell us how voting was going on in the districts during the second half of the day? What percentage of the residents turned out to vote?

In the afternoon the number of people who wanted to vote did not fall. People came to make their choice. More than 55.6% of the total number of residents of Chechnya voted. If we take different districts, the highest turnout was at the Zavodskoi district of Grozny with 98.6%, Oktyabrsky and Promyslovsky districts with 83.6% and 85.9% respectively. The highland districts of Chechnya were not far behind. In the Sharoi district, for instance, the turnout was

93.2%, and in the Vedeno district, one of the most troubled areas, it was 82%.

What was the reaction of the population of the republic to the preliminary results?

The results speak for themselves. They show that people made their choice. The turnout shows that Chechen people are serious in their attitude to the future of the republic. Everybody was prepared for this election. They wanted to elect their president in a democratic way, to take the peaceful road, and to feel that they are full citizens of the Russian Federation.

Were there any cases where what might be called 'dirty tricks' were used?

No. I can say with confidence that the behaviour of all seven candidates was very correct, and they conducted their campaigns according to extremely high standards. This was noted by the population of the Republic, by observers, and by journalists. There were no insults, no slander, everybody in public speeches spoke only of himself and his programme.

What was the situation in the Republic on the day of the election, and how do you characterize it today? There were intelligence reports that violent acts were possible on the part of illegal armed groups.

Fortunately, apart from some shooting incidents at three polling stations during the night of 4/5 October nothing occurred illegal.

And what about the declarations of Maskhadov's supporters?

In my view it was just bluff.

Chronicle of Events 9 October to 28 October 2003

9 October 2003. In the afternoon in the district of Yandar in Ingushetia, representatives of the Ministry of Internal Affairs of Ingushetia attempted to apprehend a group of unidentified armed individuals. The group resisted using their weapons. After shooting one member of the group was killed and the remaining three were arrested. The prosecution authority of the Nazran district initiated criminal proceedings and an investigation is currently underway. It turned out that the man killed in the shooting was Zelimkhan Saayev from Grozny.

According to operatives he had been the organizer of the explosion in Tushino on 5 July and the terrorist attack on the Tverskaya Street in Moscow on 9 July.

The identity of one of the detainees was established. He turned out to be a Grozny resident, Khasan Suleimanov, who was also a participant in the terrorist attacks in Tushino and on Tverskaya Street. This information was relayed by the Interfax agency from a source within the Ministry of Internal Affairs of Ingushetia. According to the same source the members of the group were relieved of a homemade explosive device, approximately 1.5 kilograms of plastic explosive, two Kalashnikov machine guns, an automatic pistol with ammunition, an anti-tank hand grenade, camouflage uniforms, and approximately $6,000 in cash.

In the Goi-Chu district of Urus-Martan, in the course of combat between armed formations of the Chechen Republic of Ichkeria and federal military troops, Musa Magomedovich Dudushev, born 1983, was killed. At about mid-day a large number (several hundred, according to local residents) of siloviki arrived at the western outskirt of Goi-Chu. They arrived in two or three armoured troop-carriers, a KAVZ bus, and Ural and UAZ-452 vehicles, and assumed a position in woods near the road between the Goi-Chu and Martan-Chu settlements. At around 3 pm erratic shooting began. According to Goi-Chu residents the shooting resembled a skirmish and stopped after about 10 minutes. At 6 pm shooting began again and went on for three or four minutes.

Some time later it became known that relatives were unable to find Musa Magomedovich Dudushev, born 1983. Approximately at 4 pm he had been at home stocking up hay with a neighbour but then he left without saying anything to anyone. When the twilight fell the troops took off and left. On the morning of 10 October Dudushev's relatives resumed the search for Musa, but without success.

On 11 October high school students from the Goi-Chu district found a piece of paper on which was written in capital letters, 'Musa Dudushev died in the shooting. His body is lying under a wild pear-tree 300-400 metres into the woods. Please, let Musa's family know'. Dudushev's relatives were immediately informed of the note. They found Musa's body lying under a wild pear-tree. Next to the body there were chunks of sausage, Snicker wraps, a military discharge note, a kit-bag, etc. The clothing included camouflage trousers and a military cap. The body was riddled with gunshot wounds and part of the skull was missing.

On the same day an operative brigade from the Urus-Martan police, headed by its chief, made an investigation and afterward the body was buried in the local cemetery. The following information was distributed by the press service, 'Law-enforcement authorities established that in the course of combat with federal forces an active participant of armed formations of the Chechen Republic of Ichkeria, Dudushev, born 1983, was killed. His body was found in woods between residential areas of Komsomolskoye and Tangi-Chu of the Urus-Martan district in the course of inspection of the combat site. Food stuffs, medica-

tions, and a grenade fuse were found with the body. The facts are being investigated by prosecution authorities.'
Memorial Human Rights Centre

9 October 2003. At about midday, fighters of Chechen resistance groups attacked a Russian motorized column on the southern outskirts of the village. A short column consisting of an APC, a Ural truck and three UAZ 452 military vehicles (so-called 'tabletkas') headed for Vedeno through Serzhen-Yurt. As soon as it reached the northern edge of the village, there was a powerful explosion, which damaged the APC. Shooting lasted for about 50 minutes. During that time, the Russian soldiers received considerable reinforcement from Shali – about ten units. According to unconfirmed reports, several Russian policemen were killed and injured. During the fighting, the inhabitants of the southern part of the village hid in houses and basements. There were no reports on casualties among the civilian population.

According to the inhabitants of Avtury, Shali, Serzhen-Yurt, Bachi-Yurt as well as of some villages of Kurchaloi district, the Russian military-police agencies became more active after the election. Arrests were taking place nearly every day, including at night time.
Russian-Chechen Friendship Society

10 October 2003. At approximately 3 am representatives of Russian law enforcement agencies forcefully detained and took away Adam Alkhazurovich Dadayev, born 1980. Adam Dadayev had lived in Rechnaya Street in the Alkhazurovo district of Urus-Martan. During the detention his younger brother was beaten up. Dadayev's relatives petitioned the prosecution, administration, and law enforcement authorities of the Urus-Martan district inquiring of the fate and whereabouts of their family member but the authorities responded that they knew nothing of the detainee.

Heavy shelling in the area of Bamut and the woods adjacent to the Stary-Achkhoi district went on from 0.20 till 6.50 am. The explosions shook windows in all of the neighbouring settlements: Achkhoi-Martan, Stary-Achkhoi, Yandy, Sernovodsk and Assinovskaya.
Memorial Human Rights Centre

11 October 2003. At dawn representatives of the Russian law enforcement agencies detained a resident of the Gekhi district of Urus-Martan, Zaina Gaitamirova, 32 years old, who lived at Budennogo, 54. She was taken to the Urus-Martan police department. 24 hours later she was passed over to the head of administration of the Gekhi district and she was able to return home. The reasons for her arrest are still unknown.
Memorial Human Rights Centre

11 October 2003. In the centre of Kurchaloi, there was a clash between local policemen and fighters of a unit under the command of the Yamadaev brothers. According to local inhabitants, skirmishes between policemen and Yamadaevs' people lasted for about 40 minutes and resulted in losses on both sides. The cause of the fighting not known.
Russian-Chechen Friendship Society

11 October 2003. A Ural type military lorry moving in a Russian motorized column on the highway of the Staropromislovsky district of Grozny, was blown up by unknown persons. The dead and wounded included policemen. Urgent investigation by the Perekhvat (Interception) unit at the site of explosion brought no results. The injured were taken to a military hospital in Khankala.

A UAZ vehicle was blown up by an unidentified roadside explosive device not far from the Severny market in Grozny. Two servicemen died and another was wounded. Further information is not available and is strictly controlled by the respective services.
Russian-Chechen Friendship Society

12 October 2003. Troops of the sapper-engineering brigade were shot at from an empty apartment block located in the Beryozka quarter of Staropromyslovsky district of Grozny at the Staropromyslovskoye highway. The shooting occurred as the sappers were moving down the road. None of the troops was injured. The next day the area was inspected by military troops and police officers of the Staropromyslovsky district. Most of the ruined buildings and deserted apartments were inspected. Closed doors were forced open.
Memorial Human Rights Centre

12 October 2003. In the morning the body of an unidentified man was discovered at the crossroads leading to Sernovodsk village and the Baku-Rostov highway. According to residents of Sernovodsk heading for the town of Sleptsovsk, people, fearing that the body was mined, called for a sapper group. The body was not identified because nobody dared to approach it until sappers came.
Russian-Chechen Friendship Society

13 October 2003. At 9 am in the Staropromyslovsky district of Grozny a representative of the operative investigation bureau (ORB), Dzhalaudi Mezhiyev, 50 years old was killed near his home as he was setting off for work in his Volga. Unidentified individuals wearing masks and camouflage attacked him from behind shrubbery in the ruins of former school No 11. Mezhiyev died of the wounds. Dzhalaudi Mezhiyev had been a highly respected member of the local community.

Vakha Khalidovich Arsamakov, head of the Sernovodsk district, was shot at with automatic weapons as he was leaving his house at about 4.25 pm. Arsamakov had left his house, No 1 on Rechnoy lane, boarded his official vehicle (a white VAZ-2105 with shaded windows and without license plates) and headed for his office. As the vehicle approached the footbridge across the Sunzha river (next to Dadayevs' and Shengiriyevs houses - three houses down from Arsamakov's house) three unidentified individuals opened fire with automatic weapons at Arsamakov's car from behind a large tree. Arsamakov was wounded in both feet, in the hip, and one bullet hit his spinal cord. After the shooting the assailants disappeared. Passers-by called an ambulance which took the wounded man to the Central District Hospital in the Ordzhonikidze district. Sunzha police have started an investigation.

Memorial Human Rights Centre

14 October 2003. A resident of the Alkhan-Yurt district of Urus-Martan, Aslan Salaudinovich Akayev, born 1984, living on Kagermanova Street, was kidnapped some time between 3 and 4 am, presumably by representatives of the Russian law enforcement agencies Akayev was sitting with associates not far from the local mosque. A VAZ-2107 vehicle drove up and several armed men wearing camouflage uniforms and masks emerged. Without introduction or explanation they forced Aslan into the vehicle and drove away. Local residents are of the opinion that he was taken in the direction of Grozny.

Memorial Human Rights Centre

15 October 2003. Aslan Vesedov, a resident of Serzhen-Yurt village of Shali district, has reportedly been released. He had been arrested at his home on 9 October by soldiers of a pro-Moscow Chechen special unit shortly after a Russian APC was blown up in the village. Vesedov was released on 13 October. There is no report on the place of detention or on his exposure to violence while in custody. It should be pointed out that Vesedov was subjected to groundless arrest by the RF enforcement agencies in the course of special operations and has been exposed to physical violence – he sustained several fractured ribs.

Russian-Chechen Friendship Society

15 October 2003. A special operation targeting several households was undertaken in the Roshni-Chu district of the Urus-Martan. At dawn the area was surrounded by military machines and the roads leading to it were blocked. Local residents on their way to the district centre were not allowed pass checkpoints set up in the outskirts of the district.

In the course of the special operation the troops searched the houses of Said-Selim Akuyev, Shakhid Eniyev, Segirat Bersinkayev, Rukman Tatayev, and Bislan Ibragimov on Ordzhonikidze Street. In addition, unauthorized searches were conducted in the houses of Khamzat Ibragimov and Baizan Dadashev on Lenin Street and that of Dara Mudarov on Nuradilov Street. The troops focused on searching gardens and out-buildings.

Abat Adamovich Amagov, born 1959, living on Rechnaya Street, was detained but released shortly afterwards. The reason for his detention remains unknown. According to local residents they were allowed to move freely within the district limits and the troops treated them politely. The troops did not explain who they were or why they were conducting searches. By about 10–11 am the mop-up operation was over and the roads were unblocked.

Adlan Musayevich Israilov, born 1981, was beaten and kidnapped in the Chernorechye district of Grozny by three unidentified individuals (all in masks, one clad in a military uniform, the others wearing civilian clothes) who had driven up to him in a white VAZ-2107 vehicle with dark tinted windows.

At around 3 pm Israilov and his friend were passing by the temporary placement centre located on Vyborgskaya, 4 when a VAZ-2107 drove up to them. A man wearing civilian clothes and a mask got out, armed with an AKSU machine gun. Pointing the gun at Israilov he spoke in Chechen and ordered them not to move. The young men were frightened and they broke into a run. The stranger shot in the air. Adlan halted. Then the stranger approached him and hit him with the butt of his gun which made him fall down. A second man wearing a camouflage uniform and a mask got out of the car and joined in the beating until Israilov lost consciousness. The incident was witnessed by a large number of people – forced migrants staying at the temporary placement centre.

According to Israilov masks were put upon him in the car. They took him to some woods and started to beat him, and then to a basement that seemed to be a bomb shelter. Adlan spent two days there. On the first day he was being beaten up. On the second day his mask was removed, he was fed and interrogated. A man wearing a mask spoke to him in Chechen. He said that Israilov could be sent to prison and stay there until he was very old. He was told he should hand in his machine gun. Adlan responded that he did not have any weapons and had nothing to be afraid of.

At the end of the second day they put a mask on him again and brought him by car to Chernorechye. Adlan was released not far away from where he had been kidnapped. According to Chernorechye residents Grozny prosecution officials inspected the place of the incident on 16 October. It is not known if criminal proceedings have been initiated.
Memorial Human Rights Centre

16 October 2003. Representatives of law enforcement agencies wearing masks were checking compliance with passport regulations in the central market of Grozny. The troops arrived in UAZ and UAZ-452 vehicles. They did not introduce themselves but the market merchants assumed that they were representatives of the Zavodsky district police and Chechen special task police fighters. The troops inspected documents, mostly those of young men. On the whole this passed without incident although the appearance of troops in masks initially caused some panic. Information on detainees is not available.
Memorial Human Rights Centre

17 October 2003. Sharani, brother of Movlady Baisarov head of Kadyrov's personal security unit, was blown up in his vehicle together with four associates in Pobedinskoe in Grozny rural district. According to witnesses Sharani and his people were in the middle of Friday prayer at the local mosque. After leaving the mosque and boarding the vehicle they had managed to drive only a few dozen metres when the car exploded. It has been con-

firmed that Sharani died in the explosion. Nothing is known about the condition of his associates.

Adam Alkhazurovich Dadayev, born 1980, who lived in an unnumbered house in Rechnaya Street in the Alkhazurovo district of Urus-Martan, was dumped in the northwestern outskirts of the Goiskoe district. He had been detained by representatives of Russian law enforcement agencies on 10 October 2003. According to his neighbours Dadayev was severely beaten following the detention, several of his front teeth were knocked out. He was very drunk: apparently he had been forced to drink. It is not known where he had been kept or what he had been accused of, if anything. Neither he nor his relatives provided any comment on the incident.

Memorial Human Rights Centre

18 October 2003. Isa Imranovich Aliyev, born 1979, who lived at 3 Tovarny Lane in the Katayama district of Staropromyslovsky, was killed in the course of a special operation at around 6 am. According to the head of the criminal police of the Staropromyslovsky district, Ruslan Gelayev, his fellow officers had been observing Aliyev for a long time and planned to arrest him. But they had nothing to do with the special operation. Aliyev gave armed resistance to the arrest and wounded a representative of the operative investigation bureau who later died in the hospital. A mop-up operation took place in the Alkhazurovo district of the Urus-Martan. From early morning temporary checkpoints had been set up on roads leading to the district by law enforcement agencies who inspected vehicles and let them proceed only after a thorough inspection and documents check.

The targeted mop-up was carried out with participation by the Urus-Martan district military authority, Urus-Martan police, and troops from the military unit located on the eastern outskirt of Urus-Martan (a battalion of internal forces of the RF Ministry of Internal Affairs). The troops did not wear masks and coordinated all actions with the district administration. Neither the local administration nor the residents were aware that the special operation was observed by representatives of the district prosecution authority. According to head of the district administration the troops treated local residents politely. However, they conducted unauthorized searches in some residents' houses.

Said-Emin Dudayev of Partizanskaya Street was detained in the mop-up operation. According to the head of the Alkhazurovo administration in the course of a search in Said-Emin's house the troops found a pair of camouflage trousers with pockets filled with ammunition. The detainee was taken to the Urus-Martan police. Later in the evening, due to intervention by the head of Alkhazurovo district administration, Dudayev was released and was allowed to go home. The mop-up operation was over by noon.

Memorial Human Rights Centre

19 October 2003. A military column consisting of armoured and UAZ vehicles entered the Zumsoy village of Itum-Kalinsky in the evening. Representatives of the Russian law enforcement agencies, law enforcement agencies of the Chechen Republic, and federal mili-

tary troops accommodated themselves in the village school. On the same day information passed through the village indicating that the group had apprehended two young men (Alik Bachiyev aged 28 and Shirvani aged 30) in the Bugaroy district (five kilometers away from the Zumsoy village). When arresting Shirvani the troops severely beat up his aunt. Alik Bachiyev was detained while he was unloading hay in his courtyard.

The military troops brought with them Mikhail Musikhov, aged 16, and Lema, aged 18. Together with Lema's mother they were travelling from the Ordzhonikidzevskaya village of the Republic of Ingushetia, where they had lived as forced migrants, to Zumsoy. They were apprehended at a temporary checkpoint when entering Zumsoy by representatives of the Shatoi FSB department. Local police officers managed to free Lema's mother but later she was detained again and kept at the Shatoi district police station until she was released two days later. During the special operation Mikhail and Lema were led around the district. They were released on 20 October. The reasons for their detention remain unknown.

On the next day troops and representatives of law enforcement agencies drove up to the house of Vakhid Makhambetovich Mukhayev. Almost all, except for two RF law enforcement officers, were wearing masks. Without any introduction the officers broke into the house and inquired, "Who is Vakhid?" When Mukhayev identified himself the troops started to beat him up – they kicked him and hit him with the butts of their machine guns. Attempts by other family members to put an end to the outrage provoked more violence. Swearing, one of the troops kicked Vakhid's mother, 82 year old Alpata Mukhayeva, and knocked her to the floor. Zara Akhmatkhanova, his wife, was beaten up with the butts of machine guns so severely that she had to seek medical assistance at the local hospital. One of the troops grabbed Vakhid's 13-year old daughter, Khazan, by her throat and started to strangle her. Troops intermittently fired their machine guns in the house. A four-year old boy in the house was so frightened he foamed at the mouth.

Then the troops pulled Vakhid outside and threw him on the ground. When he was lying on the ground they shot and wounded him – while videotaping it all. Together with Vakhid Mukhayev they detained Shadid Aldamov, aged 28, and Beslan Azieyv, aged 27, who in response to the shooting had run out of the neighbouring house of the district iman, Mukhadi Hadjiyev, where they were staying as guests. All detainees were taken to the local school – the troops' temporary location.

In the afternoon relatives of the detainees met with Artur Khachaturov, prosecutor of the Itum-Kalinsky, Sharoi, and Shatoi districts. He advised them that the detainees were being kept in the school building and that there was no need to worry as nobody was going to go missing. The prosecutor did not say what the detainees were accused of, nor why the detention had been conducted in violation of the Russian law. Eltsat Makhabetovna Mukhayeva, sister of Vakhid Mukhayev, pointed out that Vakhid was wounded when being arrested but Khachaturov denied the fact saying, "This had probably happened when he attempted to escape". At the end of the interview the prosecutor assured detainees' relatives that they would be released in the evening after they had been checked. But nobody came back.

A military doctor who attended the interview unofficially informed Malika Khamzatova, Vakhid's daughter-in-law, that Vakhid had been taken to a hospital suffering from a gunshot wound, but did not specify which hospital. On 21 October the troops abandoned the district together with detainees. It was not until the next day that a representative of the Shatoi district prosecution authority announced that those who had been detained in the districts of Zumsoy and Bugaroy were being kept at the FSB facility of the Shatoi district. He did not specify what they were being accused of. As of the beginning of November nothing was known of the fate of the detainees.

Memorial Human Rights Centre

21 October 2003. At around 7 am on the outskirts of Sernovodsk district residents saw unknown young men planting mines on the road leading to the Rostov-Baku highway in the direction of the Assinovskaya village. Residents of the Naberezhnaya Street demanded that they stop. The young men disappeared in the direction of the tractor brigade of the Chilayev state farm. Witnesses reported the incident to the police but no police officers arrived to inspect the site in question. Two hours later a column of vehicles and armoured troop-carriers of federal forces passed down that road.

At around 5 pm representatives of the Russian enforcement agencies in masks broke into the Elmurzayevs' house on the Nagornaya Street of the Starye Atagy district of the Grozny. The troops had arrived in two armoured troop-carriers and an Ural truck. Having opened fire from machine guns and smashed the gate with an armoured vehicle the troops broke into the house yelling "Where are the weapons?" the troops severely beat up Movla Elmurzayev, born 1980, and then opened fire above the bed of the elderly head of the Elmurzayevs family whose leg had just been amputated. The troops broke furniture and destroyed bedding. When leaving they shot at the house with their machine guns and with the artillery weapons of the armoured vehicle – causing substantial damage to the house. When the troops were gone Elmurzayev junior was taken to the district hospital in a serious condition. Residents, together with the head of the local administration, petitioned the commandant's office. But the military HQ denied having anything to do with this crime.

Memorial Human Rights Centre

22 October 2003. According to preliminary reports, unidentified individuals armed with machine guns murdered an unidentified young man in the Leninsky district of Grozny near the former Rossia cinema. The news of the murder immediately reached the central market where people from different districts often come together. There was word that the murdered man had been a resident of the Vedeno district. Having heard about it Vedeno residents went to the murder site. It is not known if the dead man has been identified.

Unidentified individuals in black uniforms and masks arriving in UAZ and UAZ-452 vehicles kidnapped Ruslan Baitayevich Saipuyev, born 1983. According to Khadizhat Saipuyeva,

Ruslan's mother, he had arrived that day from Ali-Yurt district in the Republic of Ingushetia where his family has been living since the beginning of military operations and where his cousin, Said-Emin Dudurkayev, was in hospital. Saipuyev was kidnapped when he went to the hospital to see his cousin.

At around 7 pm in Pobedinskoe in Grozny rural district representatives of a Russian law enforcement agency detained and took away two brothers Said-Rakhman, born 1979, and Said-Khasan, born 1977, Dudurkayevs. The reasons for the detention are not known.

According to the brothers' mother the strangers (7–10 people) wearing masks and camouflage uniforms arrived in a grey UAZ-452 vehicle. Said-Rakhman said that having heard the noise in the courtyard he stepped outside and saw the military troops and his brother lying on the ground. Said-Khasan yelled to his brother, "Run and get help from Kadyrov's people!" (a subdivision of Kadyrov's security service is stationed in this district). Having heard that, the strangers seized the Dudurkayev brothers, pulled their clothes over their heads, shoved them into the UAZ vehicle, and took them away. Their mother was never offered any explanation.

According to Said-Rakhman they were on the road for about 10 minutes. In the vehicle nobody touched them or asked them any questions. Although the troops did say over the radio, "Everything is OK, we have two boxes, one large and one small." Presumably the UAZ stopped in the vicinity of the 36th quarter of the Staropromyslovsky district of Grozny. There Said-Khasan was transferred to a different vehicle (his brother insists that, judging by the noise produced by the engine, it was a VAZ-21099) and driven away. Some time later the car containing Said-Rakhman also started to move. Then the vehicle stopped again and the kidnappers ordered Dudurkayev to get out and return back home. He asked what they had been detained for. One of the troops said, "We had received information that you were fundamentalists". When Said-Rakhman was released his documents were returned to him but the troops retained his wrist-watch and cash.

On 28 October 2003 Dudurkayev's mother petitioned the prosecution authority of the Chechen Republic, but as of late October 2003 no information about Said-Khasan Dudurkayev had been received. After the abduction local residents blocked the road from Grozny to Goragorsk in protest, but this action did not yield any results. Local residents intended to picket the House of Government of Chechnya.

On 28 February 2000 the father of the kidnapped, Salavdi Dudurkayev, born 1948, was taken away by the military troops and nothing has been heard of him since.
<u>Memorial Human Rights Centre</u>

18 KADYROV AT THE UNITED NATIONS

Tanya Lokshina, Moscow Helsinki Group/Centre 'Demos'

To be honest, when I saw Kadyrov in Geneva, I just lost it and could not regain my composure for some time. Just imagine! I was in Chechnya before the election and managed to stay there throughout the election, and happily avoided meeting the man. Then I come here, and bam! Here he is. How can I fly all the way to the shores of Lake Geneva, to end up having this sullen, unshaven character in front of me for two days in a row, right after I have been bombarded with his picture on the election posters in Chechnya? It is sad to realize that this guy, now I choose my words carefully, is the one the Russian government deems to be its most deserving representative. This guy is good enough to be sitting right next to the Russian justice minister at a key UN human rights forum!

I thought I had gotten used to everything by now. There should be nothing that can surprise me. Still, every once in a while, the powers-that-be somehow manage to find a way to leave me dumbfounded. It seems that now that the damage has been done – he's gone and been elected – it would seem that they would want to tone it down a little, and keep Kadyrov under wraps. I mean, you don't usually go bragging about your shortcomings. You usually want to keep your skeletons where they belong, that is in the closet. And yet, they decided to drag him out. How come?

The Kremlin started putting Kadyrov forward a good while ago. Even before the Chechen election Putin had Kadyrov come along with him to the USA. At first, the Americans kept quiet: they neither reacted to the farce of the Chechen election, nor uttered a word of protest. It was the silence of the lambs. The media and human rights activists were seething, and in the end there was a breaking point. When it became known that Putin's favourite was going to Camp David to shake hands with president Bush the State Department stepped in. It was the start of a real diplomatic scandal, but the State Department held firm. Without doubt, they said, 'Kadyrov is not going to Camp David'.

Strike one. Putin stubbornly kept his batter in to face the next pitch. Next time it would be the United Nations, and Kadyrov would be Russia's representative. Putin-watchers commented that these actions are typical of Putin being defiant. This side of his character was most famously showcased in 1999. Speaking of the insurgents in Chechnya Putin said "We will grab them when they are sitting in the shithouse with their pants down," "We will break them so they are not even men any more". The use of locker-room language should not prevent us from taking Putin's recalcitrance seriously. It turns out he wasn't kidding.

Just now, the newly elected president of the Chechen Republic is on the political travelling circuit once again. Russia demonstrated the Muslim features of the federation's brotherhoood by sending Kadyrov (along with the always colourful Murtaza Rakhimov) as an observer to the Islamic Conference in Malaysia. Another scandal took place at that conference, as hospitable Mohathir said things that one would presume would lead Russia to think twice before attending that party next time. One may wonder what Kadyrov had to do with it? After Geneva in 2003 one cannot help suspecting some mystic influence, some sort of cosmic destiny...

It turns out that the second pitch, at the UN, is not a strike. The powers-that-be regained faith in their batter when he was blessed by the popular mandate of the people in the election. I guess they expected that the election would rehabilitate Kadyrov in the eyes of the West, and they would throw him soft ones. At least doors would not be slammed shut in his face when he arrived.

In Geneva, Putin's oracle is poised to perform. Kadyrov was third on the Russian list for the diplomatic mission, right after minister Yury Chaika and Mr Leonid Skotnikov (local diplomatic mission). The fact that Kadyrov got in the door means that he will get to first base with the pitch. But it is not clear if the intention is to walk him, or if he will be allowed to hit the ball of his own accord.

Amidst doom and gloom Kadyrov sits silently at the presidium while the Russian report was reviewed at the Human Rights Committee's 79th Session. The committee's experts have many questions about Chechnya; they want to know about arbitrary actions by federal troops, about disappearances, about the failure to investigate complaints made by residents, and finally they ask, 'Why was a state of emergency never introduced?' One after another, the Russian delegation members take the floor and are grilled by the international community. All try to put on a good face, at times withholding the truth, at times telling barefaced lies. Throughout, our man Kadyrov is mum. By the middle of the second day, people begin to worry that there will not be an opportunity to hear from the people's leader from Chechnya.

So I whisper to a colleague sitting beside me, "Do you think he will even open his mouth at all? This silence is making Kadyrov look odd. If this is how it is going to be, why even bother to bring him here in the first place?". "Don't you get it!?" says my colleague "they are never going to give him the floor". The second he opens his mouth they would be in so much trouble that the Russian delegation would never hear the end of it. The only reason they brought him here was now that they'd elected him, they have to get the world used to seeing him so they can accept him."

My friend proved to be right and wrong at the same time. He clearly overestimated the wisdom and foresight of the delegation, because the floor is eventually given to Kadyrov. Whether Kadyrov insisted upon this himself or the Russian delegation just came to realize that two days of having Kadyrov act like a mute would look weird – we do not know. But when the mighty Kadyrov opens his mouth, there really is so much trouble that the Russian delegation found it impossible to dig itself out of it. The scandal is glorious, a real blooper. Kadyrov bunts the ball right into the pitcher's mitt.

What follows is Kadyrov's speech - his first in an international forum in the capacity of the 'legally elected president of Chechnya.' I would like to thank our veritable statesman for speaking nice and slowly; I was able to make an almost verbatim transcript as he droned on like a tired woodsman hacking through a thick tree with an axe. The text requires referential commentary, so please see my parentheses that aim to clarify anything said by dear Akhmat-Hadji. Here it is: The speech of Akhmat-Hadji Kadyrov at the 24 October 2003 session of the Human Rights Committee in Geneva.

"No one is more concerned about the citizens of the Chechen Republic today than I am. Many different games are being played in Chechnya these days, and all the time, it is ordinary people who suffer. These are the people who on 5 October of this year, gave me their full support to do everything within my power to improve the situation [*This phrase just makes my flesh creep - over the past several years the means Kadyrov used to established himself in Chechnya are so scary that it is painful to try to imagine what horrors 'everything within his power' would entail*]. It is true that we have had violations and abductions [*many of which the honourable speaker and his entourage are directly associated with*]. But it is wrong to subject me to any sort of inquisitorial process here. We have a common task, and it is not to criticize each other, but rather to come up with solutions. The information that you have received from NGOs is one-sided, so keep this in mind when you shape how you interact with us.

"Yesterday here I spoke with a fellow Chechen, a woman here at the Conference, and asked her, "Why don't you tell us what the bandits are doing? Why is the Council of Europe making us negotiate with thieves and criminals?" [*The Council of Europe required more than just negotiations with Maskhadov, but the other requirements seem to have slipped the newly elected president's mind.*

[*But who is the interlocutor, the aforementioned 'fellow Chechen woman?' It was a Chechen journalist with whom Kadyrov had a conversation the day before. In front of the camera the newly elected president managed to talk about even more interesting things! She was so good at getting him to talk, that she should work for him. In fact, she was so good at getting him to talk, that she might even work for the others. What were the last words from Kadyrov during that remarkable interview? None other than, 'What do you want? Don't you understand that we cannot fight the Russians now, we have no weapons!' Now back to our scheduled programme.*]

"I would like to ask the committee chairman to send his special representative to accompany me to each of the settlements for displaced persons in Chechnya and Ingushetia. [*At this point, Kadyrov creates a big problem for the Russian delegations because up to this point Russia had refused to allow UN rapporteurs into Chechnya. Every time the UN asked to be allowed in, Russia would say, 'not now, not now,' or they would make excuses about being unable to guarantee security. 'Maybe, another time,' they would say. And here after many refusals, Kadyrov is saying, 'Sure, go ahead, make my day.' How will Russian diplomats get themselves out of this one?*]

"And if he finds anyone who feels that they have been forced to return to Chechnya then I would be happy to stand here before you and accept the full criticism of this body. This will not happen, however, because you have all been told a pack of lies. The only truth in these allegations is that there are some that do not want to go back to Chechnya. Those who do not want to return are waiting for Basaev and Maskhadov. They are families who have sons, fathers, and cousins in bandit groups, and they are actively creating rumours that Chechnya is a place to which people have to be forced to return.

"All violation of citizens began with illegal infiltrations into the Chechen-Ingush Republic. All crimes dating from that period will be thoroughly investigated, and for this I will put together a special commission. Nobody else but I am the guarantor of human rights in Chechnya. [*According to the Russian Constitution the president of Russia is the 'guarantor of the RF Constitution, rights and freedoms of the human being and citizen', and, Chechnya, as repeatedly mentioned by the Russian delegation in attendance at the Conference, is a subject of the Russian Federation. Kadyrov is effectively defying Putin's authority. I do not know whom the Chechen people would prefer as their 'guarantor'. Taking into account the fact that Kadyrov's men are more dreaded in Chechnya than federal forces, I think Chechens might just be feeling they would like to pull for Putin - at the very least he is geographically more distant than the despot in their own back yard.*]

"More than 80% of the residents cast their votes in my favour, and I must live up to their trust. And the NGOs who seem to be against me, where were they while I have been making things better over the last three years? I invite them to come and have a look around and talk with me openly... [*Where have the*

NGOs been, indeed? Perhaps something prevents them from having access to all parts of Chechnya. Perhaps, a hard-wired desire for self-preservation. Perhaps these people would prefer to stay alive rather than openly challenge the now-elected president?].

"How come they can travel all the way to distant Switzerland and visit various international bodies, but they won't come to Chechnya, and let me in on what is going on? Please come! If these people know something, let me get them on the multilateral crimes commission. [*There is a classic line by Jaroslav Gashek, 'You think this Commission will help you? The hell it will help you!' Our colleagues from Chechen NGOs understand this completely.*]

"Chechnya is no longer the republic it was prior to 23 March 2003. Then we did not have a constitution or any kind of order. Chechnya was governed by bandits. [*Now this seems strange, perhaps the Speaker forgets that he has been in charge of Chechnya since June 2000. How wonderfully self-critical!*] In the beginning I was with Dudayev. Then I stood with Maskhadov. I expected that each would eventually do something. After the first Chechen war, federal forces gave up and left Chechnya to Maskhadov. All this did was open doors to criminal elements. These elements came into Chechnya, swallowed us up, and then kept going, all the way to Dagestan. We lived in the midst of a pure criminal order. If any of my countrymen had any kind of savings – 15 or 20 thousand dollars – he would be immediately robbed and thrown into a pit. I alone realized that I had to stop them. No one stood with me. I have been fighting them since late 1996. Many of my loved ones have been killed! [*All Chechens have lost loved ones in the fighting – but few, like Kadyrov, are personally responsible for the deaths.*]

"Today Chechnya is part of the Russian Federation. [*OK. This is today. But what about in the future, what does Kadyrov think it should be? Don't worry, our spokesman will soon explain his thoughts.*] The people have spoken on this topic. It was not me, nor Yandarbiev, nor Maskhadov, the people themselves decided. [*Much has already been written about WHO and HOW this question was actually decided.*]

"On 5 October, the election was held. Government is functioning and in place, and now will be responsible for human rights. [*It is interesting that the presi-*

dent is so confident in the ability of his governmental bodies, and believes that they will act in an independent, fair manner, benefiting the people.] I want to thank the Committee for having us here, but I do not want the Russian delegation to which I belong to have to assume the role of defendant before so many accusers. We are Russian citizens. And I will defend the rights of the Chechen Republic – I will defend as its guarantor. [*Note, that what he is going to defend is the 'rights of the Chechen Republic' – not human rights in Chechnya. That might spell future trouble for the federal centre.*]"

His fervent speech over, Kadyrov rises and leaves, taking with him Sultygov, Putin's representative on the rights of citizens and human beings in the Chechen Republic. And that's when all hell breaks loose.

Prior to the speech, the experts of the Committee had formulated their questions about Chechnya in a reserved and diplomatic manner. After this speech they forget all about politesse and speak as if they are free from the chains of etiquette. The previous speaker clearly left an indelible impression on the crowd.

I have attended a number of UN forums in the past, but I had never before heard the kind of comments that I then heard. First to speak is the Finnish expert, Sheinin. He first notes that Kadyrov's lofty platitudes and claims to respect the Human Rights Committee have not facilitated dialogue. And, he continues, the Russian delegation basically fails to show any desire to conduct open discussion on the interconnection between matters such as Chechnya and Nord-Ost. Kadyrov's speech had shown a refusal to discuss any such connections. Sheinin finally said that turning committee hearings into an arena for a public relations event for domestic consumption was simply unacceptable in principle. By the standards of the United Nations, such an angry retort is the equivalent of dropping a large bomb. The diplomatic scandal has begun.

Then Virushevsky, the expert from Poland, started. He cites Sultygov's bizarre claim in September that NGOs were working for the terrorists, and admonished the Russian delegation that this was not the way to treat NGOs. Finally came the British expert, Mr Rhodley, a former special UN rapporteur on torture. He noted that he had not wanted to address the matter, but now after listening to the speech of the honourable spokesperson for the Russian Federation, Mr Kadyrov, he deemed it necessary to do so. And so he asks the following question, "Here we have extensive testimony provided by NGOs, media, and others that violations took place in the course of the 5 October election in particular they pertained to voter turnout. Can you tell us here today of any official observers or representative of any international organisations, who in fact characterized the election as fair and democratic?"

Needless to say, the response of the Russian delegation was feeble. Neither the Council of Europe, nor the OSCE had agreed to observe the presidential election in Chechnya. The fact there were no observers is as bad as if there are observers and they don't like what they see.

And so, what happens in the end? Initially none of the committee's experts were going to speak about either the Chechen election or the newly-elected president. Nor had they been ready to tackle talk about the fact that Russia was avoiding straightforward discussion of Chechnya. Or to discuss the idea that Russia's policy in Chechnya perpetuates terrorism. Such topics were not going to be mentioned publicly. But then along came Kadyrov to end restraint. They took this opportunity, and ran all the way home with it.

Maybe this episode will make Russian authorities think twice before taking Kadyrov with them on away games in the future. The international community can and will turn a blind eye to the 'elected' president of Chechnya, but only as long as they are not forced to look at him closely. At this point even diplomats cannot act quite diplomatically.

One would also like to hope that the international scandal brought about by our hero will prompt the Kremlin to ask itself: was it right to put Kadyrov where he is? Is it right in general to insist on tackling the Chechnya issue in a forceful fashion? Things might not change, but hope springs eternal...

PS: In its Concluding Observations of 6 November 2003 the UN Human Rights Committee, in particular, noted the following:

"13. The Committee remains deeply concerned about continuing substantiated reports of human rights violations in the Chechen Republic, including extrajudicial killings, disappearances and torture, including rape. The Committee notes that some 54 police and military personnel have been prosecuted for crimes committed against civilians in Chechnya, but remains concerned that the charges and sentences handed down do not appear to correspond with the gravity of the acts of human rights violations. The committee is also concerned that investigations into a number of large-scale abuses and killings of civilians in 1999 and 2000, in the locations of Alkhan-Yurt, Novye Aldy and Staropromyslovsky district of Grozny, have still not been brought to a conclusion. The committee acknowledges that abuse of and violations against civilians also involve non-state actors, but reiterates that this does not relieve the state party of its obligations under the Covenant. In this regard, the committee is concerned about the provision in the federal law 'On Combating Terrorism' which exempts law enforcement and military personnel from liability for harm caused during counter-terrorist operations.

"The state party should ensure that operations in Chechnya are carried out in compliance with its international human rights obligations. The state party should ensure that abuse and violations are not committed with impunity *de jure* or *de facto*, including violations committed by military and law enforcement personnel during counter-terrorist operations. All cases of extrajudicial executions, enforced disappearances and torture, including rape, should be investigated, their perpetrators prosecuted and victims or their families compensated (articles 2, 6, 7 and 9).

"23. While acknowledging the difficult circumstances under which the presidential election was held in the Chechen Republic on 5 October 2003, the Committee expresses concern at reports that this election did not meet all the requirements of article 25 of the Covenant.

"The state party should ensure full compliance with article 25 in its efforts to restore the rule of law and political legitimacy in the Republic of Chechnya."

The full text of the concluding observations of the Human Rights Committee on the Russian Federation are given at:

http://www.unhchr.ch/tbs/doc.nsf/(Symbol)/622c5ddc8c476dc4c1256e0c003c9758?Opendocument. UN references: 06/11/2003. CCPR/CO/79/RUS. (Concluding Observations/Comments).

19 PERFECT STILLNESS ZONE

Tanya Lokshina, Moscow Helsinki Group/Centre 'Demos'

(Note: Some names of people and places in this chapter have been changed)

Just two weeks after the 'first president of the Chechen Republic' was elected by his people in accordance with the Chechen Constitution approved by the March referendum, Kadyrov was speaking in Geneva, at the hearings on Russia of the UN Human Rights Committee. In his emotional speech, the former mufti repeatedly underscored that it was the Chechen people of all peoples who having returned Chechnya to the Russian Federation, and having elected Kadyrov himself as president had made their ultimate choice. And he, being president "will stop at nothing for the sake of the Chechen people". In conclusion he uttered an ambiguous phrase, "We are Russian citizens. And I will uphold the rights of the Chechen Republic".

The promise of the newly elected leader to stop at nothing and his many reminders that Chechnya is a region of the Russian Federation were permanently on my mind. Two months and two days after Kadyrov's election, Chechens as well as other citizens of Russia were supposed to take part in the federal parliamentary elections. Will this subject republic of the Russian Federation join in with the other 88 in one ecstatic motion? Will crowds of Chechens rush to polling stations to vote for Putin's creation, the United Russia party? Or will they get the United Russia imposed upon them as was the case with Kadyrov on 5 October 2003? Will there again be deserted streets, empty polling stations, abandoned market places, and not a single car on the roads? (I am not a very emotional person but the October election impressions are imprinted on my memory for ever.)

It is not just elections that matter. Two months is a sufficient lapse of time for the former acting president to display his presidential abilities. What has changed in these two months? What has happened to Kadyrov's eagerness to stop at nothing? And what will be the reaction on the part of a people exhausted by the war?

I heard a lot in Chechnya on the eve of 5 October. About the inevitability of mass riots if the Kremlin imposed the hated Kadyrov on the republic. About the equally inevitable growth of anti-government activities. And about the consolidation of anti-Kadyrov forces.

At the same time I hear about the depleted vigour and resources of anti-government rebels. About the impossibility of living with such a president – or of countering him. And about the inevitability of a further exodus of population.

Both scenarios appeared to be equally feasible. Apprehension dominated the tense atmosphere prior to the October election. 'Something-is-going-to-happen-something-is-going-to-happen' was the message flashing in people's eyes. Shooting started right after sunset on 4 October and during the night the shooting turned into a continuous roar. Even the rare and short pauses caused unease. 'Let-Kadyrov-die-a-president-something-will-happen-it-cannot-fail-to-happen-in-a-little-while...'

Time passed but nothing changed. The wave of violence did not ebb but nor did it escalate. News reports were featuring the same roadside explosions, clashes between 'federals' and rebels, rebels against Kadyrov's personal guard, murders of Chechen policemen by 'unidentified gunmen in camouflage', killings of ordinary people by 'unidentified people in camouflage' and not wearing camouflage, people vanishing into thin air. Generally speaking – the usual routine reports.

Kadyrov made speeches. He demanded early withdrawal of the federal forces. He made promises. He promised compensation. He promised to rebuild. He promised to investigate all the crimes committed since the early 90s. He promised to do away with the rebels. He promised the New Year without Basaev. But the federal forces remained where were. Compensation payments were suspended rather than accelerated. And they became a target for Moscow audits. Crimes still awaited investigation. One-legged Basaev was still hobbling at large.

From time to time, our colleagues from Chechnya would give me a call. To a trite question, "What's happening down there?" I would get "Nothing special, everything as usual." I'd say, "How come nothing has changed?! It just cannot be the case!" "Come to Chechnya and you will see." "OK. I'll definitely be there for the parliamentary elections."

On the morning of 6 December, the day before the parliamentary elections, I noted changes on the Chechen border at the familiar checkpoint. The slogan 'Glory to Russia – Russian National Unity,' a bit blurred from autumn rains, was now complemented by a fancy-looking new one, 'Any road shall be open to those who travel hand in hand with United Russia!'

I bumped into problems from the very onset. It must have been the very early morning that made my face show that I am not one to go hand in hand with United Russia. My journalist credentials from the presidential administration, a nice-looking duly stamped laminated card with a Russian flag on it, that had literally saved me and a few colleagues from the law enforcement people during Kadyrov's election, now unexpectedly triggered enhanced vigilance on the part of guards:

"So, you are a correspondent, are you? Correspondents must be accompanied by personal security guards."

"I am my own personal guard."

"That's not how it is done."

"OK. In that case, my driver is my guard."

"Journalists' guards must be either police or FSB."

While I was monotonously explaining that I hadn't been warned and that as far as I knew hiring police or federal security personnel as private bodyguards hadn't quite become common practice, and that no official press-tour with proper guards, as in October, was now available. Then a stoutly-built, plain looking, short bulge-eyed woman wearing an odd blue-grey uniform came out of the booth. Her heavy eyelid make-up matched her uniform perfectly. She eyed me suspiciously. She came up very close and started explaining that correspondents could not get through. Absolutely no way.

"It's for your security, in fact."

"No need, thank you. I can take care of myself."

The scene lasted for about twenty minutes and it was only the power of being a nuisance that gave me the upper hand.

"Please, let me through, it is not a big deal," – I sang like a whining barrel-organ – "If you don't, I will get through anyway. It is not my first visit. There are other roads to Chechnya. You had better let me in right now or else I will explain to the whole of Russia that the Kavkaz-1 personnel disrespect freedom of speech and persecute journalists."

Not that I managed to impress them with such threats. Over the past four years Kavkaz-1 had gained quite a reputation of which the guards themselves were well aware. My threats could only have appeared relatively trivial. I doubt that I managed to touch their hearts – they just got sick and tired of me.

"All right then. We shall make an exception for you. Go ahead."

With a sigh of relief I got into the car. While passing through the checkpoint I asked the driver,

"What is this woman on about? There were no female officers at the 'Kavkaz' before."

"Apparently you haven't been here awhile."

"Not for two months."

"Women appeared at checkpoints about a month ago. To search girls passing through checkpoints. They are afraid of female terrorists."

People said nothing has changed. Perhaps these are trifles.

We are entering Grozny.

The driver turns on the radio. We learnt that a special operation had been carried out to find criminals among the local law enforcement agencies (the so-called 'were-wolves in police uniform'). Five thousand employees of various law enforcement agencies were investigated. The investigation revealed that 250 people used amateur IDs ('amateur' is probably a local euphemism for a forged ID, though I am not sure). Unfortunately, no criminals were discovered.

Radio reports said that Kadyrov had presented a five-year plan to rebuild Grozny which will result in a renovated Grozny and newly-built neighbourhoods. ("In four years there will be a garden city here," as a famous Russian revolutionary poet once promised... well, five years in this case... but who's counting?).

The road is familiar. I look from left to right and see exactly the same wretched ruins as two months earlier. Maybe they patched something? Maybe they put a couple of new bricks somewhere? I had had the illusion that Kadyrov as president – for self-promotion and for the sake of propriety – would surely busy himself with the renovation of Grozny. How can there be talk of establishing a peaceful life while the capital remains in ruins?

The illusion was dashed within minutes. Not a piece of flesh had appeared on the city's carcass. They may have been developing a five-year plan for two months. But they had not started real work.

Apart from rebuilding houses there is the promised compensation for lost housing and property – 300 and 50 thousand roubles respectively. Fourteen billion roubles were allocated from the federal budget. So far about 27 millions have reached Chechnya. Kadyrov, who had met Putin shortly before 5 October in the seaside resort of Sochi, ponderously explained to the Elder Brother that he had issued orders that "nothing should be stolen".

On the eve of Kadyrov's election compensation started to be paid – with a 30% or 50% kickback to the appropriate bureaucrats. Theft is theft, but a bribe is something different. People are used to paying for favours. They are happy to get something.

It was a crude yet effective pre-election move. Right after the October election the payments stopped. What's the hurry? People had been waiting for a long time and they can wait some more. For, say, another five years. Indeed, a five-year period is the best term. We are so used to it.

Now off to Shatoi.

It is a long way. The road is definitely not what you'd call smooth, and in some places it is reduced to nothing. In the past, while in Chechnya, I had seen the mountains only from afar. Now I am overwhelmed by their surreal beauty which no words can express. A breathtaking abyss, ancient towers on steep slopes... it's stunning. Makes one forget about the steep bumpy road, the inevitable APCs at the side of the road, the huge helicopters diving at us, the countless soldiers. We keep on moving up, higher and higher. I can see nothing but the mountains.

Reality catches up with me only at the approaches to Shatoi. Namely, at the Tambov checkpoint. I am regaining my consciousness and my voice. "What in the world is this?!"

It is just a checkpoint manned by police commissioned from the Tambov region. Something is out of the ordinary here. Not the checkpoint itself – which is normal, but the glorious guards. They did not rush at passing vehicles. Nor did they shoot or threaten anyone. Nor were they hampering movement. They did nothing that we saw at Kavkaz-1.

They didn't even demand money. If they had been doing that the situation would have been simple, clear and normal. Everybody knows that at such-and-such checkpoint they charge ten roubles per person, 50 roubles per vehicle. Insurgents if they show up have to pay in hard currency. Basaev should keep clear of such places – unless he's prepared to go bankrupt…

The Tambov guys by contrast were very kind-hearted. They were drunk as monkeys; so loaded, in fact, that *homo erectus* was not exactly the word to describe them. They could hardly stand, let alone walk. Soldiers is hardly the word either. What words could adequately describe four men wearing dirty camouflage pants and underwear tops with bulging expressionless eyes who are fulfilling their patriotic duty in the mountains? One is still carrying his rifle under his arm; the rifles of others have fallen on the ground.

"Good God!"

My companion comments from the back seat:

"They are not God; they are the celebrated defenders of the motherland. Anyway, these guys are meek, they do not bully anyone. I wish all the checkpoints were like that! There is a commandant Bondarenko here in Shatoi. He drinks like a fish. When drunk he often closes down the checkpoint. In September a wild boar was blown to pieces by a mine. Bondarenko's drunken response was to close the checkpoint for three days. You had to walk or wait for a miracle."

A welcoming greeting hangs over the checkpoint, 'Tambov Police wish you a happy journey'. Further down the road there is a sign 'The distance to Tambov is 1781m'. OK, guys, you'd better walk home through the forest. This Tambov wolf is hardly a comrade of the Chechen one... and he is not an impediment either.

Having returned to Grozny from Shatoi we learned that the previous day two village administration heads had disappeared in the Vedeno district. And while we were admiring the beauty of the mountains two young men were arrested in the village of Duba-Yurt. One had been amnestied earlier. Grozny is watching Operation Retaliation. For the past few days whole neighbourhoods have been surrounded, people get stopped for ID checks. It is a search for rebels, and for people who have any connections with them. That means they can grab anyone at random. Special attention is given to young women.

On 7 December at eight in the morning we left to pay visits to candidates' headquarters and polling stations. For me, after the presidential election, it is a routine procedure. But everything looks different today. Two months ago, Grozny appeared to be a desert – no people, no vehicles. You could feel the tense silence. The city's inhabitants had left the city, certain that 5 October would bring trouble.

I wouldn't say that today the city is full of life, but it is quite different from the city in silent October. You can see normal lazy Sunday activity. Market places and shops are open. There are vehicles in the streets.

"Do you see those three cars without licence plates?" My companion indicates passing cars. "If there are no licence plates it means they are Kadyrov's guards. Here they are again – overtaking everybody. And another two cars... There are so many!"

Fences, poles, houses, ruins are decorated with election material. Two parties which are visibly present: United Russia (who doubted that?), and, less common, the People's Party, whose candidates are a little wealthier. Here is 'Maigov – our deputy,' and 'Khasbulatov – our deputy.' And Musaev, and Elmurzaev... But the dominant figure is of course Akhmar Zavgaev, Kadyrov's absolute favourite, and brother of the notorious Doka Zavgaev, Chechnya's ruler of the past. By the way, Zavgaev's posters in terms of printing quality are as good as Kadyrov's during the presidential election. That indicates immediately he is a serious person. Vote for him! Zavgaev's 'weightiness' is even more vividly demonstrated by billboards featuring Kadyrov and Zavgaev together. There is no doubt whatsoever that he will be a winner among single member constituency candidates.

Khasbulatov, all doom and gloom, is found in his headquarters building. He explains to me in a very aggressive way that he is not going to talk to us because he knows the electoral law better than I do, and there is no point in thinking him stupid. He says that the law prohibits him from saying a word. I was to find out what he means but he is already raging about information received from reliable sources regarding false ballots to be thrown in favour of Zavgaev. Of course nobody knows where and how many but it will definitely happen. You call that news!? I shake hands with Bekhan Khasbulatov and hastily say goodbye wishing him good luck with a broad smile. We both realize he hasn't a chance.

From Khasbulatov we move on to Maigov who until recently was Alsan Maskhadov's representative in Moscow. On the eve of the parliamentary elections Maigov went to see Kadyrov to try to curry favour and demonstrate his loyalty, but it won't help him win a parliamentary seat – at least not this time around.

Maigov himself was not in but his chief of staff, Ibragim Umar Hadjiev, is a good substitute. He tells us of rumours that extra ballot boxes full of votes in favour of Zavgaev are ready. He says that in the Grozny and Urus-Martan district administrations, bosses explained to their subordinates that they must vote for Zavgaev if they want to keep their jobs. The election mood has been far from optimistic from the very onset. When asked about the outcome, people answer "It's the same as the presidential election. It does not depend on us. There is no point in voting." Maigov's team have therefore worked to increase the turnout to promote their candidate. But the turnout is not expected to exceed 50%. "Starye Atagi, Urus-Martan, Duba-Yurt and other hardest hit villages will be more active, but in general – not more than 50%." Here, the chief of staff's smooth speech stops and his eyes become nostalgically vacant, "You know in 1997 it was very cold, people were freezing but spent hours in queues to the polling stations. There had been nothing like that even when Lenin died."

We move on. Next on the list is Musaev.

His headquarters are next to the 'Three Fools' monument in Peoples' Friendship Square. The monument displayed fighters for revolution – three proud commissars growing from a concrete column. A Slav in the centre with a Chechen on one side and an Ingush on the other. A structure typical of Soviet consumer art. In Kharkov, Ukraine, there is a huge rock with five revolutionaries along the perimeter. Kharkov inhabitants, taking account of a building nearby, say, 'the five are carrying a refrigerator from a pawn shop.'

Grozny wits also invented far from politically correct names for the Three Fools monument that formally symbolizes the friendship of peoples. To a common Russian epithet 'One Gikalo [a Ukrainian name] and two jackals', Vainakh brothers responded with 'Two mountain eagles carrying a drunken Ukrainian.' During the first Chechen war, one of the commissars lost half of his head. During the second, a bomb demolished half of the monument. Looking at the wreck standing in the middle of the square today it is difficult to see how the Three Fools name was given. But the state of the monument does indeed symbolize the current friendship of peoples in the Russian Federation.

There is a checkpoint near the Three Fools monument. A tipsy police captain, Mikhail by name, has had a couple of shots "to celebrate the elections". He fulfilled his civil duty and had another drink. According to Mikhail, all the employees of the law enforcement agencies voted. They were ordered to vote for United Russia and Zavgaev.

We said goodbye to the talkative captain and headed for Alaudi Musaev's headquarters. He is not there, but his staff are singing the same song about administrative resources, about lack of ballot papers at some polling stations, about the lack of inspectors' signatures on the lists in the ballot boxes, and so on. The Staropromyslovsky district was the one most complained about. Maigov's people also spoke badly of it. Evidently it is truly part of Zavgaev's domain.

Then, we talk to candidate Gersolt Elmurzaev. He says he wishes people in Chechnya had more opportunities to express their opinions. He maintains that the population lacks interest in the elections – they do not believe the results could be fair. Elmurzaev and his team have been trying to convince people to come out and vote. He also estimates that the turnout will not exceed 50%.

"Another one promoting election participation," my companion shrugs her shoulders when we are leaving the headquarters "But what's the point? Our United Russia falcon Yamadaev delivers plenty of propaganda. He was yelling on TV the other day, "Everybody must go to the polling stations! Everybody must vote! There are only two parties. One is United Russia, and I am behind it. The other is Al-Quaeda!"'

"Tell me. Yamadaev is an inveterate bandit, right?"

"Quite so."

Another propaganda slogan across the street, 'Those who like order and dignified life – Vote for United Russia with all your heart' catches my eye. Not just vote, but vote with all your heart? OK. Let's take a look at the polling stations. I wonder how voting 'with the heart' is done.

The polling station visit is brightened up by absolutely gorgeous weather. For three days running it has been 8°C with a blue sky and warm spring sun. If it weren't for the long nights I would not believe it is December.

We visit six polling stations one after the other. We see half a dozen voters or so at a time. Not many, but more than in October. All the election commission heads complain of a low turnout. By 11 am it has averaged about 10%. But they add that morning is not the best time. There'll be many more people in the evening.

We know that story by heart. At the Kadyrov election, wherever we went in the morning we were told that the main flux would be in the afternoon. In the afternoon we were having the story about people coming to the station in the evening, and in the evening we were told that most of the voters had shown up in the morning…

Some of the conversations are interesting enough to put on record. At one of the polling stations, Larisa Borisovna, chair of the election commission, a school teacher of course, complains earnestly that 470 military servicemen are registered with the constituency: "And the military let us down a bit. During the presidential election they really let us down – they actually openly stated that they refuse to vote! There should be somebody to teach them to behave!"

This, indubitably, has been the oddest complaint against the military I have ever heard in Chechnya. It took me some effort to keep a neutral expression on my face, and I asked:

"The situation with the military is clear, but what's up with the civilian voters? They are letting you down, are they?"

"Well, people are angry. You know how we keep on voting. We were voting in March, in October, we are voting today, but life is not getting any better. We did not have jobs then and we don't have jobs now. People will come and vote because there is some hope left. And besides, voting doesn't hurt. Life is calmer than in October. People aren't as suspicious of elections as they were then, they are not so scared. This weekend far fewer people left the city as compared with the previous elections…"

"And what was the October turnout?"

"Well, I don't remember. About 90%."

"But you said that a lot of people had left the city at that time!"

"Well, it doesn't matter. Today we will have about 80%. Many strongly support their candidate. Take Akhmar Zavgaev. When I hear his name I feel nostalgic. We associate everything with him, with his last name, that is, our wonderful past, sweet recollections. Beautiful city… kind people…no war, no hatred… I am sorry I have to work. If you wish you may talk to the observers. Here is Ludmila, she is from the United Russia party."

Ludmila smiling shyly, touches her silk headscarf.

"Ludmila, is your party popular in Chechnya?"

"United Russia enjoys a lot of support. No other party has such support. United Russia sends people to hospitals for treatment, supports families, sends pilgrims to Mecca. Donates money to build mosques. Frants Klintsevich, the party leader, has been here since 2001. He is well-known. He helps ordinary people; he visits villages even in the mountains. And Yamadaev is number two in the party. He is really big here, you know."

From the Staropromyslovsky district we move on to the Lenin district. On the way I note new optimistic slogans: 'Voting for United Russia Is voting for Chechnya revival!' 'United Russia means unity of words and actions!' The latter is redolent of unchallengeable policies, secret decision making and denunciation of any dissent. And all of a sudden bright graffiti on a half-ruined wall: 'No to lies and dirt! Yes to truth and honesty!' Huge multi-coloured sharply-angled letters that painfully scratch the heart.

At another polling station only about a hundred people of 1800 registered voters have voted by noon. Aset Isaevna, chairperson of the election commission, principal of the school that's housing the polling station is concerned about the low turnout.

"Fifteen hundred people came here to vote at the presidential election back in October. Today, God willing, 500-600 will show up. The houses are empty, people have left. You see, the day before yesterday, some terrible mop-up operations were conducted. If it hadn't been for the mop-up people would surely have come. I convened a parents' meeting this week in school, and all the parents of my pupils maintained that they would vote. And all of a sudden this mop-up operation!"

Aset looks about 50 years of age. A tired face. Huge black circles under her eyes. Curly hair escapes from under her headscarf, she tucks it back in nervously.

"But on the whole, you mustn't misunderstand me. United Russia is very popular here. Because it is closer to Putin. Putin and the Parliament are together. A lot of people in Chechnya rely on Putin today – they hope to get compensation, to see Chechnya rebuilt. They hope he will do something to make their life easier. If it is not him, who else?"

Aset suddenly steps up close to me and starts whispering hurriedly and emotionally: "You know how tired we all are? It is impossible to live this way! And for so many years! You have come here and you stayed overnight, right?

Don't even try to tell me you weren't scared? And that's how we feel every night. I can't sleep at all. I am so afraid for my son. When will it end?"

I wish I could answer the question. I squeeze her hand and talk platitudes. I tell her that I understand everything but cannot change it. And that there are other people in Russia who also realize it, who feel ashamed and try to do something but fail.

"Do you come here often?" asks Aset suddenly.

"Not in the past, but this year it's my third visit…"

"Please, come again. And bring others with you. Those who are not afraid. If more people see what our life's like… But perhaps you'd better not; it is such a risk to bring people here. But you should return. You've already done it a few times anyway. Thank you!"

"What for?"

"For not being afraid. For not being indifferent."

I am so ashamed at this point that my one and only wish was to become invisible. I rush out. Kids are running around an empty swimming pool. Two young girls are filling their buckets with water at a water supply hydrant, talking to each other and giggling. Next to the school there is a large building, a temporary lodging centre. The People's Party has offices in the building occupying part of what was formerly a dormitory-hostel of the Chechen-Ingush state University. In December 1999 Basaev turned it into a stronghold. The school which I have just left was occupied by Khattab. And federal tanks were approaching from across the road.

That's it. I've had enough of the Grozny polling stations. Time to go to the country. But before we move on it makes sense to talk to people in the streets. Such attempts fail in the villages – there is no hiding there, people are scared. But inhabitants of Grozny, judging from my past experiences, don't mind having a chat.

"Well, I don't think people will say anything to you on the street", my local colleague says.

"Why not? In Grozny in October I was talking to people at random. No problem. And back in September…"

"That was a different time. But today people have become reticent and reserved. Let's go to a market place. If we want to find someone chatty, that is the place to go."

We are walk to the market place. I make a few desperate attempts to start a conversation. No dice. Everybody smiles politely and turns away. In October I heard a flow of jokes about the election of the president who had already been elected, curses about Kadyrov, rhetorical questions about the best country to go to if enough money was pooled to buy plywood, and make a helicopter…

My colleague is trying to play the mediator. She goes up to people explaining in Chechen that I am a Moscow journalist wishing to speak to people about the elections and life in general, no names will be mentioned, everything is absolutely safe. She gets monosyllabic answers from people who immediately turn away. Only one woman says in a very low voice over the counter, and without looking me in the eye, "You want to hear about elections? We had elections in 1997. People got up at dawn to line up to vote. I queued for seven hours myself. My feet were numb with cold but I kept on waiting in line… And now… There is nothing to talk about. And what kind of life we have? You can see for yourself. You'd better go…"

"Sorry," my escort is apologizing for her fellow-Chechens. "Times are bad now. Everybody is afraid of saying something wrong – what if someone overhears? Those mop-up operations in the city… Special operations is what they call them now, but there is no difference. Not long ago a French journalist came here, an acquaintance of mine. She couldn't believe her eyes! People had changed so much! They have nothing to hope for now, that's why they keep mum."

On the counter nearby – a heap of cassettes of different colours. A dashing song resounds in the air, 'At dawn a company of soldiers moves on… I believe in the goodness of your soul, my sergeant!'

People in this city do not believe in anything now. How many years will it take? What has to for these people to regain trust?

Now we are going to the village of Varandy. There isn't much traffic. A ruined house enclosed by a galvanised iron fence catches our attention. On the fence we read an inscription painted in white, 'This is my house. Everything is going to be all right! Sveta.' A smiling face is drawn next to the optimistic message. Where is this Sveta now? Can she still hope that everything will be all right?

Varandy feels very cosy. The village is small. There are only 387 voters. Near the polling station is a flower-bed surrounded by a low fence made of artillery shell cases. Young guards, smiling shyly, ask if I would be photographed with them.

"We rarely have guests from afar. But when people come we always take photos – them and us together. We'll make extra copies of the pictures to give to you when you come back."

Of course I agree. Why should I offend these them? We stand at the edge of a steep bank. The boys ask me to remove my headscarf "so that everyone understands you really are from Moscow". Four young men wearing the invariable camouflage and holding on to their assault rifles. I am in the centre smiling. The fifth guy is taking a picture. Then, he joins our little group and changes places and passes the camera to one of his mates. The procedure is repeated five times so that each of them is in the frame. So we end up with five pictures. Then they thank me politely and ceremonially show me to the voting place.

"It is only 3 pm but 82% have already voted. By the evening, the turnout will be 100%!" the head of the election commission, Birlant by name, happily reports. "It is always like that here. No problem. These are my third elections."

There is a whole range of Kadyrov calendars on Birlant's desk under the desktop glass. Noticing what I am looking at Birlant proudly explains. "They are left over after the presidential election. Would you like one?" "No, thank you. I already have a few October leftovers. Do tell me which party is the most popular among villagers. Varandy being so small, you probably know everything about the electoral preferences of your fellow-residents."

"What do you mean 'which party'?!" Birlant replies "United Russia! It is the only party! The one and only! United Russia means 'together with the president!' And if we are together with the president – then everything will be OK."

Someone taps me on the shoulder. A small crowd has gathered behind my back. They take me to the corner of the room: "She is not telling the truth. We have more than one party. The other one is the People's Party. All of us voted for it."

"Why did you vote for this particular party?"

"Well, because it is for the people."

A little investigation indicates that none of the four active supporters of the People's Party I am talking to have any idea who's on the party's list. Nor are they aware of the party's programme. I ask if they are aware that General Troshin, one of the butchers of Chechnya, is one of the top three in the People's Party. My inquiry meets complete lack of understanding. They just keep on saying that if the party's name is 'People's Party' that means it is for the people and everyone must vote for it.

Having said goodbye to hospitable Varandy we make up our minds, while it is not yet dark, to drive even higher. In this other village (I will not disclose the name) there are 770 voters. Four hundred have allegedly voted by the time of our arrival.

The polling station is hosted by the local school. A large room with huge windows, bright with afternoon sun. On the wall a huge poster from October election times with Kadyrov smiling against a background of high mountains. Putin's office-type portrait in a nice frame is on the same wall.

We are greeted by the election commission chair who is naturally the school's principal, Nina. She is a good-looking, fair-haired girl. Pretty face with fine features. A shiny mink coat thrown over her shoulders. Nina greets me as happily as if I am her next of kin.

"Oh, you are a journalist, aren't you? Come in please! We are almost colleagues! I am a philologist myself. It is so nice to welcome you here! We have so few guests!"

She bombards me with questions about Moscow, what's on at the theatres, concerts and exhibitions. I feel sorry for the girl who is obviously bored to death in this village in the middle of nowhere. Forgetting that I am pressed for time, I try to quench her cultural thirst. Two old men come up to the desk with their papers asking where they are supposed to put tick-marks. Nina blushes, jumps to her feet, and takes the old men to the booth explaining something to them. Then she returns to me.

"I am sorry. You know what old people are. They don't have a clue about voting. The lists are so long. So many options to choose from. How can this be explained to them? It is the same in all the villages, not only here. Old people just can't understand what is required. They come to polling stations demanding that someone explain where to tick-mark the papers. Generally speaking, everybody votes for United Russia. It is so popular because there are no other parties. A year ago, the United Russia was the only party in Chechnya. No other parties. Not a single one.

"To be frank, I hate this United Russia. But everybody, especially young guys, join the party. There is nothing else they can do. They have to get around somehow. At checkpoints, a United Russia party membership card serves as a badge that gets you through. If they are detained in the course of some special operation they show their party cards, and that sets them free. And sometimes party activists get money from United Russia. That's why everybody wants to join."

Nina keeps on chattering but red circles start to pulse before my eyes. I know about money, about Klintsevich and Yamadaev, about hand-outs to mullahs, and about everything else. But party cards used as passes at checkpoints! This simply hadn't occurred to me. A loyalty certificate reminiscent of denazification in postwar Germany, but reversed. This is beyond cynicism, beyond good and bad. If you are for United Russia you are cleared to survive. The rest are doomed to extinction. What did the Kavkaz-1 slogan say? 'Any road willl succumb to those who travel hand in hand with United Russia!' Apparently, that means what it says. What the slogan did not say is the fact that if you are not travelling hand in hand with United Russia you can expect to come to harm. But this seems to go without saying. Only strangers like me have to work this out. Insiders know it. Each and every person in Chechnya must be well aware of it.

So far only in Chechnya. Is this just the beginning? Soon the whole of Russia will face it. Will it creep all over the country like many other things? Like the uncontrolled arbitrary rule of law enforcement agencies that are immune from punishment. Will each of us have to have a United Russia membership card carried close to the 'heart' that you have to listen to when electing United Russia candidates?

"Oh, here is my father!" Nina stands up hurriedly. "He is the head of the local administration. He must have learned that you are here, so he is coming to talk to you. Please, do not tell him what I have told you about the United Russia. He is a big wheel in the party and is trying to make me join. But I refuse; I just hate United Russia."

Nina takes me to her father and makes the introductions. The hale old man shakes my hand with a vengeance and starts a speech. It seems as if he is speaking at a rally:

"I am Said-Emin, the village administration head. The whole village and I stand together with the United Party. I am a party member and this whole village…"

"Excuse me," I interrupt him cautiously, "What kind of a party is this United Party? You must mean United Russia?"

"We have only one party – the United one. We are tired of Zhirinovskys-the-clowns, Zyuganovs-the-communists and the likes. The United Party is the party of the president. The party which must come to power. We need to fight against oligarchs and werewolves in police uniform. People who left the village in 1991 haven't all returned from the forests, but the law will soon reign here. Chechnya has not yet created itself but soon the time will come. We, as well as the whole of Russia, are tired of old parties and we trust no one. We support the United Party!"

The speaker is swinging his arm as if he is slashing at an enemy with a sword. I feel a bit chilly even though the room is well heated…

"In 1999 I advanced shoulder-to-shoulder with General Shamanov and General Troshev. On 7 February 2000, together with the Russian Army, I led my people out of the village and brought them back by the end of the month. Since 1999 the village hasn't had a single person killed or disappeared!"

"Haven't you had any mop-up operations here in all this time?"

"We've had plenty. But I was in charge and didn't let them take our people. I negotiated and got issues resolved. I even managed to save some people from the neighbouring villages of Duba-Yurt, Chiri-Yurt, and Starye Atagi, people who had been detained and beaten up. Our village is at the wolf's gate. The Russian army was stationed here. I celebrated General Verbitsky's birthday with him. I was an honoured guest at his table. Being a remote village, we lack attention. But in 2000 we managed to get connected to water, gas and power supply lines. I was personally involved in that, sitting on top of a tank. I spent the whole war on a tank. I am everything here. The president presented me with a Volga car because the whole village voted unanimously in the October election. And today we'll be voting unanimously. It cannot be any other way."

The worthy mayor is dragging me to the window and I have ample opportunity to admire his shining brand new Volga which apparently substituted for his combat tank.

"And here are my letters of award for the election and for the referendum. The president appreciates me. Take a look!"

How could I miss them! On the wall, under the ceremonial portraits of the royal twins – Putin and Kadyrov – are two fancy letters of award, one for exemplary organisation of the referendum, and the other for equally wonderful organisation of the October presidential election.

"What do you expect of the new president whom you were supporting so ardently at the election?" I ask.

"We expect that the new president will have Russian troops pull out and returned to barracks. Right after the referendum I started saying to the soldiers, "I have conducted the referendum. I am a Russian Federation citizen. But you commit outrages and you have no right to do so! We are waiting for compensation payment. So far only two persons from the village have been paid. Houses should also be rebuilt."

"Aren't people tired of waiting?" I said. "Kadyrov started demanding the federal forces' withdrawal immediately after his election. He promised that the troops would pull out very shortly. But the troops remain. He also promised that compensation would be paid speedily and honestly. But today compensation payments are suspended.

"We believe that Kadyrov will deliver on his promise. Hope dies last", states Said-Emin optimistically and cordially invites me to dinner. I refer to the late hour and the need to go back to Grozny and politely decline his offer to stay overnight. I notice disappointment in Nina's eyes. The girl wanted to talk about Moscow theatrical and book novelties till late at night. I still feel sorry for her but not to the extent of accepting the mayor's hospitality. It was not easy to escape but escape I did – with Putin and Kadyrov looking at me venomously from the wall.

I ask the driver to pull up just after we have left the village and passed the bridge. We linger on the bridge for about five minutes absorbing the mountains, the rushing stream underneath coloured pink by the sunset, the crystal cold air.

By about 7 pm we are back in Grozny. Thank God, the electricity is not off tonight. Angry and tired we drop down in front of the TV set. A smiling hostess of Chechnya news chatters happily: "Today, on 7 December, the air has been warmed by the sun as if reflecting a festive mood among voters. Most of the people hope that their party will be elected to the state Duma and their candidates will uphold their own (sic) rights there with dignity!"

Sometimes a slip of the tongue may be so full of meaning!

We are already aware that United Russia and Zavgaev won in Chechnya. Which implies that Kadyrov is the real winner again. They are all the same. Nobody doubted this. (Later we came to know exact figures: 79.9% voted for United Russia and 50.7% for Zavgaev with a turnout of 88%). When the population on paper is a few hundred thousand more than in reality, it goes without saying that the turnout is overstated. But people did vote. They were cornered. They had no hope. Voting can't hurt you. If you don't vote... who knows...?

In addition we learn that at the federal parliamentary elections no democratic party made its way to the state Duma. Russians supported not only United Russia, but also Zhirinovsky with his Liberal Democratic Party and Rogozin with his Rodina (motherland) block. United Russia and fascists. Together with the president. Nice combo. Any discussion would be pointless at this point. My colleague shrugs and goes to the kitchen to fix us dinner.

On her way out of the room she puts an old Soviet film on the video. It is *The Captive of the Caucasus* that several generations of Russians have adored. Five minutes later I watch with utter fascination as a Russian friend and a Chechen, my colleague's husband, laugh at the uncomplicated adventures of the protagonist, a sweet young and awkward Russian student, in the safe and benevolent Caucasus. Maybe this unaffected and good-humoured film continues to inspire people with never-ending admiration because of its nostalgic unreality?

The night is tranquil. Last night we heard very little shooting too. What a contrast to those few nights I had spent in Grozny in October.

Next morning the weather suddenly changes. Ice-cold drizzle envelops the city. Passing by the House of Government, we see a crowd of women. We get out of the car to have a look. They are the mothers and wives of those who disappeared. They are waiting to see Kadyrov. They have been gathering here every Monday and Wednesday for several months. It is Monday today. They are promised that Kadyrov will receive them at some point. And hope is known to die last.

We also learn from them that the mothers of two young men who had disappeared on the eve of the election in Duba-Yurt erected a barricade with the help of their relatives, blocking the bridge not far from the village. They pledge to stay put till they get their sons back. I have several hours before the departure, so we've got the time to go and talk to the protesters.

But when we reach the place there is no one there. Only the barricade made of boards and old tyres still blocks the far end of the bridge, and a small fire is still smouldering. The pickets may have just left. Maybe not for long. Over the barricade we see a narrow white banner. *'Return our sons!'* the red letters scream on the thin faded cloth. I come to the bridge to take a couple of pictures. A bus is approaching the bridge from the highway. It is overcrowded. The bus pulls up at the bridge. It cannot go any further.

People, mostly women with small babies and heavy bags, get off the bus and walk with heads lowered down the bridge shivering in the piercing December wind. They are not dismantling the barricade, though two men could easily do it in five minutes. They look at the barricade frowning and mutter something disapproving about those who have erected this obstacle on their path. The mothers of the disappeared blocked the road out of sheer desperation and helplessness. Today their own neighbours scorn them because they suffer as a result of the helplessness and desperation of the mothers. It is impossible to condemn the people who have to drag their feet on slippery slopes slouching to hide from the wind. There is nothing left but the feeling of shame and pity.

A Chechen taxi. I am going back to Ingushetia.

Actually, this is a 'taxi' in name only. In fact, it functions as a mini-bus with a bit of additional comfort, in other words a car for four passengers. A hundred roubles per person and in an hour and a half you are in Nazran.

The radio is on full blast and pop music floods the ears. Two girls sharing the back seat with me are discussing something in Chechen with great animation, and munching popcorn. I know this road inside out and from time to time notice something new. This time I see a rusty piece of iron attached to a tree with a crooked inscription: 'Are you still fighting? In that case we are coming. Special Task Force.' Another 500 metres down the road, there is a flashy election poster, 'Peace, Order, Goodness and Strength – that's what United Russia is'.

I know that in the past two months a lot has changed. The war is over. But in its place, something sticky, troubled, criminal and dark has crept in. This something, this swamp-like substance, no matter how strange it might seem, is more scary than the war itself. A war has an end, it implies negotiations, settlement. But this swamp devours everything has no discernible end. It may last for ever. And that is really frightening.

Nazran. Ingushetia.

A small cosy kitchen. Five o'clock tea (well, it's more like seven o'clock, but who cares). I am sharing the United Party anecdotes with a bunch of Chechens. The guys are roaring with laughter.

"Every time you go in, you return with some crazy stories. Though anything is possible. Remember that mop-up operation in Serzhen-Yurt in 2001? The feds take 500 roubles per head and off you go, right? Males only, of course, say from 15 to 55 years old. But if a man is bearded or wears dirty pants, that makes him suspicious, and they charge a thousand, otherwise they take the man away and that's the end of him. So, an old woman, dirt poor, managed to borrow 500 roubles from her neighours to pay for her grandson. By that time she had lost all her sons – only the grandson survived. Despite the bribe the feds decided to pay her a house visit. Just in case – maybe they thought somebody else was there, or wanted to find something worth confiscating. But the house was literally empty. So they counted 200 roubles and gave the money back to her saying, "Do you think we are some kind of looters or what!"

The laughter sets the table shaking. Some tea spills on the tablecloth.

"No need for you to wipe the table. You are a guest. Just listen here. During the first war hostilities reached Gekhi – that's my village – a lot of people got killed... and kids...All hell was breaking loose and I was running around looking for my young son but couldn't find him anywhere. All of a sudden a neighbour says to me, 'The dead have been taken to Urus-Martan in a truck. Your son was among them. I saw him. Don't look for him any more.' At first I did not believe her. Then, I came back to the house. Nobody there but near the doorway I noticed my son's boots and I thought that it was the end of him. But he returned home the next day! Yes, they had loaded him on the truck together with the corpses, but he had come to. And he walked back home. That's it. Only his hand had been shot through. And there I am seeing him and screaming, 'Couldn't you put your boots on?!'"

Laughter fills the kitchen. It spills through the open window outside. Our hilarity catches up with the children who are playing in the yard. It is so infectious that soon everybody in the yard is laughing. Well, should they cry? Or what?

'Magas' Airport. Ingushetia. Waiting hall.

I am dragging a bag full of papers that my colleagues and some other people asked me to pass over in Moscow to important and not so important officials. I am already accustomed to this heavy feeling – yes, I will hand them over.

And even accompany them with adequate covering letters. And I will make sure that each document reaches the addressee. But I fear that it will be all down the drain. I feel guilty yet again and the routine quality of the emotion makes it more difficult to bear. I feel guilty because I am leaving. I have escaped once again. But what about those who live in that situation every day? What right do I have to leave when my friends are staying? When anyone is staying?

The traditional thirty-minute delay. The bar counter. I put my bag by the high stool.

"Oh, I remember you. Fifty grams of vodka mixed with orange juice, right? You come here often. Do you like Nazran?"

On the plane a guy sitting next to me tries to start a conversation. At first I only mutter something politely without raising my eyes from the book that I am reading. But after about twenty minutes I cannot resist his talkativeness. A smiling thin young man of about twenty-five with the most biblical name, Adam, is going to Moscow for two weeks leave. He is from Grozny where he works in the police force. When he landed the job "life became easier." Though some time ago he had to "join the party".

"Which party?" I ask, barely feigning innocence.

"What do you mean 'which party'? We have only one – the United."

"You mean United Russia don't you? And what's this 'I had to?' Why did you have to?"

"Don't you know? Don't you know that the party membership card gets you anywhere? They let you pass as if you are their best friend."

"Hold on, you are a policeman, right? They must let you pass without any problem."

"Come on! How can you compare! This morning there was a kilometre-long line at the Kavkaz checkpoint. But the moment I waved my membership card they almost carried me through."

"You mean to say that a United Russia membership card works better than a police ID?"

"A hundred times better. And what's more – if you are a party member they cannot fire you."

"You mean?"

"I mean exactly what I said. The party has to give its approval. In the autumn three pals of mine were kicked out. They wrote a complaint and filed it with the party leader. Tough luck that he was away at the time. But when he came back a month later he showed them who was the boss! 'Who, damn it, allowed you to fire my people? I should expel them first, and then you may show your powers! But unless I give my blessing don't stir things up.'"

"So? Did they take them back?"

"That is not the word to describe it! They got a month's pay for the time they were off!"

"Well, that's a real leader! But who is this real leader of the United Russia – Klintsevich or Yamadaev?"

"Yamadaev, of course!" All of a sudden a glint of suspicion appears in the eye of this friendly, talkative neighbour of mine. "How do you know?"

"I don't know. I am just asking a question."

It must be noted that my rather impressive knowledge of the latest Chechen realities, including such specific things as how bad the power supply had been in his native district of Grozny for the past week, did not bother the guy at all. On the contrary, he seemed excited about it. But now he starts mumbling something about how sleepy he feels after a night on duty. He says, "Sorry", turns to the window and closes his eyes.

Moscow. Vnukovo Airport.

For those arriving from the Caucasus the arrival procedure is as strict as for foreign guests. Even more severe, in fact. Passport control is not enough. Get your baggage X-rayed and walk through a metal detector. Thank God, my colleagues sent a taxi to pick me up and the driver patiently endured the long wait. On my way to downtown Moscow I am practically glued to the cell phone monotonously calling all those whom I promised to call first thing upon arrival. "Yes, I am fine. Just fine. All the rest is pretty disgusting." I am reluctant to say another word but one friend or another manages to make me utter a few complete sentences. The driver perks up with apparent interest.

"You must be a journalist, aren't you?"

"Something like that. Why?"

"You see, I am trying to understand what this United Russia is all about. They won the elections. But I just don't understand what they are. And no one can explain. Maybe you will?"

"Why not! I have just learned this myself and I'll be glad to tell you. 'Peace, Order, Goodness and Strength' – That's what United Russia is! An exhaustive explanation, don't you think?"

Chronicle of Events: 1 Dec 2003 to 8 Dec 2003

1 December 2003. At 2.20 am in the district of Gikalovsky of the Grozny region representatives of an unidentified federal law enforcement agency abducted two local residents: Zelimkhan Khamidovich Bachaev, born 1977, of Teplichnaya Street, and Omar Isaevich Demilkhanov, born 1977, of Teplichnaya, 6-1. The houses were surrounded by troops who had arrived in four armoured troop carriers accompanied by UAZ and Ural vehicles.

Zelimkhan and his wife, Elita, were woken up by knocks on the entrance door. Then five or six armed people in masks and camouflage uniforms stormed into the house. They demanded that the Bachaevs get out of bed and produce their passports. Elita showed her papers but it turned out that Zelimkhan had his father's passport. The woman said that the passports had been misplaced by accident. Bachaev's father lived next door to them and she said she would go there and fetch her husband's passport. The troops beat her up although it was impossible not to notice that she was pregnant. Then they entered the house of Zelimkhan's mother and father, beat up his parents and took away his passport. After that, without giving Bachaev a chance to get dressed, they took him outside and put him in an armoured Ural vehicle. Bachaev's next door neighbour, Omar Demilkhanov, was also taken away.

Relatives of the abducted men saw the military column heading towards the Starye Atagi district. They immediately attempted to seek assistance from the commandant's office near their house but there was no response to their petition. Later, in a private conversation, the commandant's office admitted that they had seen the abduction but they had no ordered to intervene and they could not do anything without an order.

On the morning of 1 December the parents of the abducted men petitioned the prosecutor's office and the police department of Grozny rural district. In order to get the attention of authorities, residents blocked the road leading from Grozny to Shatoi. The picketing site was visited by the prosecutor of the Grozny rural district and the deputy military commandant of the republic, Ibragim Suleimanov.

On 2 December the relatives of the abducted went to Grozny to petition the government of the Republic of Chechnya, but they were not allowed to enter the government's building. An official came out of the public reception room and recommended that they should seek assistance at the prosecutor's office.

On 3 December residents of the Gikalovsky district went to town and organized a picket at the governmental compound. Security guards attempted to chase them away but did not succeed – a journalist from Grozny television, Zulikhan, began to videotape what was going on. She was detained and taken inside the compound territory but was soon released minus her videotape.

Some time later a representative of the governmental administration who did not introduce himself came out but was unable to say anything intelligible. At the same time the picketers managed to have a word with the deputy military commandant of the republic I.Suleimanov. Suleimanov promised that he would give them a concrete answer as to the fate of the abducted men within the next ten days. After that the mothers of Bachaev and Demilkhanov were invited to enter the governmental compound. On the same day the abductors released Bachaev and Demilkhanov. Both had been severely beaten. It turned out that all that time they had been kept on the territory of the former mill on the outskirts of Stariye Atagi where the district police department and a subdivision of troops of the RF Ministry of Internal Affairs are stationed.

1 December. Representatives of the Urus-Martan police detained a resident of the Goity district of the Urus-Martan, Kati Isaevich Khadizov, born 1975, of Mutsaev Street. Several hours later he was released. No sooner did he return home than representatives of law enforcement agencies came for him again; without introducing themselves or providing any explanations they took him away again in the direction of Urus-Martan.

Kati was released on the next day, 2 December 2003. It is not known where he had been kept once arrested for the second time, nor is it known which law enforcement agency had detained him and on what grounds. According to local residents it was clear that K.Khadizov had been beaten up. However Kati himself has not mentioned having suffered from violence when in custody.

2 December. Early in the morning Koltsova Street in the Staropromyslovsky district of Grozny was blocked by representatives of law enforcement agencies who arrived in an armoured troop carrier, and Ural and UAZ vehicles. All day long they stood outside not answering local residents' questions as to the purpose of the operation. After asking who

lived there they entered the house in which Dzhokhar Dudayev's sister had lived earlier. The house is ruined and currently uninhabited while Dudayev's sister lives in a different part of Grozny now. The troops also visited another house located at Koltsova 150 where the family of Muradovs live. The troops asked the women who lived in the house who else lived there and having received an answer left the property without ever explaining the reasons behind their visit.

It is not known why the troops spent the entire day on this street. They had their lunch delivered to them in the course of the day. In the evening they left the district. Street residents spent the entire day under a great deal of tension.

2 December. In the afternoon, in Grozny, representatives of an unidentified law enforcement agency detained Magomed Adamovich Sultanov, born 1979, and took him away. The passenger route No 15 minivan in which he had been returning home was pulled over for documents inspection not far away from the checkpoint on Khankalskaya Street. Magomed's parents heard about what had happened from one of the minivan passengers.

It became known later day that law enforcement agencies of the Chechen Republic were conducting a special operation, 'Djamaat,' in several residential areas. According to some sources two other young men whose whereabouts are also not known were detained in a similar fashion. Two days earlier, on 30 November, in a Grozny downtown shooting, Magomed's younger brother, Abubakar, had been seriously wounded. He was detained under observation of the law enforcers in Gudermes hospital No 2.

Magomed's detention was not the last shock that the Sultanov family suffered. The same day, before anything was known of the detention of the elder son, representatives of an unidentified law enforcement agency drove up to their house in an UAZ vehicle with the licence plate number A 0107-95. Soldiers blocked off the area and some entered the house and demanded from Sultanovs' daughter, Petimat, the whereabouts of her brothers, Abubakar and Magomed. Without getting an intelligible answer from the frightened girl the troops left the house. Young people who lived next door were subjected to interrogation.

On 3 December 2003 Adam Edilovich Sultanov, the father of the detained brothers, petitioned the Memorial Human Rights Centre requesting assistance in the search for Magomed Adamovich Sultanov.

2 December. Resident of the Gekhi district of the Urus-Martan, Elsa Adievna Gaitamirova, born 1973, of Budenny Street, 31, received a writ stating that she was to report to the Urus-Martan police on December 2, 2003. On December 2 she went to Urus-Martan but never returned. Her mother, Roza Khasanovna Gaitamirova, tried to find her daughter. Representatives of law enforcement agencies do not deny the fact that Elsa is in custody but they refused to discuss what she is accused or where she is being kept.

4 December. In Grozny representatives of unidentified law enforcement agencies of the Chechen Republic beat up a young man driving in his car past the central market. Accord-

ing to the officers the young man had not complied with their order to pull over. They opened fire, targeted the car wheels, and when the car with shot-through wheels stopped the driver was dragged out of the vehicle and severely beaten up. Passers-by who attempted to interfere were prevented from doing so by officers' threats.

5 December. At 3.50 am a military column consisting of four armoured troop-carriers, several Ural trucks, and several UAZ jeeps entered the Duba-Yurt district Shali. The troops surrounded the house of the Bersanovs on Podgornaya Street, stormed inside and captured Said-Khussein Bersanov, born 1978. His mother and grandmother rushed to his rescue but were beaten up. The grandmother suffered the most – her arm being seriously injured. Handcuffed, Said-Khussein was taken outside without having been given a chance to get dressed, was pushed into a military vehicle and taken away in an unknown destination.

Sultan Adamovich Khadzhimuradov, born 1964, living on Sheripov Street, was taken away in the same fashion. His relatives pursued the captors and saw that the military vehicles passed through the checkpoint at the Chiri-Yurt district and headed towards Starye Atagi. The next day relatives of Bersanov and Khadzhimuradov petitioned the police, prosecutor's and commandant's offices of the Shali district.

On 6 December residents of the Duba-Yurt district blocked the road near Chiri-Yurt district, near the bridge over Argun. They were accosted by Sergei Ovchukov, chief criminal investigator of the Shali police department. To the question of a Memorial representative as to whether he could confirm that the detainees were being kept by military troops stationed near the Starye Atagi district he said that he did not have access to that territory. Ovchukov clarified that check point representatives were not authorized to inspect military vehicles and that they could not always check troops' documents. The residents continued picketing the road and kept it blocked on 7 and 8 December.

In Assinovskaya, during an inspection for mines at polling stations for the election of deputies of the state Duma of the Russian Federation, representatives of the Sunzha police department found a landmine in the courtyard of school No 3. Sappers were summoned from the commandant's office. All polling station representatives and school teachers were evacuated from the school building; there were no children in the school as the classes had been cancelled from 4 December until the end of elections. Examination found that the landmine had been made from an artillery shell and was filled with nails and bolts. The sappers could not neutralize the landmine and detonated it on the spot. Nobody was injured. It is assumed that the terrorists had intended to set it off on 7 December, the day of the elections.

Approximately at 6 am a special targeted operation began in the Sernovodsk district. Houses were inspected by representatives of Russian law enforcement agencies who had arrived in armoured troop-carriers and UAZ vehicles. The troops examined houses on M.Mazaev, Kutalov, D.Bedny, M.Gorky, and Bolnichnaya streets. Vehicles and one armoured troop-carrier were also observed in the Sernovodsk upper district. Nobody was arrested. On Kutalov Street the troops searched house No 30 that belongs to Shakhid Ibragimov. They asked to see Aindi Ibragimov, father-in-law of 'Abdul-Sabur' Khas-Magomed Islamov who had been killed in a shooting earlier. In the Sernovodsk district representatives of operative investigation bureau No 2 of the Ministry of Internal Affairs (ORB-2) arrested Said-Khussein Madievich Azarsanov, deputy of the district mullah, and took him away directly.

In the afternoon ORB representatives arrived at the Sunzha police department where the officer-in-charge introduced himself as Arbi and said that he was from Urus-Martan. Then they headed towards Kalinin Street where S.-Kh.Azarsanov lives. According to Sovdash, Azarsanov's wife, armed people arrived in several vehicles in the afternoon and asked for her husband. She told them that he was at a funeral in Grozny. At around 5 pm representatives of ORB-2 came back. This time S.-Kh.Azarsanov was at home and preparing for prayer. The officer-in-charge took him aside. Sovdash overheard that her husband was requested to go with them after prayer to the Sunzha police department where he would be questioned and then released. She intended to go with him but was told that there was no room in the vehicle. Sovdash rapidly followed the vehicle on foot. She saw that the vehicles did not go to the police but headed towards the Rostov-Baku highway. She told her relatives what had happened.

The next day they asked for S.-Kh.Azarsanov at various law enforcement agencies and found out that he was being kept at the ORB. On 7 December the iman of the Sernovodsk district, A.Gayev, and several district patriarchs went to the Ministry of Internal Affairs. They were allowed to speak with Azarsanov and give him a parcel. He informed them that he was being treated courteously and had been promised that he would be released after the election. He was not however released even in the second half of December. Apparently S.-Kh.Azarsanov was detained because he is the father-in-law of the liquidated field commander, Arbi Baraev.

6 December. At 11.10 pm the polling station at Sernovodsk School No 1 was shot at. Firing by automatic weapons came from the park adjacent to the school and went on for two minutes. As a result of the shooting the windows of the room in which the voting station was located were damaged. At the time of the shooting the voting station was being guarded by the police. Nobody was injured.

7 December. In the Prigorodnoye district of the Grozny rural district two teenagers were killed by a landmine: Yanars Baudinovich Mutaliev, born 1989, of Stroitelei Street, and Islam Rasulovich Khabuev, born 1988, of 7 Pushkina Street. In the afternoon Mutaliev and Khabuev received their parents' permission to go out for a walk. At approximately 3 pm not far from the district, in the area known among local residents as Basi, the sound of a powerful explosion was heard. Nobody paid much attention, but in the early evening relatives

of the children concerned about their prolonged absence went out to look for them. On that evening they did not find Yanars and Islam.

On 8 December residents found the bodies of the children in the area where the sound of explosion had come from the day before. The teenagers were killed on the edge of the zone that had been mined at the outset of the second Chechen by federal forces with assistance of front-line aviation units. The spot is a significant distance from the Grozny-Prigorodnoe highway and its mining was absolutely pointless. No security measures had been undertaken to protect the local population. The mined area was not fenced off from residential areas nor identified in any way with signs.

Cattle of Prigorodnoe residents had been killed on this territory repeatedly. One day 32 cows that happened to wander off in that direction were killed simultaneously. The fear of mining meant that residents had almost no pasture land left for their cattle. The mined territory is adjacent to the Oktyabrsky district of Grozny. People and animals have also been killed there. Local residents have repeatedly petitioned the authorities requesting that the mined zone be isolated but their complaints and petitions remain unanswered.

Relatives of the dead children, together with the precinct police officer-in-charge, petitioned the military troops stationed near the district requesting that they ensure a safe passage to the site of the explosion. The troops refused to participate, stating that they needed authorization from the commandant's office of the Grozny rural district. Realizing that it was useless to count on any assistance from the military, the relatives accompanied by the precinct police officer made their way to the site of explosion at their own risk and retrieved the bodies of their children. Yanars and Islam were buried at the local cemetery after a group summoned from law enforcement agencies had completed their own investigation.

On 11 December a number of information agencies reported that two teenagers, residents of the Prigorodnoe district, had been killed by the explosion of a landmine that they were trying to plant. Relatives of the dead children were outraged by this blatant lie of Russian information agencies.

7 December. At night, in Gudermes, not far from the office of the commission for election of the deputy of the RF state Duma, unidentified individuals murdered a local resident, Yunus Yakubov, who had represented the United Russia political party in the capacity of an election observer. He was shot on his way home.

8 December. A targeted special operation was conducted in the Gekhi district of the Urus-Martan. According to head of the district administration 5–6 vehicles, including armoured troop-carriers, took part in the operation. Some of the representatives of law enforcement agencies were wearing masks. The district was not closed off and people could leave its boundaries unobstructed.

The inspection focused on Shkolnaya and Zarechnaya streets. Representatives of law enforcement agencies checked derelict buildings and conducted unauthorized searches in several inhabited houses. The head of the district administration is of the opinion that representatives of law enforcement agencies who conducted the operation had grossly violated the order that specified that in any such operation the military should first notify the local administration and coordinate their actions with them. The special operation went on for several hours. Nobody was detained.

8 December 2003. In the evening, in the Leninsky district of Grozny representatives of one of the law enforcement agencies of the Chechen Republic conducted an armed assault of the temporary placement centre for forced migrants located at 47 Kirova. At around 7 pm three UAZ and several VAZ-21099 vehicles drove up to the temporary placement centre. A large group of troops in masks came out of the vehicles and headed towards the temporary placement centre entrance. They disarmed the security guards at the entrance: the two of them had one pistol and a radio between them. Security guards working at this temporary placement centre are not provisioned with automatic weapons following several attacks undertaken against Grozny temporary placement centres with the view of procuring weapons.

Then the armed individuals beat up the security guards and headed towards the second floor hitting everyone who they happened to encounter on their way. Threatening with weapons they forced the temporary placement centre residents to squat with their hands behind the back of their heads. They hit those who failed to comply with the butts of their machine guns knocking them off their feet. These actions were accompanied by rude cursing in Russian. The armed people who installed themselves in the temporary placement centre neither identified their agency nor explained to anyone the purpose of their visit. The troops distributed themselves throughout the entire temporary placement centre building beating everyone they happened to encounter on their way regardless of whether it were a man, a woman, or a child.

Below are several examples:

Akhmed Saluev, aged 40. Threatening with weapons, the troops threw him on to the floor and beat him up for his attempt to help a 60-year old woman who had lost consciousness from fear.

Said-Magomed Chibilyaev, aged approximately 60, was hit heavily on the shoulder with a machine gun butt for refusing to lie down on the floor.

Khava Takaeva aged 22. Soldiers hit her in the face when she stepped out of her room having heard the noise in the building. They then forced her to go back into her room poking at her with the barrels of their machine guns.

After forcing open the door to the rooms of the Dakaevs family, the troops forced Akhmed Dakaev out and dragged him towards the crowd of other people. His sisters, Luiza, aged

18, and Elina, aged 15, tried to find out what was going on but the troops hit them in their faces and pushed them back into their room, hitting them with butts of their machine guns.

Zargan Mutaeva, born 1961, was hit in the face when she attempted to pass to A.Dakaev his passport in case there should be an inspection.

Imani Visaitova, aged 12, who was in the corridor on the third floor at the time, tried to reach her room when she saw the strangers in masks, but when the troops reached her one of them hit her in the face with his hand and shoved her to the side with the barrel of his machine gun so violently that she was thrown and hit herself against the wall. The girl remained in a state of shock for some time.

Later a representative of the temporary placement centre administration in charge of residents' registration came out of her room in response to the noise. The troops ordered her to lie down on the floor but she vehemently refused to comply. She declared, "I can see by your eyes that you are Chechen." After that the troops ordered her in Chechen in a more civilized manner to go to her room .

No longer hiding the fact that they were Chechens the troops began to leave the temporary placement centre. None of the residents was detained. The security guards received their pistol back and were ordered to stay put. Official authorities of Chechnya did not respond to the incident in any way. According to the victims nobody came to see them afterwards, neither from law enforcement bodies, nor from the television, nor from the presidential administration, The incident was simply ignored.

The temporary placement centre residents petitioned president A.Kadyrov and one of the leaders of the United Russia party, F.Klintsevich, asking that they should be protected from the arbitrariness of the law enforcement agencies. These petitions remained unanswered.

This was not the first armed attack on this temporary placement centre. On the night of 26 May 2003 the centre was surrounded by armoured cars and a large number of soldiers from the Khankala military base. The troops broke into rooms and captured young people who happened to be in. The captives included several girls who the troops wanted to take away with them. Fortunately, a group of Chechens – representatives of a special designation division – who were visiting relatives and spending the night at the centre interfered. Having realized that it would be impossible to take away the captives without running the risk of being punished the troops released them all.

<u>Memorial Human Rights Centre</u>

20 THE WAR IN THE CAUCASUS AND PEACE IN RUSSIA

Alexander Cherkasov, Memorial Human Rights Centre

The second war in the Chechen Republic has been going on for more than four years. Throughout this period Chechnya has seen an endless series of war crimes and crimes against humanity. During the initial months of the combat, the crimes took the form of blanket non-selective bombings and shellings, in which thousands of people were killed. The total death toll of the first war of 1994–1996 is estimated at about 50 thousand civilians, and of the second war – from 10 to 20 thousand.

For several years so-called mop-up or cleansing operations were carried out in towns and villages of Chechnya. These operations involved massive non-selective violence, 'disappearances' of people, and sometimes mass killings. It is impossible to say how many people were detained, beaten up, tortured and abused. Even more were robbed and humiliated. It is impossible to say how many women were raped.

There have been relatively few mopping-up operations during the past year but 'disappearances' and extra-judicial executions continue. People are detained at night and taken away by gunmen in camouflage and riding APCs. The total number of the 'disappeared' during the second war exceeds 3,000 – and that is from official sources.

It should be noted that Chechnya is a small territory – just one thousandth that of Russia. The current ratio of Chechen population to the population of Russia is about 1:250. Russia itself does not have an enviable historical record with regard to the scale of deaths in wartime, nor with regard to governmental oppression in peacetime. The situation in Chechnya can be put into some kind of perspective by pointing out that over the past decade Chechnya, in terms of the proportion of the population killed or disappeared, has lived through the equivalent of half of the second world war and the whole of the period of Stalin's repression.

Yes, terrorists exist; they commit crimes, crimes against their own people. The evidence is provided by the explosions in Znamenskoe, Mozdok, and Moscow, and in the hostage-taking in Dubrovka in 2003 (and in Beslan after this book was written, Eds). Does that mean that the authorities' statements about the 'counter-terrorist' operation' in Chechnya are meaningful?

It has to be understood that the Russian authorities give words Orwellian meanings. Counter-terrorism is a word that has come to be used to avoid recognition of political problems and as a pretext for state terror. Denial of the existence of separatism as a political aspiration supports the use of counter-terrorist terminology as cover for a war against separatists. In fact such problems are political and ought to be tackled by Russia politically.

A 'counter-terrorist operation' might be expected to mean a highly selective operation. The objective of an operation labelled as counter-terrorist should be, first and foremost, to save human lives, and then to capture or destroy terrorists. But the hierarchy of values of Russian law enforcement agencies is not focused on saving lives. Law enforcement agencies try to achieve their goals at any human cost. The evidence of this is the scores of thousands killed in Chechnya, the 130 people who died in the Nord-Ost tragedy and the many hundreds killed in Beslan.

Orwellisms such as 'counter-terrorist operation' can be found in almost every governmental statement on Chechnya. They speak of 'targeted hits' that in fact were blanket and non-selective bombings and shelling. They speak of 'humanitarian corridors' that were corridors of death where the roads were continuously bombed and shelled.

The authorities speak of restoring constitutional order, but in reality a legal vacuum has been created in Chechnya. Law enforcement agencies have been given the opportunity to operate in an even more cruel and uncontrolled ways than in Stalin's times. The Russians have even invented a new word – siloviki (the powerful ones) – to describe former KGB men and military officers who, with tacit governmental approval, attack, arrest, detain and kill. Crimes in Chechnya, by siloviki and by others, go unpunished. Victims' claims are not accepted. Relatives' protests about disappearances are ignored. Only a few dozen cases have been considered in Chechen courts of law. Only a few perpetrators have been sentenced. The scale of lawlessness cannot but help provoke new crimes.

Russia is waging a war and whatever is happening in Chechnya influences the life of the Russian Federation as a whole. Personnel of the law enforcement agencies from other regions go to Chechnya. The experience of uncontrolled and unpunished violence cannot but leave its traces. The experience of routinely violating the law also leaves its scars. Russia itself is threatened by lawlessness and the return of a totalitarian past that has already settled on one thousandth of its territory.

What is to be done? We should use each and every opportunity to talk about crimes and the impunity of the perpetrators. We should stress that leaders of democratic countries must not make friends with the spiritual successors of Molotov and Ribbentrop.

Big bloodshed goes hand in hand with a big lie. The Russian mass media provided practically no coverage of the second war in Chechnya, or to be more precise, practically no truthful coverage. The media reproduce official press releases but do not in the case of Chechnya report matters of life and death. Such matters are described with the use of official lies. Some journalists and outlets do cover important events and try to write the truth. But such publications are marginal. There is no place in the media for the nationwide debate on the problem of Chechnya that is so desperately needed.

How did this happen? The second war started with seemingly accurate reporting. In Dagestan, after the invasion by Basaev detachments in August/September of 1999, the Russian military, for the first time in decades, were operating as, and were perceived as, liberators. Journalists and their audiences wanted good news and they got what they wanted. There was euphoria about a small-scale victorious war. But when the war moved on into Chechnya strict censorship was imposed. At first it was censorship by the public, 'How could you write bad things about our glorious army?'

Then, blatant lies were substituted for information. For instance, on 21 October 1999, tactical missiles tipped with ball-scattering cluster warheads killed more than a hundred people and wounded hundreds more – most of them in the market place. The then chairman of the government of the Russian Federation, Vladimir Putin, said at a news conference, "I can confirm that an explosion did take place in Grozny in a market place. But I would like to draw the attention of the press to the fact that it is not just an ordinary market. We are facing a weapons market here - that's the way it is referred to in Grozny. Actually it is a weapons warehouse, an arms supply base. This place is one of the headquarters of the bandit detachments. We do not rule out the possibility that this explosion resulted from clashes between rival groupings."

Such 'truthfulness' remains a distinguishing feature of our president.

Then came police censorship. The RFE/RL journalist Andrei Babitsky was detained by Russian law enforcement officers, and went through 'filtration' in Chernokozovo. It was said that he had then been handed over to Chechen resistance forces, but in fact he was handed to a detachment controlled by the FSB. He managed to get to freedom, but was quickly arrested again on the basis of a forged accusation. After that, only the most foolhardy journalists continued to write objective reports about what was happening in Chechnya.

The second war in Chechnya started the current dominance of 'good news' in all the media outlets. Independent TV channels NTV, TV-6, TVS were either liquidated or became subject to control by various methods. Other victims followed. Within a few years, a comprehensive mopping-up operation was successfully completed in arena of the mass media.

Objective information is non-existent, not only on Chechnya, but on many other problems vital for Russia. Objective information has been replaced with silence, meaningless words and official lies. Only very few journalists and outlets raise important problems and dare to tell the truth. But they are marginal. Almost no important problems are discussed publicly.

We need solidarity and pressure. First, it goes without saying that independent outlets, independent journalists and non-governmental organisations must be supported. Such support will help them to get out of their marginalised state. If we can help them get in touch with European NGOs and mass media, they will gain a forum that is at least a substitute for discussion. This could be an avenue of escape from their marginality in the Russian information environment.

Second, it is essential to bring some pressure to bear upon Russia both with a specific slogan, 'Stop lying about Chechnya', and with demands for restoration of freedom of speech.

Third, our colleagues – human rights activists from democratic countries – should exert pressure on their politicians engaged in various negotiations with their Russian counterparts: 'If they tell lies about Chechnya, how can we trust them in other things?'

Through their control of information the Russian authorities acquired tools for the manipulation of the political environment. The second Chechen war made Putin – at the time a little known bureaucrat – president of the country.

In the autumn of 1999, Russia got a leader who, in contrast to the lethargic and unsteady Yeltsin, displayed some response to current events, who was saying something and actually doing something. The details appeared to be of no significance. Putin met the popular need to have an authority in power. The liking was mutual but perverting – as is commonly the case with power relationships.

In the autumn of 1999, in the atmosphere of counter-terrorist hysteria created by explosions in residential buildings in several Russian cities, to show any doubts about the policies of the powers-that-be seemed completely out of the question. Yabloko was the only political party that did so and its rating plummeted immediately. Supporting the war was likened to supporting Putin - and the other way round. As a result pro-Putin parties won a majority in the state Duma – the lower house of the Russian parliament. In March 2000 Putin himself became president.

However it is impossible to win two election campaigns separated by four years under the same slogan of a 'small-scale victorious war'. That is why in the course of the election campaigns of 2003 and 2004 the word Chechnya has always come linked with the word 'settlement'. But 'settlement' is another word from Orwell's vocabulary. Instead of a political process we are dealing with a puppet theatre.

The federal side, as emphasised, referred to separatists as terrorists. That provided a rationale to cease any dialogue with Aslan Maskhadov, president of the Chechen Republic of Ichkeria, recognized by Russia in 1997 when Yeltsin was receiving him at the Kremlin. No negotiations were held. Instead of talks with separatist leaders the Russian authorities offered a 'dialogue' with their own protégé, Akhmat Kadyrov. Instead of an amnesty for rank-and-file members of armed Chechen groups, the authorities came up with an offer for them to join the personal guard units of Kadyrov himself, under his guarantees of their loyalty.

The results of the 2002 All-Russia census were presented as proof of the normalization of the situation. In October 2002 the Census in Chechnya found 1,088 thousand people, many more than prior to the second Chechen war, but that figure is actually an indicator of the scale of disaster – the product of double counting of some of the massive refugee movement. The RF state Committee of Statistics operated with a figure of 815 thousand for the same year. Just two months earlier officials in Chechnya had been using a different, more realistic figure of 600 thousand.

The double counting in the Census was actually used as a propaganda resource. The hundreds of thousands of 'dead souls' that were part of the overstatement of population were used to overstate the size of the electorate – in the March 2003 'referendum' on the Chechen Constitution, in the October election for Chechen president, and in the federal parliamentary elections of December 2003. But the big lie in this case does not sully the truth. The use of inflated population figures makes the falsification of the election statistics more obvious. The 83% majority reported for the presidential election of October 2003, for example, implies that 380 thousand voted for Kadyrov – a figure that is implausible in the light of the exodus of population and is quite inconsistent with other official statistics.

The elections in Chechnya give a glimpse of a controlled democracy – a model of what may now be being imposed on the whole of Russia.

In accordance with international standards, conducting elections, referenda, or censuses during a war or a state of emergency is impossible. But the Russian authorities claim that they are not waging war. They are carrying out a 'counter-terrorist operation.' The state of emergency was not declared officially, though *de facto* it's been in place for years. As a result, terror *per se* has become the key element of the election campaign.

The election results had been programmed, everything was controlled from the Kremlin. Real opponents, that is the separatists, were at an opportune moment removed from the list of candidates. In the course of the 'election campaign' Chechens loyal to the Kremlin who could successfully compete with Kadyrov were erased from the list. Khussein Dzhabrailov was threatened, Aslambek Aslakhanov was offered a lucrative position, and the last one – Malik Saidullaev was withdrawn from the race on the basis of a court decision. That's it. The mopping-up operation in the political arena was over, only the extras remained. The extras were subdued by federal propaganda as well as by a variety of local pressures.

The meeting of Kadyrov and Putin that was telecast by all channels is a form of propaganda specifically prohibited by the Russian election law. And the pre-election trip by Kadyrov to the United States? (That was not crowned with a handshake - president Bush got squeamish...). We don't have to add that such promotional actions for other candidates in the Chechen presidential 'race' were unthinkable.

How much does all this differ from the overall situation in Russia? Shakespeare wrote about the world being a stage and people being players. But Russia has become a puppet show, where the creative freedom of the actor is supplanted by the controlled dance of the ventriloquist's dummy. Opponents – parties or individuals – are removed from the political environment under false pretexts, only clowns remain. Terror remains an extreme measure in the political process – but the Chechnya example demonstrates how easily an appetite for terror comes in the course of a meal. Pressure on recalcitrant actors is a common practice. Courts in Russia make the 'necessary' decisions at the 'right' time. For the favoured candidate – any kind of promotion, including meetings with the president with talks about a rain of gold pouring into the region if that candidate wins. 'Alien' candidates face confiscation of election materials. The predetermined victory of Valentina Matvienko in the gubernatorial election in St.Petersburg provides a parallel case to that of Kadyrov in Chechnya.

What's to be done? We must use every opportunity to remind people in Russia and abroad of the farce of Kadyrov's election. Such reminders are for the benefit of Chechnya, Russia and the West.

The problems of Chechnya are an extreme version of the problems of Russia. The negative experience gained in Chechnya threatens to spread throughout Russia. These are becoming European problems and problems for the whole international community. Refugees from Chechnya are not a major problem. Refugees are often a valuable resource – like the Jewish refugees of the last century who became scattered throughout the world. The problem belongs primarily to the Russian authorities whose ruling style may be being borrowed by those in power in other countries. There is a danger of mutual reinforcement of totalitarian solutions to what has already being labelled a war against terror. This threat should not be underestimated. It should be countered here and now.

RECENT BOOKS ON CHECHNYA

Gall, Carlotta and Thomas de Waal (1997) *Chechnya: A Small Victorious War*, Pan Books.

Lieven, Anatol (1998) *Chechnya: Tombstone of Russian Power*, Yale University Press.

Dunlop, John B (1998) *Russia Confronts Chechnya: Roots of a Separatist Conflict*, Cambridge University Press.

Gall, Carlotta and Thomas de Waal (2000) *Chechnya: Calamity in the Caucasus*, New York University Press.

Nivat, Anne (2001) *Chienne de Guerre: A Woman Reporter Behind the Lines of the War in Chechnya*, PublicAffairs.

Politkovskaya, Anna (2001) *A Dirty War: A Russian Reporter in Chechnya*, Harvill Press.

Evangelista, Matthew (2003) *The Chechen Wars: Will Russia Go the Way of the Soviet Union?* The Brookings Institution.

Goltz, Thomas (2003) *Chechnya Diary: A War Correspondent's Story of Surviving the War in Chechnya*, Thomas Dunne.

Politkovskaya, Anna (2003) *A Small Corner of Hell: Dispatches from Chechnya*, University of Chicago Press.

Meier, Andrew (2004) *To the Heart of a Conflict*, W.W.Norton.

Tishkov, Valery (2004) *Chechnya: Life in a War-torn Society*, University of California Press.

Orr, Michael (2005) *Russia's Wars with Chechnya, 1994-2003*, Osprey (Essential Histories Series).

ON-LINE RESOURCES

The Moscow Helsinki Group website at http://www.mhg.ru/ is a major archive with good search facilities and many pages in English – including an earlier version of this book.

Memorial Human Rights Centre website at http://www.memo.ru includes many reports on events in Chechnya and international activities related to Chechnya. In English and German.

The Caucasian Knot a partnership project of the Memorial Society website at http://www.eng.kavkaz.memo.ru/ gives news and background information with promise of expansion of coverage of Chechnya.

The Chechnya section of the Kavkaz-Center Islamic News Agency at http://kavkazcenter.com/ or http://kavkaz/org.uk gives hourly reports of events in Chechnya in Turkish as well as Russian and English. There are many contributions from a Muslim perspective.

A seemingly official website at http://www.chechnyafree.ru tells in Russian and English of Chechen culture and other peaceful aspects of the law abiding majority of the Chechen people.

Johnson's Russian List at http://www.cdi.org/russia/johnson/default.cfm gives almost daily reports in English about Russia mostly from non-Russian sources, and may well give more reports on Chechnya than the Russian press. The list includes occasional reports on Chechya edited by Stephen D. Shenfield – for example, Issue No. 29, January 2005, *Chechnya and Russia, a post-Beslan symposium*. Johnson's list accepts contributions from individuals so supports discussion.

An email discussion list in English at http://groups.yahoo.com/group/chechnya-sl/ established in 1995, has about 800 members with several hundred messages every month. Based on individual contributions. Moderation by Norbert Strade, based in Denmark, maintains coherence.

INDEX

This index has been made automatically. For reasons made evident on pages 40-41 of Chapter 3, the aim has been to include at least the family name for all individuals mentioned in the text. We apologise for any misspellings and for any names that have been missed.

Abalayev, 65
Abdul-Wahid, 74
Abkhasia, 34
Achkhoi-Martan, 38, 48, 56, 57, 59, 74, 75, 77, 101, 117, 128, 130, 132, 171, 175
Adam, 158, 214, 218, 254, 258
Adayeva, 87
Ahmatukaev, 131
Akhmatov, 113, 118
Akuyev, 216
Al Qaeda, 23, 240
Alaudinov, 99
Alavidze, 173
al-Barami, 181
Aldamov, 219
Alexeeva, 118
Ali-Atgeriev, 83
Alihadjiev, 82, 83
Aliyev, 218
Alkhanov, 17, 70, 114
Alkhan-Yurt, 84, 91, 93, 96, 123, 180, 216, 230
Amadaev, 112
Amaev, 77, 78
Amagov, 98, 216
amnesty, 43, 76, 83, 103, 269
Anasov, 168
Argun, 38, 50, 131, 162, 167, 171, 172, 259
Arsakhanov, Abdul Kerim, 17, 70, 128, 140, 169, 172–174, 179, 209
Arsakhanov, Buvai-Sari, 129
Arsanukaev, Mukhamed, 17, 86, 120–125
Arsanukayev, 64
Askhabov, 78
Aslakhanov, Aslambek, 11, 17, 44, 48, 49, 66, 75, 80, 84, 87, 89, 95, 103, 107, 111, 118, 120, 125, 183, 184, 270
Assinovskaya, 41, 87, 88, 97, 99, 140, 149, 170, 179, 187, 188, 191, 220, 259
Astamirov, 87
Atsaev, 114, 148
Aushev, 17, 20, 198
Avtorkhanov, 32
Azarsanov, 260
Azieyv, 219

Babitsky, 158, 267
Bachaev, 256, 257
Bachiyev, 219
Badalov, Ruslan, 185–189
Baisarov, 217
Balyan, 42
Bamut, 214
Baraev, 260
Bart, 179, 183, 185–189
Barznukaev, 74
Basaev, Shamil, 9, 15–18, 34, 43, 63, 65, 82, 83, 114, 226, 232, 236, 243, 266
Bashirov, 47
Batalov, 101
Baucher, 173, 180
Bella, 183, 187
Bersanov, 259
Bersinkayev, 216
Birlant, 245
Bislan Umarov, 41
Biybulatov, Khusein, 17, 49, 50, 70, 71, 75, 87, 117, 142, 144, 151, 179, 211
Boltiyev, 70
Bonetti, 140
Borisovna, 241

Bugaev, Abdula, 16, 17, 50–53, 56, 75, 87, 118, 142, 144, 152, 168, 175, 179, 211
Buraev, Shamil, 16, 18, 48, 50, 56–59, 71, 73, 75, 87, 111, 117, 142, 144, 151, 175, 178, 179, 211

Camp David, 130, 222
census, 12, 21, 35, 190–197, 205–209, 210, 269
Central Election Commission(s), 41, 42, 70, 78, 114, 117, 147, 169, 171, 172, 208, 209, 210
Centre Demos, 12, 25, 56, 91, 106, 122, 150, 157, 162, 183, 222, 231
Chaika, 132, 223
Chechen Committee for National Salvation, 29, 86, 90, 99–101, 112, 113, 116, 129, 130, 171, 185
Chechen State TV and Radio, 118
Chechen TV, 77, 129, 157
Chechnya Election Commission(s), 44, 45, 48, 63, 74, 77, 117, 119, 125, 128, 129, 140, 170, 172, 173
checkpoint, 39, 41, 47, 70, 88, 91, 112, 131, 134, 186, 188, 189, 233, 234, 236, 237, 239, 254
checkpoints, 39, 40, 141, 147, 148, 162, 180, 187, 188, 234, 236, 247
Cherkasov, 18, 30, 190, 264
Chernyaev, 85
Chibilyaev, 262
Chiri-Yurt, 41, 86, 116, 160, 176, 249, 259
Chizhov, 140
CIASSR, Chechen Ingush Autonomous Soviet Socialist Republic, 17, 21, 50, 53, 191
CIS, Commonweath of Independent States, 21, 32, 41, 114, 117, 172
civil rights, 12, 205
civilian casualties, 34, 198, 201–204
cleansing, 54, 199, 206, 264
cleansing operations, mop-ups, 21, 22, 200
Communist, 34
Council of Europe, 115, 117, 225
Council of PACE, Parliamentary Assembly of the Council of Europe, 229
counter-terror, 44, 49, 55, 56, 63, 65, 66, 69, 106, 114, 118, 199, 205, 230, 265, 268, 269

CSU, Chechen State University, 21, 67, 118, 129

Dadashev, 216
Dadayev, 214, 218
Dagestan, 15, 17, 18, 21, 30, 35, 63, 65, 82, 131, 188, 205, 227, 266
Dakaev, 139, 170, 262, 263
Danilenko, 209
Danish Refugee Council, 115, 116, 198, 207, 208
Dashoukayev, 72, 73
de Waal, 273
Demilkhanov, 256, 257
Deniyev, 180
Dikayev, 100
disappeared, 30, 35, 40, 83, 99, 103, 105, 111, 121, 122, 180, 182, 199, 203, 216, 220, 237, 248, 251, 252, 264
Djantaev, 119
Dokamaldaev, 168
Dovletukaev, 118
Duba-Yurt, 100, 176, 237, 238, 249, 251, 259
Dudaev, Dzhokhar, 15, 18, 20, 32–34, 52, 83, 193, 227, 258
Dudayev, 218
Dudurkayev, 221
Duma, 34, 43, 48, 49, 66, 75, 76, 89, 96, 111, 115, 145, 146, 171, 190, 208–210, 250, 259, 261, 268
Dzantiev, 131
Dzhabrailov, Khussein, 11, 18, 35, 48, 75–80, 84, 95, 107, 118, 120, 124, 125, 183, 184, 270
Dzhamaldaev, 46
Dzholaeva, 161

Edelkhanova, 70
Edilkhanov, 77
Election Commission(s), 6, 7, 11, 17, 36, 62, 70, 71, 76, 78, 80, 84, 89, 114, 117, 119, 120, 126, 144, 145, 152, 165–179, 209, 240–246, 261
electorate, 38, 58, 73, 125, 191, 208–211
Elmurzaev, 102, 237, 240
Elmurzayev, 220
Elzhiev, 57, 75
emigration, 193, 194, 195, 209
Eniyev, 216
Ermolov, 30
Eskirhanov, 77

European Union, 42, 128, 140, 181
Farisov, 171
Federal Migration Service, 193, 195, 197, 201
forced migrants, 113, 149, 179, 189, 190, 193, 195–200, 205, 207, 217, 219, 262
FSB, Federal Safety Bureau, 20–30, 31, 47, 73, 77, 101, 219, 220, 233, 267

Gafuraev, 114
Gaidar, 33
Gainutdin, 64
Gaitamirova, 214, 258
Gakayeva, 129
Gall, 273
Ganayev, 130
Gantamirov, Beslan, 18, 46, 48, 75, 77, 78, 113
Gayev, 260
Gelayev, 218
Gelman, 202
Goragorsk, 37, 39, 221
Gorbachev, 32, 96
Gorky, 101
Grozneftegaz, 48, 75, 116
Grozny, 15, 18, 21, 22, 33, 34, 38–49, 56, 65, 67, 71, 75–80, 86–95, 100–107, 114, 116, 118, 119, 122–126, 129–131, 139–141, 147–152, 158–162, 169–173, 178, 194, 200–205, 209–217, 220, 221, 230, 234–239, 243, 250, 251, 254–258, 260–262, 267
Gryzlov, 18, 44, 74, 172
Guchigova, 113
Gudermes, 45, 64–66, 76, 94, 102, 147, 148, 175, 258, 261
Guldiman, 9
Gunukbaev, 86

Hadjiyev, 219
Harmam, 140
Human Rights Committee, 35, 223, 224, 228–231
Human Rights Watch, 149, 201, 203
humanitarian aid, 39, 128, 131, 186, 198, 200, 206–208
humanitarian corridors, 199, 203, 265

Ibragimov, 216, 260

Ichkeria, 15, 19, 21, 25, 40, 42, 51, 54, 61, 65, 68, 81, 82, 99, 102–104, 113, 124, 132, 149, 157, 173, 180, 193, 196, 208, 213, 268
Idigov, 74
IDP, Internally displaced person, 21
Iliyasov, 205
Ilyasov, 141
iman, 21, 57, 64, 219, 260
Ingushetia, 15, 17, 21, 22, 26, 33, 39, 87, 101, 113, 131, 140, 149, 150, 153, 155, 165, 179, 183, 185–191, 192, 195, 198–201, 205, 206, 212, 213, 219, 221, 225, 252, 253
intelligentsia, 21, 53, 60, 67
international observers, 46, 114, 171
investment, 32, 42, 68
Irbaiyev, 102
Isaevna, 242
Isigov, 98
Islamov, 88, 260
Israilov, 70, 217
Ivan the Terrible, 196, 201

jihad, 64, 66, 120
Judd, Lord, 186, 205, 207

Kadyrov, 5, 6, 9, 10, 11, 12, 15–18, 20, 25–27, 35, 38, 43–52, 55–77, 82–88, 92–99, 102–106, 111, 113, 116, 117, 120–130, 134–146, 149–152, 157, 165–176, 179–185, 200, 211, 217, 221–240, 244–246, 249–251, 263, 269, 270
Kadyrov, Ramzan, 10, 66, 129
Kagirmanov, 107, 108, 110
Kaimov, 78
Kalamanov, 66, 195, 197
Kasyanov, 62
Katraev, 76
kavkaz.memo.ru, 29, 36, 44, 50, 53, 59, 60, 66, 67, 75–87, 88, 89, 97, 104, 113–120, 128–133, 140–143, 147–149, 170–174, 179–181, 211
Kavkaz-1, 39, 91, 233–236, 247
Kazantsev, 66
KGB, 19, 21, 80, 265
Khabuev, 260
Khadizov, 257
Khadzhimuradov, 259
Khaidukayev, 172
Khambiev, 65, 147

Khanbiev, 149
Khanchukaev, Avkhat, 18, 48, 50, 56, 67, 75, 87, 114, 118, 144, 151, 179, 211
Khasbulatov, Ruslan, 18, 44–46, 75, 237, 238
Khattab, 18, 63, 65, 137, 243
Khayauri, 86
Khazakhstan, 15, 22, 64, 67, 96
Kheda, 124
Khildikhoroev, 101
Khurikova, 141
Klintsevich, Frants, 19, 112, 119, 242, 247, 255, 263
Kravchenko, 45
Kremlin, 25, 26, 27, 44
Kurchaloi, 38, 64, 65, 94, 129, 178, 214, 215

law enforcement agencies, 22, 33, 65, 77, 88, 90, 96, 114, 119, 130, 172, 194, 200, 203, 205, 206, 214–221, 234, 239, 248, 256–266
lawlessness, 10, 11, 145
Lebed, 15, 19, 65, 204
Lieven, 273
Lokshina, Tanya, 19, 25, 56, 91, 106, 122, 150, 157, 162, 183, 222, 231

Madagova, 102
Magamaev, 102
Maigov, 19, 82, 180, 201, 237, 238, 239
Makhauri, 87
Manilov, 204
Maskhadov census, 196
Maskhadov, Aslan, 9, 15, 16, 19, 20, 42, 43, 49, 58, 65, 68, 81, 82, 83, 88, 97, 113, 114, 117, 118, 132, 149, 157, 158, 180, 193, 196, 208, 212, 225–227, 238, 268
Memorial Human Rights Centre, 12, 18, 29, 30, 46, 47, 76–78, 87, 88, 100–103, 112–116, 119, 139, 141, 148, 172, 177–182, 185, 190, 202, 203, 214–221, 258, 264, 274
Merzaev, 119
Mezhiyev, 215
Migiev, 75
migration, 186, 189, 190, 193, 195, 197, 200, 204
Mikhailov, 31
Milan, 44, 75, 96

Mnatsakanyan, Alexander, 5, 6, 19, 37, 134
Mohathir, 223
Mokhchaev, 159
mop-up, cleansing, 21, 22, 43, 101, 199, 216, 218, 242, 244, 248, 253, 264, 267, 270
Moscow Helsinki Group, 12, 19, 25, 28, 56, 91, 106, 107, 118, 122, 123, 150, 157, 162, 170, 175, 183, 222, 231, 274
mosque, 102, 128, 140, 160, 216, 217, 241
Movlatov, 49
Mudarov, 216
mufti, 22, 58, 64–66, 74, 231
Mufti, 64, 65, 171
Mukhayev, 219
Musaev, 237, 239
Musayev, 100
Musayeva, 88
Musikhov, 219
Mutaliev, 260

Nakaev, 148
Nasukhanov, 74
Nazirov, 102
Nazran, 39, 150, 212, 252, 254
NGOs, Non Government Organizations, 12, 22, 28, 179, 225–228, 267
Nivat, 273
Nord-Ost, 228, 265
Novye Aldy, 230
Novye Atagi, 40, 65
Nozha-Yurt, 38

October election, 26, 189, 228, 231, 246
Ojera, 179
Omaev, 74
OMON, 79
ORB-2, 22, 260
Ortsa, 67
OSCE, Organisation for Security and Co-operation in Europe, 9, 22, 35, 42, 115, 117, 132, 147, 179, 205, 207, 208, 229
Ossetia, 21, 22, 33, 131, 193
Ovchukov, 259

PACE, Parliamentary Assembly of the Council of Europe, 22, 35, 132, 147, 207

Paizullaev, Nikolai, 11, 19, 75, 87, 89, 104–111, 114, 117, 120, 126, 144, 179, 211
Pamfilova, 84
Pankisi Gorge, 141, 173
Parliamentary Assembly of the Council of Europe, 129
parliamentary elections, 33–35, 146, 169, 231, 233, 238, 250, 269
People's Party, 237, 243, 246
Politkovskaya, Anna, 19, 44, 140, 273
polling stations, 38, 41, 42, 45, 119, 128, 129, 132, 140–142, 145, 148, 151, 159, 162, 163, 169–177, 208–212, 231, 237–240, 243, 247
Popov, Anatoly, 19, 45, 46, 48, 68, 77, 78, 140, 181
Popov, Sergei, 102
Putin, 11, 17, 18, 19, 20, 23, 36, 42–44, 61, 62, 66, 71, 80, 81, 84, 88, 89, 95–99, 103, 111, 116–118, 121, 122, 128, 129, 138, 163, 172, 195, 196, 222, 223, 226, 228, 231, 235, 242, 246, 249, 250, 267–270

Qatar, 9

Raduev, 157
Rakhimov, 223
Rammel, 174
Ramzaev, 118
referendum, 26, 32, 36–43, 60, 61, 74, 75, 109, 115, 131, 149, 161, 167, 174, 184, 190, 208, 209, 231, 249, 269
refugee camp, 39, 179, 183, 206
refugees, 12, 21, 38, 39, 87, 116, 131, 141, 173, 179, 183, 184, 185, 186, 187, 188, 189, 190, 195, 196, 197, 198, 199, 200, 202, 205, 206, 269, 271
Rhodley, 228
RNE, Russian National Unity Party, 22, 91
Rodina, 250
Rogozin, 42, 250
RSFSR, Russian Soviet Federative Socialist Republic, 22, 33
Rubanov, 202, 204
rule of law, 25, 54, 169, 230, 248
Russian Federation, 26, 32, 35, 46, 48, 50, 59, 61, 62, 65, 70–73, 92, 97–99, 105, 112, 114, 115, 119, 122, 123, 132, 140, 145, 146, 147, 169, 180, 198, 202, 212, 226–231, 239, 249, 259, 266, 267
Russian State Duma, 119
Russian-Chechen Friendship Society, 29, 74–76, 86–88, 90, 112, 116, 128, 130, 131, 148, 181, 214–216

Saayev, 212
Saduev, Kudus, 19, 48, 75, 87, 118, 142, 144, 151, 179, 211
Saidayev, 101
Said-Emin, 218, 221, 248, 250
Saidullaev, Malik, 11, 19, 35, 44, 46, 48, 75, 78–80, 84–99, 107, 109, 111, 118–127, 143, 144, 179, 183, 184, 270
Saidullaev, Milan, 91, 93, 94, 123
Saiev, 98
Saipuyev, 220
Salaudi, 43
Saligov, 204
Saluev, 262
Sanaeva, 141
Sanarbekov, 47
Satuyev, 49
security zones, 199
separatists, 32, 34, 35, 83, 158, 265, 268, 270
Sergei Khaykin Institute, 82
Serzhen-Yurt, 73, 74, 139, 148, 180, 181, 214, 216, 253
Shabalkin, 49, 114
Shabdurasulov, 190
Shabiev, 169
Shali, 37, 50, 73, 74, 78, 100, 101, 102, 111, 116, 130, 131, 139, 140, 151, 175, 176, 177, 180, 199, 209, 214, 216, 259
Shamanov, 19, 84, 197, 198, 248
Shangareev, 171
Sharoi, 37, 211, 219
Shatoi, 130, 219, 220, 235, 236, 237, 257
Shefer, 179
Sheinin, 228
Shevardnadze, 117
Shirvani, 219
Shuaipov, 178
siloviki, 21, 22, 181, 213, 265
Skotnikov, 223
Solzhenitsyn, 32

SPS, Soyuz Pravyki Sil, 22, 57, 72
Staropromyslovsky, 130, 161, 171, 215, 218, 221, 230, 239, 242, 257
Starye Atagi, 46, 47, 238, 249, 256, 259
State Department, 173, 180, 222
statistics, 12, 141, 178, 190, 195, 196, 203, 204, 207, 209, 269
Sterligov, 96
Suleimanov, 213, 257
Sultanov, 258
Sultygov, 115, 116, 202, 228
Sunzha, 38, 77, 87, 97–101, 113, 148, 170, 179, 191, 201, 215, 259, 260
Supreme Court, 57, 71, 80, 84, 89, 92, 110, 111, 119, 120, 122, 123, 127, 143
Supreme Soviet, 32, 33, 45
survey, 44, 95, 110, 132, 202, 207, 208
Susaev, 97, 99

TAC, Temporary Accomodation Centre, 22
Takaeva, 262
Tambov, 236, 237
Tarasov, 96
Tatarstan, 33
Tatayev, 216
Temirov, 81, 82
Temporary Accommodation Centre, 183
Three Fools monument, 239
tiep, 23
Troshev, 248
Tsitsayev, 76
Tsuev, 19, 49, 75, 87, 111
Tsybaeva, 168
turnout, 35, 37, 41, 75, 162, 167, 169, 172, 175, 178, 179, 190, 208–212, 228, 238, 240, 241, 242, 245, 250
Tutakov, 82
TV, 40, 47, 52, 61, 65, 68, 71–78, 87, 88, 96, 105, 111, 115, 118, 124, 125, 137, 138, 141, 149, 153, 157–160, 165, 178, 186, 197, 240, 250, 267

UAZ, Ulyanovsk Avtomobil Zavod, 23, 40, 76, 78, 101, 102, 130, 172, 180, 186, 213, 214, 215, 217, 218, 220, 221, 256, 257, 258, 259, 262
Udugov, 157
Umarov, 129
Umarov, Ruslan, 5, 6, 20, 53, 60, 67, 104, 143

Umarov, Vicit, 40
UN, 35, 44, 117, 132, 171, 198, 222, 223, 225, 228, 229, 230, 231
unemployment, 32, 194, 206
United Russia Party, 18, 19–23, 44, 57, 91, 112, 119, 231, 233, 237, 239–242, 245–256, 261, 263
Urus-Martan, 37, 39, 77, 86, 87, 112, 113, 115, 141, 162, 165, 166, 172, 175, 180, 213–218, 238, 253, 257–261
US, 114, 117, 118, 128, 130, 173, 180, 270
Usmaev, 76

Vainakh, 23, 161, 191, 193, 194, 201, 206, 239
Vakhitov, 78
Varandy, 160, 244, 245, 246
Vedeno, 38, 74, 86, 90, 99, 112, 159, 180–182, 212, 214, 220, 237
Vesedov, 216
Veshnyakov, 114, 117, 147, 171, 210
Vesti Respubliki, 47, 78, 114
Virushevsky, 228
Visaitova, 263
Vitaev, 113
Voloshin, 76
Vozvrashchenie, 122

Wahhabis, 18, 23, 52, 58, 65, 83, 157, 166
Wakhid, 167
Wright, 140

Yabloko, 268
Yakubov, 261
Yamadaev, 65, 119, 215, 240, 242, 247, 255
Yandarbaev, 102
Yandarbiev, Zelimkhan, 20, 52, 65, 109, 227
Yanderbiyev, 9, 16
Yarov, 41, 114, 172
Yastrzhembsky, Sergei, 20, 44, 81, 82, 163, 164
Yeltsin, 15, 20, 32, 33, 34, 68, 268, 269
Yunusov, 112
Yura, 123, 124, 126

Zakayev, 20
Zakriev, 113

Zarkiyev, 49
Zavgaev, Akhmar, 20, 237, 238, 239, 241, 250
Zavgaev, Doka, 20, 32, 33
Zhirinovsky, 34, 250
Zindrina, 141
Znamenskoe, 37, 265
Zyazikov, 20, 186
Zyuganov, 248

Dr. Andreas Umland (Ed.)

SOVIET AND POST-SOVIET POLITICS AND SOCIETY

ISSN 1614-3515

This book series makes available, to the academic community and general public, affordable English-, German- and Russian-language scholarly studies of various *empirical* aspects of the recent history and current affairs of the former Soviet bloc. The series features narrowly focused research on a variety of phenomena in Central and Eastern Europe as well as Central Asia and the Caucasus. It highlights, in particular, so far understudied aspects of late Tsarist, Soviet, and post-Soviet political, social, economic and cultural history from 1905 until today. Topics covered within this focus are, among others, political extremism, the history of ideas, religious affairs, higher education, and human rights protection. In addition, the series covers selected aspects of post-Soviet transitions such as economic crisis, civil society formation, and constitutional reform.

SOVIET AND POST-SOVIET POLITICS AND SOCIETY

Edited by Dr. Andreas Umland

ISSN 1614-3515

1   *Андреас Умланд (ред.)*
    Воплощение Европейской конвенции по правам человека в России
    Философские, юридические и эмпирические исследования
    ISBN 3-89821-387-0

2   *Christian Wipperfürth*
    Russland – ein vertrauenswürdiger Partner?
    Grundlagen, Hintergründe und Praxis gegenwärtiger russischer Außenpolitik
    Mit einem Vorwort von Heinz Timmermann
    ISBN 3-89821-401-X

3   *Manja Hussner*
    Die Übernahme internationalen Rechts in die russische und deutsche Rechtsordnung
    Eine vergleichende Analyse zur Völkerrechtsfreundlichkeit der Verfassungen der Russländischen Föderation
    und der Bundesrepublik Deutschland
    Mit einem Vorwort von Rainer Arnold
    ISBN 3-89821-438-9

4   *Matthew Tejada*
    Bulgaria's Democratic Consolidation and the Kozloduy Nuclear Power Plant (KNPP)
    The Unattainability of Closure
    With a foreword by Richard J. Crampton
    ISBN 3-89821-439-7

5   *Марк Григорьевич Меерович*
    Квадратные метры, определяющие сознание
    Государственная жилищная политика в СССР. 1921 – 1941 гг
    ISBN 3-89821-474-5

6   *Andrei P. Tsygankov, Pavel A. Tsygankov (Eds.)*
    New Directions in Russian International Studies
    ISBN 3-89821-422-2

7   *Марк Григорьевич Меерович*
    Как власть народ к труду приучала
    Жилище в СССР – средство управления людьми. 1917 – 1941 гг.
    С предисловием Елены Осокиной
    ISBN 3-89821-495-8

8   *David J. Galbreath*
    Nation-Building and Minority Politics in Post-Socialist States
    Interests, Influence and Identities in Estonia and Latvia
    With a foreword by David J. Smith
    ISBN 3-89821-467-2

9   *Алексей Юрьевич Безугольный*
    Народы Кавказа в Вооруженных силах СССР в годы Великой Отечественной войны 1941-1945 гг.
    С предисловием Николая Бугая
    ISBN 3-89821-475-3

10 *Вячеслав Лихачев и Владимир Прибыловский (ред.)*
    Русское Национальное Единство, 1990-2000. В 2-х томах
    ISBN 3-89821-523-7

11 *Николай Бугай (ред.)*
    Народы стран Балтии в условиях сталинизма (1940-е – 1950-е годы)
    Документированная история
    ISBN 3-89821-525-3

12 *Ingmar Bredies (Hrsg.)*
    Zur Anatomie der Orange Revolution in der Ukraine
    Wechsel des Elitenregimes oder Triumph des Parlamentarismus?
    ISBN 3-89821-524-5

13 *Anastasia V. Mitrofanova*
    The Politicization of Russian Orthodoxy
    Actors and Ideas
    With a foreword by William C. Gay
    ISBN 3-89821-481-8

14 *Nathan D. Larson*
    Alexander Solzhenitsyn and the Russo-Jewish Question
    ISBN 3-89821-483-4

15 *Guido Houben*
    Kulturpolitik und Ethnizität
    Staatliche Kunstförderung im Russland der neunziger Jahre
    Mit einem Vorwort von Gert Weisskirchen
    ISBN 3-89821-542-3

16 *Leonid Luks*
    Der russische „Sonderweg"?
    Aufsätze zur neuesten Geschichte Russlands im europäischen Kontext
    ISBN 3-89821-496-6

17 *Евгений Мороз*
    История «Мёртвой воды» – от страшной сказки к большой политике
    Политическое неоязычество в постсоветской России
    ISBN 3-89821-551-2

18 *Александр Верховский и Галина Кожевникова (ред.)*
    Этническая и религиозная интолерантность в российских СМИ
    Результаты мониторинга 2001-2004 гг.
    ISBN 3-89821-569-5

19 *Christian Ganzer*
    Sowjetisches Erbe und ukrainische Nation
    Das Museum der Geschichte des Zaporoger Kosakentums auf der Insel Chortycja
    Mit einem Vorwort von Frank Golczewski
    ISBN 3-89821-504-0

20   Эльза-Баир Гучинова
      Помнить нельзя забыть
      Антропология депортационной травмы калмыков
      С предисловием Кэролайн Хамфри
      ISBN 3-89821-506-7

21   Юлия Лидерман
      Мотивы «проверки» и «испытания» в постсоветской культуре
      Советское прошлое в российском кинематографе 1990-х годов
      С предисловием Евгения Марголита
      ISBN 3-89821-511-3

22   Tanya Lokshina, Ray Thomas, Mary Mayer (Eds.)
      The Imposition of a Fake Political Settlement in the Northern Caucasus
      The 2003 Chechen Presidential Election
      ISBN 3-89821-436-2

23   Timothy McCajor Hall, Rosie Read (Eds.)
      Changes in the Heart of Europe
      Recent Ethnographies of Czechs, Slovaks, Roma, and Sorbs
      With an afterword by Zdeněk Salzmann
      ISBN 3-89821-606-3

24   Christian Autengruber
      Die politischen Parteien in Bulgarien und Rumänien
      Eine vergleichende Analyse seit Beginn der 90er Jahre
      Mit einem Vorwort von Dorothée de Nève
      ISBN 3-89821-476-1

FORTHCOMING (MANUSCRIPT WORKING TITLES)

Nicola Melloni
The Russian 1998 Financial Crisis and Its Aftermath
An Etherodox Perspective
ISBN 3-89821-407-9

Rebbecca Katz
The Republic of Georgia
Post-Soviet Media Representations of Politics and Corruption
ISBN 3-89821-413-3

Annette Freyberg-Inan
The Social Sciences in Romania
Research Conditions and the Role of International Support
ISBN 3-89821-416-8

Laura Victoir
The Russian Land Estate Today
ISBN 3-89821-426-5

Stephanie Solowyda
Biography of Semen Frank
ISBN 3-89821-457-5

Margaret Dikovitskaya
Arguing with the Photographs
Russian Imperial Colonial Attitudes in Visual Culture
ISBN 3-89821-462-1

Stefan Ihrig
Welche Nation in welcher Geschichte?
Eigen- und Fremdbilder der nationalen Diskurse in der Historiographie und den Geschichtsbüchern in der Republik Moldova, 1991-2003
ISBN 3-89821-466-4

Sergei M. Plekhanov
Russian Nationalism in the Age of Globalization
ISBN 3-89821-484-2

Михаил Лукянов
Российский консерватизм и реформа, 1905-1917
ISBN 3-89821-503-2

Robert Pyrah
Cultural Memory and Identity
Literature, Criticism and the Theatre in Lviv - Lwow - Lemberg, 1918-1939 and in post-Soviet Ukraine
ISBN 3-89821-505-9

Dmitrij Chmelnizki
Die Architektur Stalins
Ideologie und Stil 1929-1960
ISBN 3-89821-515-6

Andrei Rogatchevski
The National-Bolshevik Party
ISBN 3-89821-532-6

Zenon Victor Wasyliw
Soviet Culture in the Ukrainian Village
The Transformation of Everyday Life and Values, 1921-1928
ISBN 3-89821-536-9

Nele Sass
Das gegenkulturelle Milieu im postsowjetischen Russland
ISBN 3-89821-543-1

Josette Baer
Preparing Modernity in Central Europe
Political Thought and the Independent Nation State
ISBN 3-89821-546-6

Ivan Katchanovski
Cleft Countries
Regional Political Divisions and Cultures in Post-Soviet Ukraine and Moldova
ISBN 3-89821-558-X

Julie Elkner
Maternalism versus Militarism
The Russian Soldiers' Mothers Committee
ISBN 3-89821-575-X

Maryna Romanets
Displaced Subjects, Anamorphosic Texts, Reconfigured Visions
Improvised Traditions in Contemporary Ukrainian and Irish Literature
ISBN 3-89821-576-8

Alexandra Kamarowsky
Russia's Post-crisis Growth
ISBN 3-89821-580-6

Martin Friessnegg
Das Problem der Medienfreiheit in Russland seit dem Ende der Sowjetunion
ISBN 3-89821-588-1

Vladimir Kantor
Willkür oder Freiheit?
Beiträge zur russischen Geschichtsphilosophie
ISBN 3-89821-589-X

Florian Mühlfried
Postsowjetische Feiern
Das Georgische Bankett im Wandel
ISBN 3-89821-601-2

John B. Dunlop
The 2002 Dubrovka and 2004 Beslan Hostage Crises
A Critique of Russian Counter-Terrorism
ISBN 3-89821-608-X

Series Subscription

Please enter my subscription to the series *Soviet and Post-Soviet Politics and Society*, ISSN 1614-3515, as follows:

❏ complete series   OR   ❏ English-language titles
                                                  ❏ German-language titles
                                                  ❏ Russian-language titles

starting with
❏ volume # 1
❏ volume # ___
      ❏ please also include the following volumes: #___, ___, ___, ___, ___, ___, ___
❏ the next volume being published
      ❏ please also include the following volumes: #___, ___, ___, ___, ___, ___, ___

❏ 1 copy per volume   OR   ❏ ___ copies per volume

Subscription within Germany:

You will receive every volume at 1st publication at the regular bookseller's price – incl. s & h and VAT.
Payment:
❏ Please bill me for every volume.
❏ Lastschriftverfahren: Ich/wir ermächtige(n) Sie hiermit widerruflich, den Rechnungsbetrag je Band von meinem/unserem folgendem Konto einzuziehen.

Kontoinhaber: _____ Kreditinstitut: _____
Kontonummer: _____ Bankleitzahl: _____

International Subscription:

Payment (incl. s & h and VAT) in advance for
❏ 10 volumes/copies (€ 319,80)   ❏ 20 volumes/copies (€ 599,80)
❏ 40 volumes/copies (€ 1.099,80)
Please send my books to:

NAME_____ DEPARTMENT_____
ADDRESS _____
POST/ZIP CODE_____ COUNTRY _____
TELEPHONE _____ EMAIL_____

date/signature_____

A hint for librarians in the former Soviet Union: Your academic library might be eligible to receive free-of-cost scholarly literature from Germany via the German Research Foundation. For Russian-language information on this program, see
       http://www.dfg.de/forschungsfoerderung/formulare/download/12_54.pdf.

Please fax to: **0511 / 262 2201 (+49 511 262 2201)**
or mail to: *ibidem*-Verlag, Julius-Leber-Weg 11, D-30457 Hannover, Germany
or send an e-mail: ibidem@ibidem-verlag.de

ibidem-Verlag
Melchiorstr. 15
D-70439 Stuttgart

info@ibidem-verlag.de

www.ibidem-verlag.de
www.edition-noema.de
www.autorenbetreuung.de

www.ingramcontent.com/pod-product-compliance
Lightning Source LLC
Chambersburg PA
CBHW051805230426
43672CB00012B/2636